D1806809

Neo-Gothic Narratives

Neo-Gothic Narratives

Illusory Allusions from the Past

Edited by
Sarah E. Maier and Brenda Ayres

ANTHEM PRESS

Anthem Press
An imprint of Wimbledon Publishing Company
www.anthempress.com

This edition first published in UK and USA 2020
by ANTHEM PRESS
75–76 Blackfriars Road, London SE1 8HA, UK
or PO Box 9779, London SW19 7ZG, UK
and
244 Madison Ave #116, New York, NY 10016, USA

© 2020 Sarah E. Maier and Brenda Ayres editorial matter and selection;
individual chapters © individual contributors

The moral right of the authors has been asserted.

All rights reserved. Without limiting the rights under copyright reserved above,
no part of this publication may be reproduced, stored or introduced into
a retrieval system, or transmitted, in any form or by any means
(electronic, mechanical, photocopying, recording or otherwise),
without the prior written permission of both the copyright
owner and the above publisher of this book.

British Library Cataloguing-in-Publication Data
A catalogue record for this book is available from the British Library.

ISBN-13: 978-1-78527-217-2 (Hbk)
ISBN-10: 1-78527-217-9 (Hbk)

This title is also available as an e-book.

Dedicated to those readers who love to feel their hair standing up on the back of their necks

CONTENTS

ACKNOWLEDGEMENTS

Thanks to Robert J. Moore, who granted us permission to use his painting *Proof of Life* on our cover.

We are so grateful for the pioneering work in the Gothic by Fred Botting, David Punter, Andrew Smith and Montague Summers; followed by the twenty-first century scholarship of Ellen Brinks, Glennis Byron, Markman Ellis, Maggie Kilgour, Diane Long Hoeveler, Catherine Spooner, Dale Townshend and so many others who have helped us understand more about ourselves through their analysis of Gothic literature. As for neo-Gothicism, we are grateful for the frontrunners Nadine Boehm-Schnitker, Marie-Luise Kohlke, Susanne Gruss, Christian Gutleben and Diana Wallace, who have offered significant insights as to why we, as post-postmoderns, like to look at the "Victorians in the rearview mirror," a phrase borrowed from Simon Joyce.

We want to express our great appreciation for the contributors of this volume: Geremy Carnes, Martin Danahay, Carol Davison, Jessica Gildersleeve, Karen Livett, Karen E. Macfarlane, Jamil Mustafa, Ashleigh Prosser and Nike Sulway.

Thanks go to Liberty University student Avery M. Powers, who worked as an intern and helped with proofing this manuscript.

Ayres would like to thank the generosity of Penn State's library, which loaned her hundreds of books and articles in order to do this project.

Maier's enthusiasm for this project was conceived in discussions with University of New Brunswick students who love a good scare: Belinda Balemans, Genevieve Crowell, Connor DeMerchant, Rachel Friars and Jessica Raven. BOO! For introducing her to her love of the art of chilling the blood, thanks to Glennis (Stephenson) Byron. For his mentorship, Donald MacPherson, her grade 12 English teacher, whose haunting voice she still hears. Her gratitude to Gido, and of course, most importantly, for letting her borrow Frankie Stein, her love to Violet—always always.

Introduction

NEO-GOTHICISM: PERSISTENT HAUNTING OF THE PAST AND HORRORS ANEW

Brenda Ayres and Sarah E. Maier

You notice the turreted pink elephant as you pass the Tube entrance at The Elephant and Castle. You consider yourself a scholar of the Gothic, so the irony of the statue is not lost on you. "I wonder […] what an elephant's soul is like," you quote to yourself from *Dracula* and chuckle.[1] Then you remember the elephant and castle that appeared in margins of several Gothic manuscripts on display at the British Library. No wonder your physician is sending you to a therapist. "You are a postmodern who is not coping well in this century," he said. "You escape into the past and live inside Gothic books and movies." Forcing yourself to be polite but, after all, you do have academic pride, you refrain from informing him that we are now in the post-postmodern age. Besides, you don't know what that means, but he would probably shake his head and deduce that you are more deranged than he originally thought.

Your taxi deposits you somewhere in Walworth. Before you can close the car door, the taxi driver, with his pronounced Eastern European accent, speeds off as if he saw a ghost. Then you turn around and find yourself standing before a rickety old bridge that dares you to cross a moat that leads to two turrets, and you instantly think of Wemmick's Castle in Dickens' *Great Expectations*. You double check the address to make sure that it is the clinic that you are supposed to visit for help with your nerves. "It's probably run by someone crazier than I am," you mumble to yourself. Maybe it is a meeting place for support groups with unhealthy Gothic obsessions, beginning with the shrink in charge.

You are tempted to turn around, but the cab has left you, so you brave the crossing only to halt before a sign that reads, "Beware of Piranhas." You peer over the side and spot a frenzy of teeth and blood and hair of some hapless stray who must have ventured into the murky water.

This cannot be good for your nerves.

"Oh, it is an unusual clinic," Dr. Frankenstein had mentioned with a twinkle in his eye, which you now realise that you mistook as his confidence in your road to recovery. You gaze up at the crenellate parapet and notice that even though it is midday, bats are leisurely soaring around it, and their chatter sounds as if they are plotting your demise. You hope your Valium will soon kick in.

Hesitating before a door knocker that you know was Dickens' inspiration in *A Christmas Carol*, you are relieved to see a doorbell and decide to use that instead. When you push it, however, you hear the sound of a dying cow and remember that that was the "chime" for the Addams family.[2] Your better sense tells you to go back, but as the portal creeps open, you peer into the darkness and are alarmed that there is no receptionist, no nurse, no doctor to greet you. Still, morbid curiosity propels you inside.

The door slams behind you.

If you are intrigued with the neo-Gothic, whether reader, writer or another sort of fan, then you may be the "you" above. You share a postmodernist propensity to be "fundamentally concerned [...] with the ontological and epistemological roots of the *now* through a historical awareness of *then* (Kaplan 2008, 4). The way you cope with the present is to "turn around and step back" (Gutleben 2001, 10) and are thus trapped in the castle. "This," your colleague Christian Gutleben assures you, "is the fundamental aporia of nostalgic postmodernism" (10). Or, as another colleague, Simon Joyce, puts it, you are driving ahead while keeping your eyes on the past in your rearview mirror (2007, 3).

When that same mirror is used to look back to the Gothic from an interrogative, postmodern position, it appears that Gothicism is metamorphical, meaning it is shapeshifting: What Gothic literature was in the first centuries was very different from the Gothic during early Medievalism and morphed into something else by the middle and late "Dark Ages," and so on. By the time Horace Walpole and then Sir Walter Scott had become so enthralled with medievalism that they built Strawberry Hill and Abbortsford, respectively, Medieval Gothicism morphed into something else. Diana Wallace in her *Female Gothic Histories: Gender, History and the Gothic* argues that Gothic literature was already metafiction, *avant la lettre*, in its generation of historical text (2013, 1). The term "Gothic" implies a return to the past, or to put it into Gothic terms, the past never stays dead—it is self-reflexive because it deals with the undead in the present. Then neo-Gothicism is doubly reflexive as it reflects on the reflection of the past.

When Ralph Waldo Emerson stated, "Each age, it is found, must write its own books" (1901 [1837], 14), he could have been alluding to Gothicism because although there are elements that we consistently consider to be "Gothic," Gothicism does make real through fiction our anxieties, our hauntings our horrors—and those change from age to age. Therefore every revision of Gothicism might be called "neo-Gothic"; however, the writers of this volume emphasise that today's Gothic is radically different from any published before, and they probe its neo-Gothic attributes.

If there is one definition of postmodernism that most scholars can agree on, then it is a rejection of absolutes. If postmodernists reject the notion that there is a universal acceptance of a single denotation of good versus evil, and that morality is relative, then of course, contemporary Gothic works are going to reflect that zeitgeist, and since it is a unique perspective to human history, its expression through the Gothic is new. We are calling this zeitgeist neo-Gothicism.

Contemporary readers seem to continue to have a need for emotional catharsis through the horror evoked by those creatures and situations that terrify us and oblige us to contend with forces beyond our control. It also seems to be a human inclination to look back to a past thought to be simpler and halcyonic. Maggie Kilgour suggests a reason for the persistent presence of the Gothic past in the present, including our postmodern, if not post-postmodern era. In *The Rise of the Gothic Novel*, she theorises that *because* of postmodernism, we experience "the resurrection of the need for the sacred and transcendent in a modern enlightened secular world which denies the existence of supernatural forces, or as the rebellion of the imagination against the tyranny of reason" (1995, 3). There are those critics who proclaim us to be in the post-postmodern age, but they cannot tell us what that is other than claim that it is a longing; it is all that is left after postmodernism and its "silence, inaccessibility, elitism, and the futility of all acts of language" (Holland 2013, 16). Many of us, like Mary Holland, look to the past to recover what postmodernism negated and do not mourn for the end of postmodernism but rather "dance on its grave" (16).

If we perform any postmodern graveyard ritual, then it begins with the work done by those scholars who have focused their energies on the fictional interpretations of Romanticism and Victorianism oft collapsed under the banner of neo-Victorianism which includes neo-Gothicism. Linda Hutcheon defines "historiographic metafictions" as "those well-known and popular novels which are both intensely self-reflexive and yet paradoxically also lay claim to historical events and personages"; she further asserts that such fictions have "a theoretical self-awareness of history and fiction as human constructs (historio*graphic meta*fiction) [that] is made the grounds for [a] rethinking and reworking of the forms and contents of the past" (1988, 5; emphasis in original). Patricia Waugh distinguishes this form of metafiction as "fictional writing which self-consciously and systematically draws attention to its status as an artifact in order to pose questions about the relationship between fiction and reality" (1984, 2).

As Ann Heilmann and Mark Llewellyn have deduced from their study of neo-Victorianism, we post-postmodernists expect a revival of previous literature repackaged and rebranded for a contemporary audience to provide us with an alternate view of what the original literature offered (2010, 3–5). Any such modern revisitation of Victorianism is a "cultural and critical practice that re-visions the nineteenth century and is latter-day aesthetic and ideological legacies in the light of historical hindsight and critique, but also fantasy—what we *want* to imagine the period to have been like for diverse reasons, including affirmations of national identity, the struggle for symbolic restorative justice, and indulgence in escapist exoticism" (Kohlke 2014, 22; emphasis in original).

In the creation of this collection, the idea of the neo-Gothic sets itself apart from the neo-Victorian and the neo-Romantic. Fred Botting and Catherine Spooner continue their investigations into the contemporary Gothic in their collection *Monstrous Media/Spectral Subjects* that explores how across "pairings relationships multiply and numerous configurations emerge" that are "underpinned (and undermined) by disturbing and obscure movements of monstrosity and spectrality, of monstering and spooking, a key polarisation [that] is sustained in interrelations of political, normative systems and subjective orientations" (2015, 1–2) in technological advancements. While the term "neo-Gothic" is evoked by Danel Olson—"we need an understanding of how and why the alien will within the neo-Gothic has cast such a spell on us" and evokes its "macabre emotional territory"—he admits a definition is needed, asking, "What does the new Gothic mock, flaunt, or falsify?" (2011, xxiii, xxvii). Similarly, other authors refer to neo-Gothicism, but they do not define the term.[3]

Susanne Becker courageously attempts to define and apply the term but does so differently than do the writers of this volume. Her neo-gothicism (with a lower "g") spans "the politicized 1970s, the conservative 1980s and the millennium-ridden 1990s" (1999, 4), but in all fairness, her book was published in 1999 and did not have the benefit of newer Gothic texts of the twenty-first century. Nevertheless, for her, the neo-gothic is literature that employs the familiar Gothic but is all about "a new form of gendered writing" arising out of "a lack of orientation especially relating to everyday life, as the tradition of spheres of production and reproduction along gender lines is radically shaken" (4). We do not dispute the gender contest that persists in contemporary texts, but we do find this definition inadequate for neo-Gothicism, given, for example, the plethora of postmodern, queer readings of *Dracula*,[4] a late-Victorian novel, but one that is, to borrow Becker's descriptors of late twentieth-century works, full of "gendered subjectivity" and "anti-realism" (21), with much "excess" (147), "disguise" (225), "covert and stripped narrative" (226). In short, earlier Gothic texts navigate the murky waters of genderfication with similar narrative strategies found in contemporary texts. We do agree that many neo-Gothic stories are extremely "self-reflexive" (111, 122, 142, 260 and 287), and although they do convey au courant anxieties, unlike earlier Gothicism, many of them do not offer any solutions for the harried modern (4).

Besides, gender identification is not the only modern vexation. If familiar Gothic elements include supernaturalism, excess and Medievalism while the text is peopled by damsels in distress as well as monstrous men who exist in labyrinthian mazes of the real world and/or the psyche, then the pressing questions include if and how and why those traditional Gothic influences move forward to the present day. What are the new castles? What does monstrosity consist of now? Can a transmedia culture invoke the terrors of the internal psychological turmoil of the Gothic? How does the current political age foster a new and hyper awareness of gendered roles in these sexually charged texts of the past? Further, if nostalgia is invoked, then surely it is not to return to the past but to marshal the past to reintegrate forgotten voices, subjects, subjectivities and histories to problematize received ideas of Gothic escapism. The neo-Gothic mobilizes what is accepted as the Gothic in order to deal with a post-postmodern, sometimes posthuman, world to expose the ambivalence and banality that now greets questions of evil, to address questions of memory, violence and traumatic experience, to investigate non-linear identities as well as spectral selves and to give voice to multifaceted cultural, scientific and artistic complexities in a time of complexity. To wonder if, in all these issues, there is a "metafictional I-thou relationship with the postmodern reader" (Snodgrass 2011, 112) begins to form a focus for the reader of the neo-Gothic.

It would seem, then, that neo-Gothicism seduces us to the dark side and subtextual reverberations of past literatures, the hauntings that scientific reasoning has never been able to exorcise, the evil that scientific reasoning can never eradicate, the supernatural that scientific reasoning can never dismiss. Neo-Gothicism, in contrast to neo-Victorianism, is that which cannot be controlled, the infectious Other that cannot be scientifically or objectively contained. Perhaps Kilgour is right: just as the genre of Gothic gained popularity during the eighteenth century, beginning with Horace Walpole's *The Castle of Otranto* (1764), Gothicism is a "rebellion against a constraining neoclassical aesthetic ideal of order and unity, in order to recover a suppressed primitive and barbaric imaginative freedom" (3). Ever since this backlash to neoclassicism, writers and readers have been intrigued with the "bizarre, eccentric, wild, savage, lawless, and transgressive" (3).

At times, this retrospective neo-Gothicism is indeed about nostalgia, about struggling so much with the modern era that we look back to a time when our eighteenth- and nineteenth-century precursors—like ghosts in our present—were and still are struggling to steady themselves on the shifting sands of industrialisation, urbanisation and religious doubt. Fred Botting reminds us that the Gothic of the eighteenth and nineteenth centuries was all about looking to the past for answers to the perplex- ities of the Industrial Age (2010, 7); therefore, neo-Gothicism is looking back at a time of technological advancements, new media and cultural systems that continue dehumanization, domination and objectification practices to those who are Other to the norm. Those who are ex-centric—other than the centre of communicative fic- tional or transmedia concern—seek discussion of extremes to heighten their ideas of escape and to investigate and/or expose their situational displacement in often non- linear, fragmented narratives that revisit themes of contamination, collision, trans- gression and excess while revisiting Gothic precursors including Dark Romanticism, Victorian Gothic(s) and representations of truth therein. It is a turning back to "the nostalgia for the nostalgia of nostalgia" (Shuttleworth 1997, 262). Sally Shuttleworth is herself quoting from Graham Swift's *Ever After* when a student asks a professor about "Tennyson's misty and moated chivalric nostalgia" (1993, 254). Professor Potter recognizes in this student "the nostalgia for the nostalgia of nostalgia." He assures her that she "has come to the right place" for help, a haunted house with "spiral staircases and genuine Gothic features" (253). Swift resurrects the Gothic text from the dead, as Potter describes the fireplace as "a genuine piece of neo-Gothic pastiche, dating from Tennyson's time" (253).

Cora Kaplan explains this nostalgia within the historical context of the disintegration of the British Empire during World Wars I and II so that by the 1960s, "the Victorian as at once ghostly and tangible, an origin and an anachronism, had a strong affective presence in modern Britain" (2007, 5) and was nationalistic nostalgic for a past when Britain was the largest empire on earth. Julie Sanders reasons that "the Victorian era proves ripe for appropriation because it highlights many of the overriding concerns of the post- modern era: questions of identity; environmental and genetic conditioning; repressed and oppressed modes of sexuality; criminality and violence; an interest in urbanism and the potentials and possibilities of new technology; of law and authority; science and reli- gion; and the postcolonial legacies of empire" (2006, 161). Neo-Gothicism follows this trend established by neo-Victorianism where, "just as the Victorian novelists sought a textual resolution for the industrial problems in their new cities, perhaps we seek a textual salvation in mimicking them as a salve to our (post)modern condition" (Heilmann and Llewellyn 2010, 2). More specifically, and intrinsic to this collection, is that it is by much like exploring the "Gothic in relation to the nineteenth-century past and the period's specific cultural field that neo-Victorianism endeavours to circumvent the hypermodern, globalised and uniform presentation of the Gothic, in the process rekindling an intensely disturbing desire that unsettles norms and redefines boundaries once more" (Kohlke and Gutleben 2012, 2). That said, the neo-Gothic is not constrained by the time frame designated by the neo-Victorian Gothic.

The neo-Gothic parallels the project of neo-Victorianism except it moves back and forward in time—back to the reanimation of Romantic Ur-texts like Mary Shelley's *Frankenstein* (1818/1831) and forward with other multimedia speculations that rely on our understanding of the traditional Gothic in relation to our current cultural context. "New Gothic" or "post-millennial Gothic" are terms that do not necessarily maintain the essential relationship between the past, present and future of Gothic narratives; to be "neo" places the narratives in a necessary and elucidatory partnership with the past. Neo-Gothic is, always, a spectral revisitation of past Gothicism, but such rearticulations can help elucidate our present cultural anxieties and fears.

That said, one has got to wonder why we are so nostalgic for the Gothic; terror and horror are in the news, never mind in fiction, so to turn to the neo-Gothic must, in some way, provide a cathartic reworking of the monstrous around us. There is a need for the neo-Gothic to sort through the breaking down of once universally understood binaries between good and evil. One need only to watch the film *Crimson Peak* (2015) to be reminded that we live in a heartless, violent world, where a sister and her brother murder their mother, father, and the brother's three wives, and nearly succeed with a fourth, foiled by the brother who is finally weary of his controlling sister and her madness and opts (but not successfully) for love and life with Wife #4. The neo-Gothic attacks the "dehumanizing modern world" (Kilgour 1995, 12). Instead of feeling for the damsel in distress as we might in reading a Gothic novel, we post-postmodernists might relate more to Sir Thomas Sharpe, BT, in *Crimson Peak*: We want peace, we respond to the possibility of a new life full of hope, we want a break with our past that only haunts and torments us, but because we continue to make love to our sociopathic kin, there is no possibility that we will ever get to live happily ever after. "Whether read as a signal of obsessive postmodern anxiety about all manners of excess and hybridity (capitalist, technological, sexual, multicultural) or as a sign of general instability, degeneration or decline of distinct 'Culture(s),'" Marie-Luise Kohlke and Christian Gutleben believe that the "Gothic has permanently emerged from the crepuscular cultural unconconscious into the brightly lit mainstream"; they add, "Perhaps the most remarkable aspect of contemporary Gothic is its hegemonic power to invade all aspects of our consumer society" (2012, 2).

Neo-Gothicism is not always a door that opens into a haunted house or castle. Nadine Boehm-Schnitker and Susanne Gruss as well as others[5] have surmised that the mission of producing the neo-Victorian is to "correct" the past, or that if people are writing, reading and watching it is because they want "to change the past to suit current purposes" (2014, 2). Cora Kaplan theorises its mission to be "the self-conscious rewriting of historical narratives to highlight the suppressed histories of gender and sexuality, race and empire, as well as challenges to the conventional understandings of the historical self" (2007, 3). The neo-Gothic uses the palimpsestic nature of the Gothic to deconstruct and resituate ourselves in our alienation from the supposed stability of our received notions of technological advancement, real-world violence, political conversation(s), enforced containment, contagious ideas and other self-reflexive certainties that no longer hold.

Anxieties that have always plagued humans, as well as those that have emerged because of changing technologies, ideologies and politics, and others that have only intensified are reflected in those narratives considered Gothic. Brenda Ayres, one of the coeditors for this volume, opens with an account of the history of Gothic literature. Then she identifies the changes that she sees in contemporary Gothic narratives that are very different from any that precede it, thus coming up with a definition of neo-Gothicism.

At the bicentenary of Mary Shelley's *Frankenstein*, it is on point to evaluate her Gothic novel from a neo-Gothic perspective. The second chapter has been written by Sarah E. Maier, the coeditor of this volume. Hers is a feminist reading of the Gothic afterlives of Mary Shelley and her monstrous progeny in creative retellings of the underdeveloped women of the novel—Lady Caroline, Elizabeth Lavenza and Justine—as well as in biofictions that consider Shelley's birth, life, trauma, grief and creation(s). The neo-Gothic narratives of the past few years are, no doubt, intended as either homages or more cynically to capitalize once again on her spectral presence, but Kiersten White's *The Dark Descent of Elizabeth Frankenstein* (2018), Theodore Roszak's *The Memoirs of Elizabeth Frankenstein* (1995), Antoinette May's *The Determined Heart* (2015), Lita Judge's *Mary's Monster* (2018), along with Laurie Sheck's neo-Gothic *A Monster's Notes* (2009) allow the reader to see her female characters, and Shelley herself, beyond kneeling at the feet of powerful men. Surely, to be haunted by one's own life and its creations is worthy of its own stories.

Carol Davison's Chapter 3 advances the possibilities of revision through the neo-Gothic in her analysis of Emily Brontë's *Wuthering Heights* (1847). The last few decades have seen numerous powerful revisionings of Emily Brontë's novel that include racialising Heathcliff as black. Davison investigates such revisionings in Peter Forster's compelling and suggestive wood engravings of *Wuthering Heights* for the Folio Society (1993), Maryse Condé's *Windward Heights* (2003), Andrea Arnold's cinematic version of *Wuthering Heights* (2013), Caryl Phillips' *The Lost Child* (2015) and Michael Stewart's *Ill Will* (2018). While these neo-Victorian revisions bring forward the question of race relations and British imperialism that Brontë's Gothically insular narrative only gestures towards, it may be said that, in some senses, they minimize the masterful ability of that poetic mother-text to speak—albeit, paradoxically, in a limited narrative framework—more expansively to that question. Davison's study commences with a concise formal and ideological reading of *Wuthering Heights* and then moves to the idea of inheritance, very broadly defined— economic, biological, moral, sociopolitical, genealogical and (even) literary given how these literary offspring of Emily Brontë's work speak back to the mother-text, a process that involves an awareness of, and engagement with, other similarly strategized works.

Gothic scholar Martin Danahay has written Chapter 4 in which he contends that the anger of white men, especially American white men, is a new feature in Gothicism. He notes that Richard Mansfield's 1887 stage adaptation of Robert Louis Stevenson's *Strange Case of Dr. Jekyll and Mr. Hyde* (1886) introduces a female love interest when women are noticeably absent from Stevenson's original, turning Mr. Hyde into a sexual predator who directly threatens women. Mansfield's version rebrands Mr. Hyde as a figure of Gothic toxic masculinity, whereas Stevenson's narrative tenders "hegemonic masculinity"[6] that is threatened by Dr. Jekyll's transgression of Victorian propriety. Then Chuck

Palahniuk's *Fight Club* (1996) is an updated, neo-Gothic telling of *Jekyll and Hyde* that expresses a similar rage by men who feel their lives are thwarted by consumerism and their feminisation. The narrator is literally toxic in that he attacks conservation measures, advocates for pollution and promotes random violence. The film version of *Fight Club* (1999) popularised the term "snowflake" as a rallying cry for right-wing misogynist and racial attacks on opponents, bringing toxic masculinity into popular political discourse.[7]

Some of the most revealing works that revision the Gothic and expose the "illusory allusions from the past" (the subtitle of this collection) can be found in several multi-media platforms. The vampire, without doubt among the key players of traditional Gothic fiction and film, also plays a leading—though transformed—role in neo-Gothic narratives. These two points are evident in Jamil Mustafa's chapter in its catechism on vampirism, scientific advancement and neo-Gothicism in *Dark Shadows* (2012), Tim Burton's film adaptation of the television series of the same title; and in "A White World Made Red" (2016), an episode of the neo-Victorian television series *Ripper Street* (2013–16) that features and reimagines Bram Stoker's *Dracula* (1897) and *The Passage* (2019), a Fox television show based on the first novel of Justin Cronin's trilogy. Chapter 5 makes clear that it is the profound uncanniness, the *mise en abyme* that results from aligning these most-current iterations with their predecessors, and from tracing both sets of narratives to their common Gothic sources, that provides an ideal construct within which to understand how the neo-Gothic adapts to mesmerise its audiences—in much the same fashion as the vampire changes form, the better to lure its victims.

Chapter 6 by Ashleigh Prosser undertakes a comparative analysis of Peter Ackroyd's 1994 neo-Victorian Gothic novel *Dan Leno and the Limehouse Golem* and its recent adaptation by screenwriter Jane Goldman as *The Limehouse Golem*, a neo-Victorian horror film directed by Juan Carlos Medina and released in 2017. The depictions of London's East End can be read as a neo-Gothic narrative of textual haunting in that the movie and novel assume an urbanisation of the Victorian Gothic in the form of the golem, that is, an inanimate object brought to life. Depending on the cultural and historical context, metatextually, each recurrence of the golem plays/haunts newer texts with golems of the past. In the story and the film, London's East End is haunted by a malevolent "spirit of place" that appears to have manifested itself as a monstrous serial killer, the Limehouse Golem. Prosser examines precisely how such a neo-Gothic (re)vision is at play within *The Limehouse Golem*, a cinematic adaptation of a work of historiographic metafiction. The famous nineteenth-century pantomime turn for which the real Dan Leno was so well known and that resounds throughout both texts encapsulates not just Ackroyd's neo-Victorian Gothic vision of London's East End, but Goldman's adaptation of it too, for, as the first and last dialogue of the book says, "Here we are, *again!*"

Kate Livett's chapter is unique in its treatment of the neo-Gothic in Australian post-colonial novels through her examination of *The Night Guest* (2013) by Fiona McFarlane, *The Swan Book* (2013) by Alexis Wright (2013) and *The Engagement* (2012) by Chloe Hooper. Chapter 7 scrutinises authorial gender as well, asking how women writers have represented gender in their recent Gothic texts. Drawing out the specific uses of the neo-Gothic in texts by female authors from different cultural traditions—Vietnamese Australian, British Australian and Indigenous authors—in current posthumanism, this chapter charts the respective concerns of these texts, the effects of their deployments of Gothic tropes and narratives, and what their neo-Gothicism means.

Monsters do important work in the cultures in which they appear and proliferate in neo-Gothic narratives; our current obsessions with the walking dead, creatures, monsters and post-apocalyptic cyborgs abound; historically, they mark the boundaries of the familiar and evince the limits of categorization, of civility, of relations, of humanity. Karen E. Macfarlane's chapter notices the increased frequency of "monsters" that have been "rehabilitated" in recent adaptations. These figures—formerly labelled as "monsters"— have effectively become signs, not of otherness and transgression, but of human difference. They have become metaphors for defining tolerance, inclusion and the positive recognition of difference. In recent years, first in fiction and now on film, the zombie has begun to be rehabilitated as the object of teen affection in the novel *Warm Bodies* (2011) and in Lia Habel's *Dearly* (2011–12) series. More recently television series like *IZombie, In the Flesh* have characterised the zombie as a not only walking, but a talking undead subject. The arrival of the self-aware zombie demonstrates a refusal to uncouple the consciousness from the body and resists posthuman fantasies of disembodiment in contemporary networked culture.

Chapter 9 by Jessica Gildersleeve and Nike Sulway moves us beyond our usual understanding of a Gothic narrative to capture the anxieties created in neo-Gothic representations of dinosaurs in modern films. While they believe that the Gothic more generally has always been a genre that attends to the social and cultural problems faced in the contemporary moment, precisely because of its interest in the strange, the abject or the Other, the dinosaur narrative has a particular kind of neo-Gothic uniquely positioned to address the collapse of moral, spatial and historical boundaries. Considering the range of films in the *Jurassic Park* series (1993–2018), as well as Ray Bradbury's "A Sound of Thunder" (1952) and what was perhaps the first "dinosaur novel," Jules Verne's *Journey to the Centre of the Earth* (1864), the dinosaur exists at the limit of our neo-Gothic imagination. These works employ Gothic tropes in the most recent *Jurassic Park* film, *Jurassic World: Fallen Kingdom* (2018): the isolated mansion, the rich benefactor, the orphan child, the presence of family secrets and the haunting or stalking figure. In these ways and in a contemporary context concerned with environmental collapse, the dinosaur and its impossible presence is reinvigorated in the conservatism of the Neo-Gothic narrative not as a warning, but as a manageable problem.

In much recent criticism of the neo-Gothic, the limelight on trauma in general has come at the cost of attention to the particular trauma that originally birthed the Gothic: the loss of faith in both traditional Christian religious ideology and in the modern ideology of reason and science that had begun to gain currency among portions of the British elite in the eighteenth century. In postmodernity faith in science has weakened and this loss of faith is a major contributor to the rise in prominence of the neo-Gothic. The penultimate chapter by Geremy Carnes takes as a case study the long-running television program *Doctor Who* to better understand the resurgence of the Gothic in postmodernity not as a response to radically new circumstances, but as a return to the centuries-old doubts that gave rise to Gothic literature in the first place.

The Gothic continues to be written, read and viewed as we seemed to be compelled to resurrect horrors of the past or continue to be haunted by the horrors of the past.

Maybe this preoccupation and fascination of the Gothic is driven by our need to master our anxieties instead of letting them master us. In the first chapter of this collection, Brenda Ayres underscored the proclivity of Gothicism, but in the closing chapter, she interstitialises it with a chronic omission in Gothic/neo-Gothic scholarship, namely, the presence of Satan/the Devil/demons/evil in Gothic narratives. She proposes that the first true written Gothic tale, even if the term is anachronistic, is the Christian Bible. She interprets the Gothic through a biblical lens and suggests that neo-Gothicism is different from its precursor in its biblical representation of evil in contemporary Gothicism in books, television and other media

In any "neo" re-creation, whether monstrous, spectral or otherwise, there is a selective adoptive appropriation of what is desired or needed from the past to attempt to or correct past misconceptions or misperceptions As such, this volume traverses a vast range of neo-Gothicism, with its refracted memories, supernatural visions and spectral visitations, as a multicultural, multinational, multigender, multitechnological and intertextual phenomena, all of which are illusory in their unreality and in our presumed ability to control our terrors; they remain, always, unstable, inconstant and unknowable, the haunting of our houses and the spectral anomalies of our lives.

Notes

1 In *Dracula*, Dr. Seward is thinking about his patient, R. M. Renfield, the "zoöphagous maniac" who eats flies and spiders in order to procure their life force (1897, 66–67). Seward records in his diary that he asked Renfield to "breakfast on elephant" and then speculated on "an elephant's soul" (253).

2 The Addams family—Gomez and Morticia and their children, Wednesday and Pugsley, Uncle Fester, Grandmama, the Frankensteinish Lurch, the disembodied hand called Thing and Cousin Itt—appeared on *The Addams Family* television series from 1964 to 1966.

3 See Mary-Ellen Snodgrass, Barbara FreyWaxman, Lucian-Vasile Szabo and Marius-Mircea Crisan who evoke, but do not define, the term "neo-Gothic."

4 See Jorge Flores Real (2018), Roger Luckhurst (2018) and William Hughes (2009) to name just a few.

5 Another prominent team to theorize that neo-Victorianism corrects the past is Ann Heilmann and Mark Llewellyn (2010, 8). Peter Widdowson, in noting the plethora of historical novels today, calls them "re-visionary fiction" because they re-write the past (2006, 492).

6 Danahay quotes from Connell and Messerschmidt (2005, 840).

7 Danahay's citation for this observation is Amanda Hess (2017).

Bibliography

Becker, Susanne. *Gothic Forms of Feminine Fictions*. Manchester, UK: Manchester University Press, 1999.

Boehm-Schnitker, Nadine, and Susanne Gruss. "Introduction: Fashioning the Neo-Victorian—Neo-Victorian Fashions." In *Neo-Victorian Literature and Culture: Immersions and Revisitations*, edited by Nadine Boehm-Schnitker and Susanne Gruss, 1–20. New York: Routledge, 2014.

Botting, Fred. *Gothic*. London: Routledge, 1996.

———. *Limits of Horror: Technology, Bodies, Gothic*. Manchester: Manchester University Press, 2010.

Botting, Fred, and Catherine Spooner. Introduction to *Monstrous Media / Spectral Subjects*, 1–11. Manchester: Manchester University Press, 2015.

Connell, R. W., and James W. Messerschmidt. "Hegemonic Masculinity: Rethinking the Concept." *Gender & Society* 19, no. 6 (December 2005): 829–59.

Crimson Peak. Directed by Guillermo del Toro. Legendary Pictures, 2015.

Diehl, Digby. "Playboy Interview: Anne Rice." *Playboy*, March 1993, 53–64.

Emerson, Ralph Waldo. "The American Scholar." 1837. New York: The Laurentian Press, 1901. https://books.google.com/books?id=rAAiAAAAMAAJ.

Gutleben, Christian. *Nostalgic Postmodernism: The Victorian Tradition and the Contemporary British Novel.* Amsterdam: Rodopi, 2001.

Heilmann, Ann, and Mark Llewellyn. *Neo-Victorianism: The Victorians in the Twenty-First Century, 1999–2009.* Houndmills, Basingstoke: Palgrave Macmillan, 2010.

Hess, Amanda. "How 'Snowflake' Became America's Inescapable Tough-Guy Taunt." *New York Times Magazine*, June 13, 2017. https://www.nytimes.com/2017/06/13/magazine/how-snowflake-became-americas-inescapable-tough-guy-taunt.html.

Ho, Elizabeth. *Neo-Victorian and the Memory of Empire.* New York: Continuum, 2012.

Holland, Mary K. *Succeeding Postmodernism: Language and Humanism in Contemporary American.* New York: Bloomsbury, 2013.

Hughes, William. *Bram Stoker's "Dracula."* London: Continuum International Publishing, 2009.

Hutcheon, Linda. *A Poetics of Postmodernism: History, Theory, Fiction.* London: Routledge, 1988.

Joyce, Simon. *The Victorians in the Rearview Mirror.* Athens: Ohio University Press, 2007.

Kaplan, Cora. *Victoriana: Histories, Fictions, Criticism.* Edinburgh: Edinburgh University Press, 2007.

———. "Perspective: *Fingersmith*'s Coda: Feminism and Victorian Studies." *Journal of Victorian Culture* 13, no. 1 (2008): 42–55.

Kilgour, Maggie. *The Rise of the Gothic Novel.* London: Routledge, 1995.

Kohlke, Marie-Luise. "Mining the Neo-Victorian Vein: Prospecting for Gold, Buried Treasure and Uncertain Metal." In *Neo-Victorian Literature and Culture: Immersions and Revisitations*, edited by Nadine Boehm-Schnitker and Susanne Gruss, 21–37. New York: Routledge, 2014.

Kohlke, Marie-Luise, and Christian Gutleben. *Neo-Victorian Gothic: Horror, Violence and Degeneration in the Re-imagined Nineteenth Century.* New York: Rodopi, 2012.

Luckhurst, Roger, ed. *The Cambridge Companion to "Dracula."* Cambridge, UK: Cambridge University Press, 2018.

Mighall, Robert. *A Geography of Victorian Gothic Fiction.* Oxford, UK: Oxford University Press, 1999.

Negra, Diane. "Coveting the Feminine: Victor Frankenstein. Norman Bates and Buffalo Bill." *Literature / Film Quarterly* 24, no. 2 (1996): 193–200.

Olson, Danel. "Introduction." In *21st Century Gothic*, edited by Danel Olson, xxi–xxxiii. Plymouth, UK: Scarecrow Press, 2011.

Real, Jorge Flores. *Queer Dracula: The Perverse Father and Homoerotism.* Zurich: Universität Zürich, 2018.

Sanders, Julie. *Adaptations and Appropriation: The New Critical Idiom*, 2nd ed. London: Routledge, 2006.

Shuttleworth, Sally. "Natural History: The Retro-Victorian Novel." In *The Third Culture: Literature and Science*, edited by Elinor S. Shaffer, 253–68. Berlin: Walter de Gruyter, 1997.

Snodgrass, Mary Ellen. "Michel Faver, Feminism, and the Neo-Gothic Novel: *The Crimson Petal and The White.*" In *21st Century Gothic*, edited by Danel Olson, 111–23. Plymouth, UK: Scarecrow Press, 2011.

Stoker, Bram. *Dracula.* 1893. New York: Doubleday, 1897.

Swift, Graham. *Ever After.* New York: Vintage International, 1993.

Szabo, Lucian-Vasile, and Marius-Mircea Crisan. "Technological Modifications of the Human Body in Neo-Gothic Literature: Prostheses, Hybridization and Cyborgization in Posthumanism." *Caietele Echinox* 35 (2018): 147–58.

Wallace, Diana. *Female Gothic Histories: Gender, History and the Gothic.* Cardiff: University of Wales Press, 2013.

Waugh, Patricia. *Metafiction: The Theory and Practice of Self-Conscious Fiction*. North Yorkshire: Methuen, 1984.

Waxman, Barbara Frey. "Postexisentialism in the Neo-Gothic Mode: Anne Rice's *Interview with the Vampire*." *Mosaic* 25, no. 3 (Summer 1992): 79–97.

Widdowson, Peter. "'Writing Back': Contemporary Re-visionary Fiction." *Textual Practice* vol. 20, no. 3 (2006): 491–507. doi: 10.1080/09502360082894.

Chapter One

"THROUGH A GLASS DARKLY": THE GOTHIC TRACE

Brenda Ayres

During the 2019 Halloween season in the United States, Geico Insurance ran a television commercial that was a pastiche of recent horror movies. Four young people are fleeing from something horrible as they leave a forested area.[1] They see a house that looks appropriately formidably haunted or maybe it is the house that Hitchcock built for *Psycho* (1960). They wisely dismiss each other's proposals for hiding in its attic or the basement. The "dumb" blonde cries, "Why can't we just get in the running car?"—a sensible suggestion, but "the guy" says, "Are you crazy?" Then he offers his own insane idea of their taking refuge behind several dozens of chainsaws suspended at the entrance of a shed, which the brunette affirms as "Smart."

They scurry to the shed. To most conscious viewers, the dangling chainsaws are like a neon sign shouting, "Danger, Will Robinson."[2] Sure enough, as the group cowers behind the saws, the camera cuts to a man inside the shed, and he is wearing the iconic goalkeeper's mask, the one worn by Jason in the *Friday the 13th* movies (beginning in 1987). He shoves up the mask with a look on his face as if to say, "Can anyone be so dumb?" The voice-over concludes: "If you're in a horror movie, you make poor decisions; it's what you do."

When the four realize that they are not alone, they dash out of the shed with one of the girls yelling, "Head for the cemetery." Convenient, for they will soon be dead bodies.

All five characters are played by actors and actresses that should be identifiable to viewers from their previous performances in murder stories on television and in movies.[3] Besides the information that draws on that hypermedia, there are other intertextual references in the commercial. For example, when one character suggests that they hide in the basement of the house, we might think of *The House by the Cemetery* (1981) or *Poltergeist* (1982) or other haunted houses built into former cemetery sites thereby disturbing the dead. Besides the basement, the attic is another scary place, especially in Victorian mansions, such as told in *The Grudge* (2004) and *The Attic* (2007). And then, of course, the place *not* to *be* if you're already scared to death is the cemetery. The running car is red, the colour of power and the colour of blood; if you are fighting the supernatural, you better know about the power of the blood of Christ to "plead" against the forces of evil. As for chainsaws, they have been the weapon of choice for many films beginning with *Dark of the Sun* in 1968 and made famous in 1974 with Tobe Hooper's *The Texas Chain Saw Massacre*.

This commercial is a perfect example of neo-Gothicism. It perpetuates motifs, storytelling techniques and devices and horrifying elements from former Gothic tales; suggests heterotopias, relies upon Gothic intertextuality; and then posits contemporary themes, in this case, making a smart choice by switching car insurance. The Gothic elements are extremely relevant for marketing insurance in that most insurance ads convince you that horrible things do happen to ordinary people. Out of fear, you should purchase insurance, for only then can you find shelter under the "umbrella" (like the Travelers insurance). As the Geico clip indicates, when in an emergency, you often make poor decisions, and that is why you need insurance. Since the only feasible escape from horror in the commercial is a car, and not any car, but a *running* car, the message from Geico is that you need to buy its affordable insurance, for it will ensure that your car is always in good condition because you never know when you need to escape from … whatever.

Freud and the Gothic, or is it the Gothic and Freud? Which comes first: his nightmare/our nightmares/our literary expressions of our nightmares in the form of the Gothic and the neo-Gothic followed by psychoanalysis of the nightmare? Or do we, like the literary theorists that we are, create the analysis of Gothicism and then apply it to the nightmare? Either way, William Patrick Day is right: "No discussion of the Gothic can avoid discussing Freud […]. We cannot pretend that the striking parallels between Freud's thought and the Gothic fantasy do not exist" (1985, 177). Hence the reference from 1 Corinthians 13:12 in my chapter's title, "through a glass darkly…," that indicates that there are myriad things of the spirit world that we cannot perceive clearly as long as we are in the flesh.

Actually, Freud preferred the term "anxiety dreams" to "nightmares" (1913 [1899], 33). He thought that we were haunted by horror in our dreams that was caused either by wish-fulfilment (100) or forbidden libidinal impulses. He believed that when the ego experienced anxiety from external or internal threats (17), which were visitations of spectres of the past, in defence and self-protection, it would repress desire, and then when our ego rested and we tried to sleep, those anxieties would generate sleep nightmares (2). We seem to have a compulsion to repeat traumatic events especially in our dreams in an effort to gain mastery over them (Freud 2015 [1920], 26).

Many of the anxieties that individuals experience are the same for everyone: They may be about sex and gender, religion, conflicts in relationships, fear for the future, recurring traumatic manifestation, material provision and the like. When transferred into a Gothic narrative, whether in a book or in some other medium, even if the horrors attached to them are disturbing, readers and viewers have a sense that they can control them in ways they cannot do in their real lives. Kelly Hurley describes Gothic as "a cyclical genre that reemerges in times of cultural stress in order to negotiate anxieties for its readership by working through them in displaced (sometimes supernatural) form" (2003, 194). She also said that the Gothic has been recursive: "cyclically, at periods of cultural stress, to negotiate the anxieties that accompany social and epistemological transformations and crises" (1996, 5).

Certainly, the movie *Groundhog Day* (1993) reflected some anxieties of Phil (the Bill Murray character) that had to be replayed over and over, day after day, until his behaviour, attitude and response to incidents reached some resolution. The movie cannot be considered a Gothic thriller, but the concept of recurring anxieties plaguing our lives and reminding us that we are not in control of what happens to us, coupled with the sense of *déjà vu*, involves Gothic elements. The title itself insinuates the supernatural with the superstitious belief from the Pennsylvania Dutch that in Punxsutawney, Pennsylvania, on February 2, if a groundhog, named Punxsutawney Phil, emerges from his burrow and sees his shadow (because of clear weather), he will be so terrified that he will return to his den, which tells the savvy interpreter of signs that winter will last for another six weeks. However, if February 2 is a cloudy day, he will come out and stay, which portends an early spring.

Gothic and now neo-Gothic are like that: They are the literary nightmares of our lives from which we can never escape by just waking up, closing the book, turning off the computer or television, exiting the theatre or crawling into a hole.

Technically, "Gothicism" and "neo-Gothicism" are parachronistic terms. When Horace Walpole wrote *The Castle of Otranto* in 1764, he subtitled it "A Gothic Story." For most Gothic aficionados, his novel was the birth of Gothicism. He authenticated the story with this provenance:

> The following work was found in the library of an ancient catholic family in the North of England. It was printed at Naples, in the black letter [(Gothic script)], in the year 1529. How much sooner it was written, does not appear. The principal incidents are such as were believed in the darkest ages of Christianity, but the language and conduct have nothing that favours of barbarism. The title is the purest Italian. If the story was written near the time when it is supposed to have happened, it must have been between 1095, the era of the first crusade, and 1243, the date of the last, or not long afterwards. (III)

From the very inception of it as a literary genre, the Gothic has been reflexive, reaching back into history for answers to horrifying situations in the present. Walpole's main title evokes spectres from the past. In the eleventh century, the Latin word "castel" was just beginning to be used to describe the large fortifications being built by William the Conqueror throughout England, Scotland and Ireland. He ordered the building of the Tower of London with its crenellated parapets in 1066. Norman-style castles would become popular locales for Gothic hauntings in the eighteenth century, for, to the Anglo-Saxons in England, the castles conveyed foreign subjugation and a force of military power and strength.[4] That is exactly the reason why the four most well-known Gothic novels of the eighteenth century took place in castles where there were hauntings by powerful, supernatural Medieval ghosts. They would include Horace Walpole's *The Castle of Otranto* (1764), Clara Reeve's *The Old English Baron* (1777), Ann Radcliffe's *The Mysteries of Udolpho* (1794) and Matthew Gregory Lewis' *The Monk: A Romance* (1796). Even if designated as the first Gothic literature, they were not.[5]

The early Goths settled in the Baltic area and then migrated to the Black Sea where they seized Greece and took over Rome in 410 AD because they refused to be assimilated into the Roman Empire (Sowerby 2012, 28–29). Once in Rome, however, the Goths did not remain long. Due to internal fighting, they had no united front to withstand Justinian (483–565), the emperor of Constantinople, which is when the historian Jordanes wrote "for the first time a history of the Goths from the Gothic point of view" in his *Getica* (551) (31). "Gothic is the earliest Germanic language to be written down in full form in manuscript" dating back to the fourth century (Murdoch 2004, 149). Jordanes included the Angles, Saxons and Jutes as "Goths" (Ellis 2000, 22). By the eighth century, "Goth" was a "blanket term for any German tribe" (23).

Chaucer and Shakespeare both regarded the Goths as "barbarous" in that they brought down the Roman Empire, which, in their day, was considered the "greatest civilization the world had ever known" (22–23). However, the term "Gothic" first appeared in the seventeenth century in the reading of Bede, translating "Jute," "Eota" and "Geata" as Goth (Kliger 1952, 15). Samuel Johnson's dictionary of 1775 defines "Goth" as "one not civilized, one deficient in general knowledge, a barbarian" (quoted in Ellis 2000, 23). Likewise, Montague Summers writes that "Gothic" implies "barbarous, tramontane, and antique" (1964, 37). To Fred Botting, certainly the undisputed expert on Gothicism, the Medieval represented in those Gothic stories was a derogatory expression for "barbarity and superstition" and criticism of "extravagant fancies and natural wildness" (1996, 22). Even into the modern age, the *Oxford English Dictionary* reminds us that the Gothic is "mediæval, [and/or] 'romantic,' as opposed to classical," sometimes "barbarous, rude, uncouth, unpolished, in bad taste" as it runs amuck in the arts.

Therefore, as early as the sixth and eighth centuries, the term "Gothic" was being reinvented and redefined and could at that time be rebranded as "neo-Gothic." At first "Gothic" did refer to a geographically defined nationality of people until the early seventeenth century, and then it primarily referred to a type of architecture and to a blackletter script used in Western Europe from the twelfth through the seventeenth centuries (Dowding 1962, 5). According to the *Oxford English Dictionary*, Lord Shaftesbury was the first to use the term in reference to any literature, and that was in 1710, with this statement: "[The Elizabethan dramatists] have withal been the first of Europeans, who since the Gothick Model of Poetry, attempted to throw off the horrid Discord of jingling Rhyme" (quoted in *OED*, 3.a).

Botting theorises that it was the Enlightenment that invented the Gothic. With the period's own "reinvention" of the classics from antiquity, the Gothic was considered as something "derogatory" for its lack of reason. However, in a reaction to the dehumanising effects of industrialisation, readers nostalgically reached back to Medievalism for its code of chivalry. Gothic's mysticism signaled the anxieties of the budding stage of modernism (2012, 3). The specific anxieties Botting lists are in full swing today if not more so: "political revolution, industrialisation, urbanisation, shifts in sexual and domestic organisation, and scientific discovery" (1996, 3). In particular, the fantasies in Gothic literature "express some of the debilitating psychological effects of inhabiting a materialistic culture. They are peculiarly violent and horrific" (Jackson 1981, 4).

One of the reasons that Gothic fiction became so popular in the eighteenth century, according to Robert Geary, is a backlash to the "'enthusiastic' excesses of the Dissenters and to the supposed mystifications of Catholics" (1992, 103). By the nineteenth century, however, the Victorians wanted "assurance of the other world" (104), and therefore the Gothic "became a vehicle not only for entertainment but also the expression of the uneasy fluctuations of belief on the part of a cognitive minority no longer content with the Christian supernatural yet appalled by the new scientism whose presuppositions they sought to reject or soften" (105).

Botting further characterises Gothic writing as "excess" and describes its appearance "in the awful obscurity of that haunted eighteenth century rationality and morality" (1996, 1), contrasting with the "despairing ecstasies of Romantic idealism and individualism" and then much later to "Victorian realism and decadence" (1). Gothic characters "shadow the progress of modernity with counternarratives displaying the underside of enlightenment and humanist values" (2); Gothicism reflects a "fascination with transgression and the anxiety over cultural limits and boundaries" exhibiting "ambivalent emotions and meanings in their tales of darkness, desire and power" (2). These last listed elements from his seminal work *Gothic* (1996) could as accurately describe the twenty-first century books and films that we are now calling neo-Gothic.

In 1797 a writer complained that it was the fashion to produce novels that "make *terror* the *Order of the day*, by confining the heroes and heroines in old gloomy castles, full of spectres, apparitions, ghosts, and dead men's bones" ("Terrorist" 1802 [1797], 227; emphasis in original). The title of his essay is "Terrorist Novel Writing," when terrorism meant something different in the eighteenth and nineteenth centuries than it does today. The terror of the early Gothic was what Elisabeth MacAndrew coins as "pleasing terror" (1979, 40) or "pleasurable astonishment" (44). The terrorists that terrify today are very real people who indiscriminately kill innocent people for a political/religious cause, and there is nothing "pleasing" about it. The same can be said about school shooters and other psychopaths.

Here is a suggested recipe for "Terrorist Novel Writing," which the writer considers to be the "distorted ideas of lunatics":

> *Take*—an old castle, half of it ruinous.
>   A long gallery, with a great many doors, some secret ones.
>   Three murdered bodies, quite fresh.
>   As many skeletons, in chests and presses.
>   An old woman hanging by the neck, with her throat cut.
>   Assassins and desperados, *quant. suff.*
>   Noices, whispers, and groans, threescore at least.
> Mix them together, in the form of three volumes, to be taken at any of
>   the watering-places before going to bed. ("Terrorist" 229; emphasis
>   in original)

The author of the essay simply signed off with The "Probatum est," which is a legal term that means "It is proven." In case you are not up on your Latin, "Quant. suff." inside the recipe, in reference to the "assassins and desperados," is a pharmacological term used to refer to the last ingredient in the make-up of a prescription. The full phrase is "*quantum sufficit*" or "as much as is required," a guiding principle still for Gothic tales, although three is still considered the spiritual number of completeness. In neo-Gothic pieces, there will be murder and frequent suicides, mysterious noises and most definitely groans.

By 1818 when Mary Shelley wrote *Frankenstein*, readers relaxed somewhat in their anxieties about scientific advancement and technological innovations, but this was still prior to Charles Darwin's publications that made evolution a household word and challenged a literal reading of the creation story in the Bible. It was before an influx of sensational novels that would focus on Victorian crime that provided "Darwinian evidence of a brutish past" (Tropp 1990, 8). Martin Tropp identifies *Frankenstein* as a new form of Gothicism, one that expresses an "exhilaration at what ingenuity could accomplish and fear of what it might destroy" (8).

In his *The Fantastic and European Gothic*, Matthew Gibson argues that the emergence of the Gothic in the early nineteenth century was a conscious, deliberate act of the French, after the fall of Napoleon in 1815, to reject the classic—or what was associated with the upper class. Called "le 'Romantism,'" this movement blended the fruits of the German *Sturm und Drang* movement of Schiller and Goethe with the *couleur locale*, picaresque adventure and 'merveilleux' provided by writers such as Scott, Byron, Lewis and Maturin (Coleridge, Shelley and Wordsworth were not remotely considered by French critics until many decades later)" (2013, 1). It departed from the conventions of "unities of time, space and action" and "stretched the boundaries of the imagination." Predominantly applied to novels and sometimes known as *frénétique* and *fantastique*, the British termed it Gothic (2).

In her analysis of Shelley's *Frankenstein* and *The Last Man* (1826), Rosemary Jackson describes Gothic fantasies in terms that seem more descriptive of contemporary Gothicism when she says that it "acts out subversive desires" (1981, 96), but also conveys an "absolute negation or dissolution of cultural order" and "no faith in improvement of social conditions" (99). Another phrase of similar importance not only to Shelley's Gothicism but to neo-Gothicism is quite postmodern, and that is the "loss of absolute meaning" (101).

The Victorians reinvented Gothicism again, with similar "innovations in Gothic" that Charlotte Brontë furnishes in *Jane Eyre* (1847) and *Villette* (1853). Although she perpetuates Gothic motifs designed to evoke fear with the mysterious burning of Rochester's bed, for example, she then infuses her story with what Robert Heilman calls the "new Gothic" (1991, 50) and "anti-Gothic," exemplified, he says, by comedy, which he supports by referring to the evening when Mrs. Rochester's blood-curdling scream disturbs the sleep of Rochester's party in chapter 20 (43). This is when "a savage, a sharp, a shrilly sound" is heard "from end to end of Thornfield Hall" (Brontë 1864 [1847], 216). Ironically, Colonel Dent cries, "Where the devil is Rochester?" When he does arrive on the scene, he is "attacked" by the Misses Easton who all but strangle him in terror as if they were in a Gothic novel, "and the two dowagers, in vast white wrappers, were bearing down on him like ships in full sail" (217). Except for the parodies and mockery in Jane Austen's *Northanger Abbey* (1817), the horror in the earlier Gothic tales was nothing to laugh about.

By the end of the nineteenth century, the horror publications of Stoker, Stevenson, Wells and Wilde form what David Punter (another Gothic expert) considers to be a "Gothic Renaissance" (2012, 1). Since then Gothicism and more recently neo-Gothicism have become synonymous with non-conformity and anti-status quo. In *The Rise of the Gothic Novel*, Maggie Kilgour surmises that Gothic writing is a "rebellion against a constraining neoclassical aesthetic ideal of order and unity, in order to recover a suppressed primitive and barbaric imaginative freedom" (1995, 3). Gothicism and neo-Gothicism are subversive challenges to the societal norms of the day with tales that have been horrifying to some and delightful to others.

The Gothic had a new medium (pun intended) with celluloid followed by television. The first horror film was *Le Manoir du Diable* (1896) by Georges Méliès. Drawing from J. M. Loaisel-Tréogate's novel *Le Château du Diable* (1802), it employed many of the traditional Gothic conventions like a haunted house and witches, but it also specified that the primary supernatural presence involved demons (Jones 2018, 3). The first *Dracula* movie appeared in 1931. Based, of course, on the 1897 Stoker novel but also on the 1924 stage play of the same name by Hamilton Deane and John L. Balderston, the movie was directed by Tod Browning and introduced to the world the consummate representation of the Gothic incarnate, Béla Lugosi.

In 1934 Lugosi would be paired with the famous Gothic actor Boris Karloff, and again in 1941 with that other famous Gothic actor Basil Rathbone in two movies titled *The Black Cat*, based on Edgar Allan Poe's short story by the same name (1843). In Poe's account, an alcoholic gouges out the eye of his pet black cat, Pluto, and later hangs the poor cat. That night, his house burns down with a single wall left standing. On it is the apparition of a cat with a rope around its neck. The man adopts another black cat, and later, in a drunken rage, tries to kill the cat but accidently kills his wife instead. In his new home, he conceals her body in a wall in the cellar. When the police arrive to investigate, they hear a loud wail emitting from the wall. When they tear into the wall, they find, sitting on the wife's rotting head, the screaming black cat. His story would be adapted dozens of times for the screen and for radio programs.

As for *Dracula*, a search in www.imdb.com (the Internet Movie Database) results in 352 hits, that is, over 352 movies have been made that feature vampires. As far as people being immured in the wall is concerned, this is a standard Gothic convention that began perhaps with Sophocles' play *Antigone*, when Antigone is to be immured in a cave. The very word "immurement" comes from the Latin that means "walling in." In the first centuries of Christianity, there were anchorites who allowed themselves to be immured in tombs as a form of severe asceticism. Archaeologists and other have found skeletons in walls, immured during the Middle Ages—some voluntarily so and others not. It apparently was one way of dealing with rogue nuns and was called *vade in pacem*, which translated means "Go *into* peace" instead of "Go in peace" (Lea 1887, 444 and n488).

There have been countless Gothic tales of wall immurements, such as the fate of the nun Clara de Clare in Sir Walter Scott's *Marmion* (1808) and an abbot accused of witchcraft in William Harrison Ainsworth's *The Lancashire Witches* (1848) based on the most famous witch trials in Lancashire in 1612. It has also found its way into opera, as in Giuseppe Verdi's *Aida* (1871). The convention has continued into neo-Gothic narratives like *The Legend of the Seventh Virgin* in 1965, written by Eleanor Alice Hibbert, who used the pseudonym of Victoria Holt when writing her Gothic romances.[6] Looking to the past, the novel tells of when a nun led six novices into breaking their vows of chastity; she was walled up—a horror story—but when six novices leave the abbey and dance of joy in a meadow, thinking that they have been spared, supernaturally they are punished by being turned into stone. The horror story then becomes neo-Gothic. In the present, a woman, Kerensa, is forced into a marriage that she does not want. When she gives birth, she thinks, "The agony of the walled-up nun could not have been greater than mine" (quoted in Wallace 2013, 155 from Holt 1965, 161). Diana Wallace discusses several novels with this theme and concludes, "Historically, these texts repeatedly insist, women *have* been locked up, entombed alive, incarcerated in lunatic asylums, and thus the protagonist is justified in her fears (2013, 155; emphasis in original). Such texts give a warning to female readers that marriage is dangerous and should be taken seriously (Anolik 2016, 95)

The 2009 film of *The Haunting in Connecticut*, based on a true story, also is about corpses in the wall but is not just about a serial murderer. A family moves into a house that had once been a funeral home run by one Ramsey Aickman, who was also a spiritualist who practiced necromancy (communication with the dead). There is plenty of the supernatural, including the emitting of ectoplasm. This term refers to the expelling through the mouth of some medium of some physical manifestation that allows the spiritual to take a physical shape.[7]

Such hauntings from the wall have not been reserved just for books, movies and television; the Canadian punk band SNFU put out an album titled *And No One Else Wanted to Play* in 1985, which included the song "Bodies in the Wall" about screams from the dead buried in a wall of a house.

The neo-Gothic continues to be more popular today than ever before. It has increased opportunities to be expressed than ever before, through books, film, television, games, the internet and still other global media. Take, for example, *Goth Girl* (2009–12), a comedy-drama, written and directed by Nick Griffo, that was streamed only on the internet and geared mostly to a teen audience. Selena calls herself an "Internet blogging Gothic Goddess" (quoted in Terrace 2015, 85, from Griffo). She believes that her parents hate her and had her just "so they could come home and make someone as miserable as they are" (quoted in 85, from Griffo). She has immersed herself in Gothicism, dreaming that a "dashing gentleman" will come to her rescue, and she would prefer that he be a vampire and that they "would sleep all day and go out at night and feed upon all the cheerleaders at [her] school" (quoted in 85). The "Goth Girl" is a teen who "desperately trying to discover who she is in a world she feels she does not truly belong" (quoted in 84). She is not alone. The title of this chapter, "through a glass darkly" is taken from the Bible (1 Cor. 13:12) reminding us that as long as we live in this world, we lack understanding of those spiritual things that will become clearer to us in the next world.

Notes

1 There are several horror movies in which teenagers are being chased by the paranormal through woods, with the first coming to mind being *The Blair Witch Project* (1999). Others that have haunted forests or creepy creatures in forests are *What Keeps You Alive* (2018), *The Witness* (2017), *The Ritual* (2017), *Always Shine* (2016), *The Monster* (2016), *The Hallow* (2015), *The Witch* (2015), *Mama* (2010), *The Strangers* (2008) and *The Evil Dead* (1979). The Gothicism of haunted woods reaches far back in Western European and North American histories. There were the horror fairy tales that emerged out of Germany's Black Forest. In early British history, many of the forests were considered haunted after habitation by druids and other Celts. In early American history, there is the headless horseman that terrifies Sleepy Hallow.

2 In the 1965 series *Lost in Space*, a robot often gives this warning to Will, the youngest child of the Robinson clan, who constantly seems to get into trouble. It became a popular catch phrase in the 1960s.

3 The "Jason" character is played by David Figlioli from dozens of murder films, including six episodes of the TV series *Murder in the First* (2014–15). He, like Cregan Dow (the "Are you crazy" dude), acted in *Castle* (2009). Aaron Jennings, who suggested the attic, played in two episodes of *The Magicians* (2020) and in *NCIS* (2017). The stereotyped blonde is Carrie Wita, who appeared in *Bones* (2013), *The Mentalist* (2012), *NCIS* (2011) and *The Protector* (2011). The brunette Cali Fredrichs was in *Escape Room* (2017), *CSI* (2015) and the *Psycho Hillbilly Cabin Massacre!* (2007).

4 See Robbert Liddiard's introduction to *Anglo-Norman Castles* (2003). He credits J. H. Round (1912, 144–59) and Ella S. Armitage (1912) for this theory (6).

5 For a history of the Goths and their writing, see Herwig Wolfram (1988 [1979]).

6 By the time of her death, Hibbert had penned over two hundred books that sold more than one hundred million copies that were translated into 20 languages (Lambert 1993).

7 Jan Dirk Blom lists this term in *A Dictionary of Hallucinations* and attempts to discredit its supernatural existence (2010, 168–69).

Bibliography

Anolik, Ruth Biestock, ed. "Introduction: Sexual Horrors—Fears of the Sexual Other." In *Horrifying Sex: Essays on Sexual Difference in Gothic Literature*, 1–24. Jefferson, NC: McFarland, 2007.

———. *Property and Power in English Gothic Literature*. Jefferson, NC: McFarland, 2016.

Armitage, Ella S. *The Early Norman Castles of the British Isles*. London: John Murray, 1912. https://books.google.com/books?id=AnVNAAAAMAAJ.

Austen, Jane. *Northanger Abbey*, vol. 1. London: John Murray, 1818. https://books.google.com/books?id=UC8JAAAAQAAJ.

Barnes, Mike. "*Empire Strikes Back, Airplane* Among 25 Movies Named to National Film Registry." *Hollywood Reporter*, December 28, 2010. https://www.hollywoodreporter.com/news/empire-strikes-airplane-25-movies-65915.

Blom, Jan Dirk. *A Dictionary of Hallucinations*. New York: Springer, 2010.

Botting, Fred. *Gothic*. London: Routledge, 1996.

———. "In Gothic Darkly: Heterotopia, History, and Culture." In *A New Companion to the Gothic*, edited by David Punter, 13–24. West Sussex, UK: Wiley Blackwell, 2012.

Brontë, Charlotte. *Jane Eyre*. 1847. New York: Carleton, 1864. https://books.google.com/books?id=lSMGAAAAQAAJ.

Day, William Patrick. *In the Circles of Fear and Desire: A Study of Gothic Fantasy*. Chicago: University of Chicago Press, 1985.

Dowding, Geoffrey. *An Introduction to the History of Printing Types; an Illustrated Summary of Main Stages in the Development of Type Design from 1440 up to the Present Day: An Aid to Type Face Identification*. London: Wace, 1962.

Ellis, Markman. *The History of Gothic Fiction*. Edinburgh: Edinburgh University Press, 2000.

Evil. 2019. https://www.cbs.com/shows/evil/.

Freud, Sigmund. *The Interpretation of Dreams*. 1899. Translated by A. A. Brill. 3rd ed. New York: The Macmillan Company 1913.

———. *Beyond the Pleasure Principle*. 1920. Translated by James Strachy. Edited by Jim Miller. Mineola, NY: Dover Publications, 2015.

Geary, Robert F. *The Supernatural in Gothic Fiction: Horror, Belief and Literary Change*. Lewiston, NY: Edwin Miller Press, 1992.

Gibson, Matthew. *The Fantastic and European Gothic: History, Literature and the French Revolution*. Cardiff: The University of Wales Press, 2013.

"Gothic, adj. and n." OED online. September 2019. Oxford University Press. https://www-oed-com.ezproxy.liberty.edu/view/Entry/80225?redirectedFrom=Gothic.

Griffo, Nick, writer and director. *Goth Girl*. www.watchgothgirl.com. 2009–12.

Heilman, Robert. "Innovations in Gothic: Charlotte Brontë." In *The Workings of Fiction: Essays by Robert Bechtold Heilman*, 41–54. Columbia: University of Missouri Press, 1991.

Holt, Victoria. *The Legend of the Seventh Virgin*. Leicester: Ulverscroft, 1965.

Hurd, Richard. *Letters on Chivalry and Romance*. Cambridge, UK: W. Thurlbourn and J. Woodyer, 1762. https://books.google.com/books?id=jUgJAAAAQAAJ.

Hurley, Kelly. *The Gothic Body: Sexuality, Materialism, and Degeneration at the "Fin de Siècle."* Cambridge, UK: Cambridge University Press, 1996.

———. "British Gothic Fiction: 1885–1930." In *A Cambridge Companion to Gothic Fiction*, edited by Jerrold E. Hogle, 189–207. Cambridge, UK: Cambridge University Press, 2003.

Jackson, Rosemary. *Fantasy: The Literature of Subversion*. London: Methuen, 1981.

Jones, David Annwn. *Re-envisaging the First Age of Cinematic Horror, 1896–1934: Quanta of Fear*. Cardiff: University of Wales Press, 2018.

Kilgour, Maggie. *The Rise of the Gothic Novel*. London: Routledge, 1995.

Kliger, Samuel. *The Goths in England*. New York: Octagon Books, 1952.

Lambert, Bruce. "Eleanor Hibbert, Novelist Known as Victoria Holt and Jean Plaidy." *The New York Times*, January 21, 1993. https://www.nytimes.com/1993/01/21/books/eleanor-hibbert-novelist-known-as-victoria-holt-and-jean-plaidy.html.

Lea, Henry Charles. *A History of the Inquisition of the Middle Ages*, vol. 1. New York: Harper and Brothers, 1887. http://www.gutenberg.org/files/39451/39451-h/39451-h.htm#FNanchor_444_444.

Liddiard, Robert. Introduction to *Anglo-Norman Castles*, 1–22. Suffolk: St Edmundsbury Press, 2003.

MacAndrew, Elizabeth. *The Gothic Tradition in Fiction*. New York: Columbia University Press, 1979.

Murdoch, Brian. "Gothic." In *Early Germanic Literature and Culture*, edited by William Whobrey et al., 149–71. Rochester, NY: Camden House, 2004.

"Poltergeist-Film Series." *ListArticle*. 2018. https://www.listarticle.com/page/en/Poltergeist_(film_series).

Punter, David. "Introduction: A Ghost of a Story." In *A New Companion to the Gothic*, edited by David Punter, 1–10. Oxford, UK: Wiley Blackwell, 2012.

Round, J. H. "The Castles of the Conquest." *Archaeologia* 58 (1912): 144–59.

Sowerby, Robin. "The Goths in History and Pre-Gothic Gothic." In *A New Companion to the Gothic*, edited by David Punter, 25–38. Oxford, UK: Wiley Blackwell, 2012.

Stoker, Bram. *Dracula*. New York: Grosset and Dunlap, 1897. https://books.google.com/books?id=T1VDAQAAMAAJ.

Summers, Montague. *The Gothic Quest: A History of the Gothic Novel*. New York: Russell and Russell, 1964.

Terrace, Vincent. "*Goth Girl*." In *Internet Drama and Mystery Television Series, 1996–2014*, 84–86. Jefferson, NC: McFarland, 2015.

"Terrorist Novel Writing." In *The Spirit of the Pubic Journals for 1797*, vol. 1, edited by Stephen Jones and Charles Molloy Westmacott, 227–29. London: Kames Ridgway, 1802. https://books.google.com/books?id=p794qMLwkcYC.

Tropp, Martin. *Images of Fear: How Horror Stories Helped Shape Modern Culture (1818–1918)*. Jefferson, NC: McFarland, 1990.

Wallace, Diana. *Female Gothic Histories: Gender, Histories and the Gothic*. Cardiff: The University of Wales Press, 2013.

Walpole, Horace. *The Castle of Otranto: A Gothic Story*. 1764. Berlin: Christ: Fred: Himbourg, 1794. https://books.google.com/books?id=YZkLAAAAIAAJ.

Wolfram, Herwig. *History of the Goths*. 1979. Translated by Thomas J. Dunlap. Berkeley: University of California Press, 1988.

Chapter Two

DARK DESCEN(DEN)TS: NEO-GOTHIC MONSTROSITY AND THE WOMEN OF *FRANKENSTEIN*

Sarah E. Maier

But you, my other creature, my creature of Otherness,

Those whom so many call "monster,"

Perhaps there is still some salvation to be had from you, […]

Something of the prodigal,

now,

to me, in dream,

returning. (Punter 2018, 328)

In November of 1818, Mary Wollstonecraft (née Godwin) Shelley unleashed her creature into culture; for 200 years, there have been endless attempts to understand, adapt, film and theorise *Frankenstein* (1818).[1] This was not a "hideous progeny" (Shelley 1831, xii) easily birthed. It was the product of "a young girl" who "came to think of, and to dilate upon, so very hideous an idea" (v) that her ability to be its parent was immediately questioned.[2] Refuting assumptions that Percy Bysshe Shelley was its author, Mary Shelley asserted her writerly lineage that as "the daughter of two persons of distinguished literary celebrity" (v)—Mary Wollstonecraft and William Godwin—she was, indeed, an authoress proud of her "hideous phantom" (x).[3] Mary Shelley's declared intention was to write a story "which would speak to the mysterious fears of our nature, and awaken thrilling horror—one to make the reader dread to look round, to curdle the blood, and quicken the beatings of the heart" (ix). She remained connected to "the spectre which had haunted [her] midnight pillow" (xi) much like twenty-first century culture cannot shake her mythic character.

The assumption of most contemporary invocations of *Frankenstein* leave an obfuscation between Dr. Victor Frankenstein and "the thing" or "wretch" (Shelley 1999 [1818], 84–85) or "the filthy daemon to whom [he] had given life," who watched him from "the gloom" (103). Much has been written about how Frankenstein "saw the dull yellow eye of the creature open; it breathed hard and a convulsive motion agitated its arms" at the same time as he comprehends the "catastrophe" (85) he has created bonded in misery, and the two male characters of the novel occupy much of the imaginative and intellectual consideration of Shelley's novel. This idea of their interchangeability is certainly nowhere more apparent than in Danny Boyle's 2011 stage production of Nick Dear's adaptation of *Frankenstein* with Jonny Lee Miller and Benedict Cumberbatch alternately starring as Dr. Frankenstein and/or his creature. The ongoing focus on the masculine presences in the novel leaves room for consideration of the oft-ignored women of the text; Mary Jacobus once queried, "Is There a Woman in This Text?" (1982, 117).

Indeed, there are. While one obvious man-made female absence is due to Frankenstein's destruction of his female creature, there are three women—Lady Caroline, Elizabeth and Justine—whose importance is not belied by their seemingly marginalised presence. In addition, the central woman of the text, Mary Godwin Shelley, is recreated in the reanimating impulses of the literary biographies (biographies of literary persons), biofictions (fictional reconstructions of a literary life) and biomythographies (mythic representations of an author's life) that obscure Mary Shelley before and with her creation(s). Such narratives are tempting because the "prospect of gaining some insight into the mysteries of the artistic process is seductive […] one greatly enhanced by the biographer's [as well as biofiction writer's] and the subject's shared medium of words, their common interest in literary forms, and the particular closeness of fictional and historical narrative" (2). Shelley's own story is embodied in the biofictional reincarnations that follow the neo-Gothic development of reclaiming voice and space in the centrality of her own narrative rather than a liminal figure. This is not a consideration of Shelley's self-writings from her existing documents although they are included, at times and in various ways, in the fictional narratives that follow. These are the women for whom neo-Gothic fictional and biofictional narratives provide a voice.[4]

The Gothic "is frequently considered to be a genre that re-emerges with particular force during times of cultural crisis and which serves to negotiate the anxieties of the age by working through them in a displaced form" (Punter and Byron 2004, 39). Rosario Arias and Patricia Pulham consider the spectral in neo-Victorian fiction and how it "represents a 'double' of the Victorian text" (2010, xv); in like fashion, the Gothic text is reanimated in a double of sorts to reveal the female presence that was liminal in Shelley's text to become neo-Gothic narratives. Here, the unknown aspects of these women's character(s) see them resurrected in a form of neo-Gothic manifestation that disrupts our nostalgic visions of the past—narratives reopen, fragments are gathered and lives of fully dimensional female characters are stitched together into narratives that elucidate aspects previously forgotten or left unconsidered. In the first case, Kiersten White's *The Dark Descent of Elizabeth Frankenstein* (2018) and Theodore Roszak's *The Memoirs of Elizabeth Frankenstein* (1995) consider Lady Caroline and Elizabeth Lavenza as two women with exceptional beliefs, while in the second, Lita Judge's *Mary's Monster* (2018) explores Mary Shelley's character(s)—her own and that of her creature. In these texts, the female characters, and Mary as a character, are moved to the centre of the narratives; no longer passive victims in these neo-Gothic narratives, Lady Caroline, Elizabeth Lavenza, Justine Moritz and Shelley are reanimated as women who are displaced from their original narratives into texts created 200 years into their futures. This move defamiliarises our preconceptions of them to allow for an investigation of their significance that moves even beyond what was possible for these motherless daughters.

Chris Baldick has said that Frankenstein and his monster enjoy a status which appears to literary criticism as an anomaly, a scandal because it is a modern myth (1987, 1); such a collapse between the novel, the scandal and the myth are further disrupted when, perhaps, the scandal becomes the women—both real and fictional. In Shelley's *Frankenstein*, the early descriptions provide portraits of women who are paradoxically traditional and unconventional in presentation. Caroline Beaufort is "possessed a mind of an uncommon mould [*sic*]; and her courage rose to support her in her adversity" (Shelley 1999 [1818], 64). When her father dies, she marries Victor's father and gives birth to three children while welcoming her motherless niece, Elizabeth Lavenza, into the family. Elizabeth becomes Victor's playfellow who sees that her "imagination was luxuriant, yet her capability of application was great. Her person was the image of her mind" (65). Their differences are apparent, split along the oppositions of Enlightenment thinking where Victor "delighted in investigating the facts relative to the actual world; [Elizabeth] busied herself in following the aerial creations of the poets" while the world was "to her it was a vacancy, which she sought to people with imaginations of her own" (66). Justine Moritz, after being rescued from her mother who "treated her very ill," joins the family and learned the duties of a servant; she is neither kept down by "the idea of ignorance" nor was she expected to "sacrifice [...] the dignity of a human being" (92). Lady Caroline educates both girls and it results in strong relationships with their "protectress" (93). At age 13, Elizabeth becomes ill and Lady Caroline cares for her; the daughter survives, but the mother succumbs to the fever and dies "calmly" (72). Barely into the narrative, the mother figure's 17-year guidance of her children is over, and Elizabeth steps into her role "determined to fulfil her duties [...] continually endeavouring to contribute to the happiness of others, entirely forgetful of herself" (73).

Although Shelley further develops some aspects of Elizabeth and Justine, Lady Caroline's narrative is at an end, an unusual, thought-provoking turn in a novel by a woman. As much as the central philosophical, moral and ethical aspects of the novel have been explored as products of Shelley's historical context, there are some readers who do pause to consider possible biographies or autobiographies for the women characters. Neo-Gothic texts, while respecting their Ur-text, concentrate on images of birth, conventional femininity, male arrogance and scientific progress to interrogate the past representation of the women of Frankenstein through a lens of radical, natural and intellectual feminism to give those women a voice, consider their life stories as well as the nature of girlhood, the idea of maternal strength, the need for generational support, the overwhelming nature of grief and the strength of woman once unbound from convention.

The Dark Descent of Elizabeth Frankenstein begins by evoking both the Romantic pathetic fallacy and the trope of mournful Gothic imagery that begins the writing of the novel and the immediate atmospheric conditions best suited to any revisioning of *Frankenstein*. History tells us Byron's challenge to write a story was laid down during the summer of 1816 at Villa Diodati where "it proved to be a wet, ungenial summer, and incessant rain often confined [the group] for days to the house" after which Shelley begins to write,

"*It was on a dreary night of November*" (1831, xi; emphasis in original), so White begins her neo-Gothic retelling with "Lightning clawed across the sky, tracing veins through the clouds and marking the pulse of the universe itself" (3). In her version of the storm, Elizabeth's first-person narrative expands the events of Shelley's text. Elizabeth and Justine open the story as they travel; Elizabeth's initial observations of how she feels a strong kinship with Justine, commenting that "it was so odd that our separate origins—similar in cruelty, though differing in duration—had had such opposite outcomes. Justine was the most open and loving and genuinely good person I had ever known. And I was—Well. Not like her" (White 2018, 5). The trials and tribulations of the women are moved into the foreground of this neo-Gothic narrative that seeks to raise the women's voices and perspectives, rather than leaving them as unformed presences of their Gothic tale of origin.

It is in the "vitality" of such stories, their potentialities, "their capacity for change, their adaptability and openness to new combinations of meaning" (Baldick 1987, 4) that make these rewritings so powerful as a cultural metaphor. While the female Gothic of Ann Radcliffe characteristically contained a woman, both victim and heroine, Shelley's novel "brought a new sophistication to literary tenor, and it did so without a heroine, without even an important female victim" (Moers 1974, 24). This paradoxical vacuum is the narrative space that these neo-Gothic novels seek to explore, to revision the text from a modern cultural and social perspective, and "in the act of looking back, of seeing with fresh eyes, of entering an old text from a new critical direction" (Rich 1972, 18).

The Dark Descent of Elizabeth Frankenstein provides a narrative of a possible life of Elizabeth before and when she comes to the Frankenstein family. The reader learns that Elizabeth's birth parallels Shelley's own traumatic entry into the world when an abusive woman tells Elizabeth that it would be "better for you to have died at your birth along with your mother than to be left here with me. Selfish in life, selfish in death" (6). In many critical readings of *Frankenstein*, there is a wise reminder of Shelley's own strong "identification with her mother's memory" (Baldick 1987, 38) and the potential for reading Shelley herself as "The Monster's Mother" (Moers 1974, 24). Maternity and motherhood are fraught with guilt. Moers argues persuasively that one of the "most interesting, most powerful and most feminine" (93) aspects of the novel is "in the motif of revulsion against newborn life, and the trauma of guilt, dread, and flight surrounding birth and its consequences" causing the text to be "distinctly a woman's mythmaking" because of the "trauma of the afterbirth" (25). This novel has much of Elizabeth's descent formed by her own guilt over being the cause of her mother's death. Emotionally haunted by an early shadow cast by the death of her own mother, Elizabeth is then saved by a woman, Madame Frankenstein, who asks if she could be "Victor's special friend" (White 2018, 7) at the same time as they walk towards a holiday villa where Elizabeth believes she had lived before. Elizabeth is now existing in echo, a reverberation of who her mother might have been, who she was before her mother's death and who she understood she must be "to make him like me" (9) for her own future security. While recounting these moments of coming to the family Frankenstein with a false cloud of nostalgia to soften her story for the younger girl, Justine, Elizabeth is now a young woman who understands that "words and stories were tools to elicit the desired reactions in others, and [she] was an expert craftswoman" (11). Recognising her place is in, but not yet of, the family—"I lived with the Frankensteins. I was not one. And I never forgot it" (25)—she "*needed* Victor. And that little girl who had done what was necessary to secure his heart would still do whatever it took to keep it" (11; emphasis added). Elizabeth is keenly aware that her tenuous position in society can only be solidified by their eventual marriage.[5] No longer the passive Gothic heroine to be preyed upon by Frankenstein and/or his creature, Elizabeth asserts her agency and uses it on behalf of a young woman, Justine.

During her flashbacks demarcated in the text by italicised passages, like letters slipped intermittently between the pages of the ongoing narrative, the reader learns that Elizabeth rescues Justine from cruel circumstances. She heard the screaming of a girl child; Elizabeth's instant reaction is to run towards the girl acknowledging to the reader her dual nature, that "*in that moment, I was no longer seeing the woman in front of me. I was seeing another hateful woman with a cruel tongue and crueler fists. With a blinding flash of anger, I leapt in front of her, taking the blow on my own shoulder* [...] *I raised my chin defiantly*" (18; emphasis in original). Clearly suffering from what are now known as symptoms of post-traumatic stress disorder, both young women lean against the wall, "*breathing heavily* [...] *our breaths and hearts racing like the rabbits we were on the inside: always watchful, always afraid of attack*" (19; emphasis in original) by the monsters whom they know. These neo-Gothic narratives reflect on Elizabeth and Justine's previous fictional context; Carol Davison agrees, like Ellen Moers, that *Frankenstein* provides a "mother text" that can be used as a "refracting lens through which to interrogate established cultural stereotypes and power politics relating to gender roles and relations" clearly; one of the concerns here is the "domestic impact of patriarchal monster-makers" (2018, 180–81) who remain unchallenged thus leading to the social ostracism of abused women. As a motherless daughter, a social outcast and a mother, Shelley has a keen awareness of the other potential stories surrounding a victim than those written for social approval, but White writes them into the foreground of her twenty-first century text.

Elizabeth knows how to use her woman's knowledge. Often the object of appreciation in the eyes of men, Elizabeth silently elucidates the power it bestows on a woman; she says, "I, however, was perfectly aware of my beauty. I considered it a skill" with a "language of its own, in a way; one that translated well in different circumstances" (27) just as "*clothes were part of the role I played. And I never stepped out of character where they could see me*" (30; emphasis in original). Again, rather than assume the role of passive victim, White's non-passive, convention-challenging Elizabeth learns to masquerade, using her femininity as a performance,[6] an act of "female power through pretended and staged weakness" to enact what Diane Long Hoeveler called "gothic feminism" (1998, 7). In a deviation from Shelley's character, White's Elizabeth uses her intellect to protect Frankenstein and, by extension the family name that will give her security from scandal, by challenging factual narratives with fictional constructions. For example, when Frankenstein cuts open his little brother's arm in morbid fascination and scientific detachment to see how veins work, she creates an alternate forensic *tableaux* at the crime scene which she hopes will convince the family of her version of events. Elizabeth must control Frankenstein and, if necessary, be expendable should he act out his "intensely obsessive" (51) behaviour upon her. Elizabeth glimpses the potential monstrosity of a burgeoning scientist, a vivi-sectionist male without compassion for the rules of nature.

Frankenstein declares his reciprocal loyalty to Elizabeth in a way that is much closer to the truth than he fathoms; he tells her, "You began existing the day we met. You are my Elizabeth, and that is all that matters" (117). While seemingly in a position of male heroic Gothic protection over a victimised Elizabeth, White subverts tradition; with his brain fevers and fainting, Frankenstein is feminised because he is ruled by his hysterical emotions[7] while Elizabeth's intellectual curiosity and strength lead her to become the version of Elizabeth he sees. When opportunity presents itself to advance his education, Elizabeth encourages Frankenstein's studies with Henri Clerval so she too might "absorb the knowledge" through "sheer force of will" (41). Significantly, in a reoccurring sensual observation throughout her narration, Elizabeth makes it clear that her favourite scent is a mixture of paper, ink and leather, all components of books and/or the study of a scholar, none of which are traditionally associated with desirable femininity.

Neither is revenge. William dies; Justine is jailed and hanged; Elizabeth declares she seeks revenge and will kill the creature to protect her own future. She "dressed in all white […] my uniform. My costume, as Victor's Elizabeth" (181) but supplements her arsenal with her own funds, "my own set of pistols, and my widow's clothing" (187) when Frankenstein threatens to duplicate his work with the resurrection of Justine. She sets herself up as "both bait and poison" (212). The reader ponders Frankenstein's possible secret; in *Frankenstein*, Peter Brooks sees "an exotic body with a difference, a distinct per-version from the tradition of desirable objects" that raise the complexity of motherhood, fatherhood, gender and narrative; the monstrous body created by Victor (1995, 81). Here, instead, Frankenstein is the monstrous body, the degenerate extension of his hubristic sci-entific obsession. The scientist must not succeed in his usurpation of nature or woman-hood because of his culturally assumed objectivity; rather, in a quick shift of narrative focus, Elizabeth has underestimated her opponent: Frankenstein is the murderer of all, not his creature who retains his Shelleyan pathos. The pathology of Frankenstein's obses-sion parallels the coldness of any other psychopathic serial killer finessed through the undertaking of scientific detachment necessary to "steal the spark of creation" and then to claim to Elizabeth, "I am doing it for *you*" (230; emphasis in original).

Elizabeth's refusal to sanction his monstrosity ends with Frankenstein committing her to an asylum where they will believe that "she imagined the whole thing! And the monsters—creatures of darkness and death—that she sees in the world around her!" (232). Aided by a medical man closer to a quack than physician,[8] Elizabeth is locked away against her will in like fashion to the eponymous heroine of Wollstonecraft's *Maria* (1798). The doctor does not believe Elizabeth's recasting of her journalistic writings as an early draft of a novel. He diagnoses her belief in her own story as hysteria to be cured if she is left for her "*nerves* to resettle" (White 2018, 237; emphasis in original). Fully cognizant of her imprisonment, Elizabeth knows that the men had "stripped us of everything we were taught made us women, and then told us we were mad" (237). One of the women in the asylum garnered Elizabeth's particular sympathy because she was "locked away for daring to want a life free from pain and abuse. How mad she must have been indeed for dreaming such a thing was possible" (252).

In many earlier-century Gothic novels, the asylum trap would signal the end of the narrative unless the victimised woman could be rescued by the heroic male; in this neo-Gothic version, the women usurp the expected outcome in two ways. First, Elizabeth is not silent. She gives voice to her predicament, albeit in a scrap of writing, in a way that a Gothic heroine might not, or at least she openly expresses her understanding of it: "For all my work learning how to be what others needed, I had not realized I was already perfectly suited to this asylum. I was *exactly* who they wanted me to be. Who Victor's father and mother had groomed me to be. Who Victor had created me to be. I was a prisoner. All my life of surviving, of being someone else's Elizabeth, had led me here. And what was I left with? Who was I when I was not performing for someone else?" (239; emphasis in original). Elizabeth's predicament emphasises how strong the constraints are on both female intellect and behaviour. Her "asylum master" (235) completely disregards her writings with his common assumption that women do not have the capacity to be intellectual; in addition, he rebukes her by infantantalising her: "My dear child. Do you really think claiming that what you were writing came from your imagination does anything to prove your sanity? Indeed, if anything, it further confirms how much you need our help" (236) because clearly for a woman to claim authorship equates to madness. Second, when in Ingolstadt, Justine and Elizabeth met Mary Delgado, a young bookseller, raised by an Uncle now missing; an insightful, inquiring woman, she gains access to the asylum masquerading as a nurse. Once in, she bluntly declares to Elizabeth that it is "time to kill your husband" (247) because he is also guilty of her Uncle's death. The two women escape the asylum and retreat to Elizabeth's room in her old home where she had "walked like a ghost" (250–51). There is neither nostalgia for the past nor a desire to be rescued. In this confrontation, Elizabeth will be her own mistress not a spectral reflection of who she is supposed to be.

The narrative ends with a new trio, one no longer based on male homosociality between Frankenstein and his monster with Elizabeth as passive catalyst, but as a family of equal choice.[9] The group is formed with the self-named Adam who, although with the eyes of Henri Clerval, is "not Henry. Not really. He is part of me, but I am not him" (267) with his self-awareness that he is a sum of parts, along with Mary and Elizabeth who "would rise from the ashes, reborn" into a "little family of three" (278) by choice rather than of birth or manipulation. Mary and Elizabeth escape the obligatory hetero-sexuality of *Frankenstein* to exchange smiles and hold hands "for no reason other than that I loved her and was glad to have her with me […] curled against her in the warmth of our bed" (274). To protect her family, Elizabeth enacts the heroic role usually reserved for a chivalric male; to save them and herself, she willingly drowns with Frankenstein. In the text's one illustration, the pages go blank, then a large image shows a blackness shattered by lightning, after which Elizabeth's internal monologue tells us, "I took a breath" (287). She is reborn not as an unnatural monster coming to life from a galvanic spark but as a woman who, in sacrificial baptism and rebirth, is Elizabeth Frankenstein, now safe from the atheist human monster who drowns.

The usurpation by these liminal women of powerful roles usually inhabited by men is a neo-Gothic signature in the afterlife of *Frankenstein*. Several potentialities that come to the foreground in White's novel are extended in Roszak's *The Memoirs of Elizabeth*

Frankenstein, particularly the idea of the strength to be found in a female community that lies outside of social convention.[10] Roszak takes many liberties to craft the women's story and provides a recreated Sir Robert Walton to narrate; his clear inability to see his own patriarchal biases force the modern reader to see just how absurd they are. His "Editor's Note[s]" lay out an interpretation of facts that lead him to the conclusion that Baroness Frankenstein suffered from a "pathological condition" (Roszak 1995, 138) evident in her outrageous behaviour. Walton frames this narrative with a preface declaring his pursuit of the truth: "But *was* there more to be told than the man had himself revealed to me?" (xv; emphasis in original). An archival pursuit of evidence leads to the Gothic trope of a found manuscript that was left in the hands of Ernest Frankenstein who "admitted to possessing certain papers relevant to his brother's history" and will part with them only for money for which Walton is "eager to pay" because it is only a "small fraction of their worth" (xv) to him. It is important to remember Walton's strong affinity for Frankenstein; in *Frankenstein*, Walton often wonders what a "glorious creature [Victor] must have been in the days of his prosperity, when he is thus noble and godlike in ruin" (Shelley 1999 [1818], 232).

These papers are only part of the matter; Walton believes "there are *three* voices that must be heard if we're to understand this extraordinary history accurately"— Frankenstein, the fiend and "Elizabeth, the third and (so I thought at the time) only innocent member of the unholy trinity" (Roszak 1995, xvi; emphasis in original). Walton admits that he had decided "mercifully to suppress what [Frankenstein] told me of certain demeaning uses to which he had subjected the woman he claimed to love" believing she "in her moral weakness, might have been forced to perform" (xvii). Over time, he comes to be "steadily less certain of [Elizabeth's] moral character" (xvii) and finds evidence that Caroline Frankenstein is a "shadowy woman" who "would surely rank as the most grotesque human phenomenon" and as "depraved a soul" (xviii) as Walton has ever encountered, albeit only textually. He concludes she is—or both women are—without a doubt, "an example of female degeneracy" (xviii) he must necessarily expose.

A countercultural narrative is created in *The Memoirs of Elizabeth Frankenstein* in which Elizabeth is an orphan foundling, raised by Gipsies. Elizabeth dreams of her own birth "as if divided in two," disembodied and spectral while she watches the pain her mother endures before she dies in childbirth; she is left with the realisation that "my life has taken a life. I have come into the world a murderer" (6). Although Moers has argued that Mary Shelley used the Gothic to represent women's horror of pregnancy and mothering (1974, 91), one could argue that the horror is directed at the medical men who do not understand the process of giving and sustaining life from a natural, womanly perspective.[11] Rosina Lavenza, the midwife who had fought to use women's healing knowledge to save Elizabeth's mother but was rejected by medical men, takes in the child and tries to raise Elizabeth as one of her own but social rank and race mark their difference. Rosina is the first to show Elizabeth women's knowledge when she brings her along to teach her midwifery. Like at her own birth, Elizabeth sees a medical man seek to overpower nature and assert his invasive masculinity on a mother in crisis with the command to "strap her down" and pull out the "claw" that will rip the child from the womb (10) ultimately killing the mother. The women's patience and centuries-old sagacity of relayed experience would have saved the unnamed woman, proving that "it is a crime against God to take birth away from the women. What does he know, this […] *man*?" (11; emphasis in original).[12] This is a clear retort to Victor Frankenstein and to a medical profession that would seek to procreate without women. Rozcak has women save as well as nurture girl children, and communities of women come together to celebrate femaleness. Sandra Gilbert and Susan Gubar assert that "the womb-shaped cave is also the place of female power, the *umbilicus mundi* on of the great antechambers of the mysteries of transformation" (2000 [1979], 95); to follow that idea, Roszak's retelling shows that there can be no usurping of the providence of womanhood that could ever be successful or loving. To give birth is, literally, a woman's birth right.

It is against this unnatural turn created by the male pursuit of science only fueled by ideas of reason without the empathy of natural experience that leads to the affective correspondence Elizabeth feels for Lady Caroline when they meet. Elizabeth admits, "No language can describe what I experienced in that moment when our eyes met. The sensation was one of physical transport, as if I had been lifted from the ground by wings I did not know I possessed" (19) and their trust is instantaneous (23). Tall and commanding with eyes that were icy grey-blue, "such eyes as angels have, that can spy into one's very heart" (19), Elizabeth sees "how unusual a figure Lady Caroline cut" wearing clothes that "might have been borrowed from a man: a frock coat and flowing cravat" with a skirt that was "daringly mannish" and "drawn high enough to reveal her boots" to represent "the advanced social views of her time" (22), including those on a natural education advocated by her own mother. In appearance, thought and action Lady Caroline's gender and sexual transgressions are progressive and for the advancement of women.

Lady Caroline is an artist of female nudes, pro-woman advocate, druidic leader and lesbian lover with the belief in a female-only community that draws its strength from secret ancient lore and rituals imparted to a young woman at menarche. Turning a blind eye, Baron Frankenstein's marginal understanding of his wife's needs displaces the wise woman's studio—a feminine space of comfort and exploration—to the top of the ancient tower, away from the otherwise open reception rooms of the manor house that host his intellectual salons.[13] Alchemy is replaced by healing, a neo-Gothic recasting of the unknown as under a woman's power, not only existent as gold in men's Medieval texts.

To create a sense of discomfort with such defiant women, Walton purposely intrudes to note how he tracks her paintings as factual evidence of Lady Caroline's degeneracy; to bolster his assumption, he has an art critic declare the paintings as "little short of the pornographic if so many of the figures chosen were not physically unappealing in the extreme" (84). This view is the opposite of Elizabeth's own view of the paintings as uncanny but not the "*evil* pictures" of "*witches*" (65; emphasis in original) Victor declares them to be. The women in the paintings are naked, "realistically depicted, lounging or sprawling with no attempt at modest concealment" with some in a "transport of ecstasy" as other "wispy figures [were] floating through darkly shaded woods, garbed in pale robes that lent them a spectral aspect" (64–65), visions of women in a world outside the boundaries of conventional acceptance, a rebuttal to the scientific sense of objectivity. In stark contrast, Victor arrogantly declares himself the equal of Michelangelo "whose portrait of Adam waking into life was the model I placed about my table. I was more the artist than the scientist as I crafted flesh to bone and delved into the intricacies of fibres, veins, and muscles" (330), a man mired in the physical at the rejection of nature, unlike the women raised to the spiritual through their respectful interaction with nature. Lady Caroline perceptively comments, "*Our* art is not *their* art" (79; emphasis in original).

If Roszak's "Father was mind, science, invention: the force of revolutionary endeavor" with a lightning bolt on the family crest (120), then Lady Caroline was "Mother [...] defender of ancient springs" and the bearer of "memories of primordial ways" (121). Both Lady Caroline and Elizabeth are, in their objection to objectification, the image of the virago cast upon Wollstonecraft in her search for women's rights, or on Shelley for her desire to live life freely outside the bounds of conventional marriage. At one point, the reader understands the implicit strength embodied by the simple ability of the women to "stand together unclothed, their hair undone, standing shamelessly in the lanthorn light. Without their dresses and adornments to mark them off from one another, they became a society of equals, where one could not tell which was a woman of quality and which a woman of the meaner orders. How brave it was to remove one's clothes [...] For one must leave behind all distinction with them" (109). Interaction and procreation must be in natural balance, not manufactured through scientific experimentation.

Shedding one's clothes is to shed one's class and all conventions expected therein; these women mirror how Shelley was raised to disregard conventional expectations and to defy limitations placed on the female body and intellect. Shelley voraciously read her mother's work, sat under her portrait and visited her grave for comfort, searching for answers to questions she was never given the chance to ask. Readers, too, have many unanswered questions; as is the case with several nineteenth-century women authors, there is a scarcity, real or perceived, of biographical information about the woman and her words. Diana Wallace agrees that in the "hands of women writers, Gothic historical fiction has offered a way of 'interpreting', or symbolizing, what Luce Irigaray calls 'the forgetting of female ancestries' and of re-establishing them within 'History'" (quoted in 2013, 1). Following in metafictional fashion, neo-Gothic biofiction invites a search to "know" Shelley's character(s); in some ways, "biographical absence makes [her] artistic presence even more dramatic" (Benton 2009, 47).

Twenty-first century readers search for Mary Shelley as a revolutionary daughter, woman, mother, writer and widow. The desire to know—to learn more of who she is, what inspired her, when was she able to find the time, where was she when the idea(s) struck and why did she desire to write—leads to the temptation to fill in the answers from fragmentary clues in adaptations of her fiction, but also in biofiction about Shelley. David Lodge defines such a narrative as one "which takes a real person and their real history as the subject matter for imaginative exploration, using the novel's techniques for representing subjectivity rather than the objective, evidence-based discourse of biography" (2006, 8).[14] One should be mindful that there may be a stumbling block "for understanding biofiction has been the scholarly desire to find a way to manage, balance, and negotiate the competing and sometimes contradictory demands of biography (representation) and fiction (creation)" (Lackey 2016, 6) while Cora Kaplan fears they cannot be reconciled because the "bio" "references a more essentialized and embodied element of identity, a subject less than transcendent but more than merely discourse. It implies that there is something stubbornly insoluble in what separates the two genres and that prevents them from being invisibly sutures; the join will always show" (2007, 65). Here, in revivifying character(s), it is important that the monstrous sutures do show; these fictions do not attempt to provide a seamless understanding of Shelley, but to show how in neo-Gothic narratives, her auto/biography and her fictional creations come together to create a better understanding overall of the woman and her work.

Temptation is then combined with the potential to find answers in the author's fiction, to collapse the auto/biographical with the fictional universe in a biofiction, sometimes encouraged by the author's own words, her own characters and her character, a kind of neo-Gothic doubling of the woman writer. An oft-quoted comment on the creationary moment of her fictional creature might be seen as an act of self-mythologising, a displacement of her genius intuition onto a waking vision: "My imagination, unbidden, possessed and guided me, gifting the successive images that arose in my mind with a vividness far beyond the usual bounds of reverie. I saw—with shut eyes, but acute mental vision,—I saw" (Shelley 1831, x). Shelley moves from "a devout but nearly silent listener" (ix) to, as she claims, the victim of an image of "terror. The idea so possessed my mind, that a thrill of fear ran through me, and I wished to exchange the ghastly image of my fancy for the realities around" as she "must try to think of something else" (xi).

It is the realities of Shelley's life before and during the creation of *Frankenstein* that this biofiction, *Mary's Monster*, seeks to fill in from fragmentary documents she left behind. The female Gothic romance has become a biofictional tool for the neo-Gothic subversion of cultural expectations; the romance is not with the masculine hero-villain, but with discovering and acknowledging her own history. Death, and Shelley's intense, multifaceted grief—for her mother, her children, her lost idealism—is at the core of Judge's text. The prologue of this graphic poem begins with a direct conflation of the creature with Shelley, his large, stitched hand in the foreground while Shelley, hair unleashed and cloak flying in the breeze as she walks alone under a thunderous sky; as he watches over her, he narrates how "most people didn't believe Mary Shelley, / a teenage girl, unleashed me, / a creature powerful and murderous / enough to haunt their dreams" (1).

The creature—her creature—turns to reanimate her life in return empathy as she had brought him to life; he understands the cost she risks because society "expected girls to be silent / and swallow punishment and pain" (3). Instead of finding compassion and understanding in the new society envisioned by her mother, "she was cast out from society" while her "friends reviled her" and "her father banished her" (3). The creature admires that Shelley "did not hide. / She was not silenced" but that she "fought against the cruelty of human nature / by writing" (4). Her creature admires her determination and her compassion in the face of adversity; with gratitude, he recounts directly to the reader how

> She conceived me.
> I took shape like an infant,
> not in her body, but in her heart,
> growing from her imagination
> till I was bold enough to climb out of the page
> and into your mind. (7)

Mary Shelley, the creator, has turned to "the ghost / whose bones have turned to dust" with the creature's admittance that "it is I who live on" (8).

The birth in *Frankenstein* of a "wretch" brought into being on a lab table via male scientific intellectual pursuit results in a creature who fills Frankenstein's heart with "breathless horror and disgust" and in a terrifying image of the "corpse of [his] dead mother" with "grave-worms crawling" (1999 [1818], 85). Rather than finding conciliation and comfort for his misdeed, Frankenstein has a cold sweat on his forehead, chattering teeth and his "every limb became convulsed" (85), struggling with his disgust during afterbirth and leading to his rejection of his creature. In distinct reversal, Judge's compassionate being acts as the frame narrator to allow Shelley, his loving creator, to "reach beyond the grave / and tell you her own" (8) story.

Beginning with her exile to Scotland at 14, the switch to Shelley as first-person narrator allows her to demonstrate her intellect in the section "Herschel's Comet" where she admires "the almost impossible fact about that comet/was that it was discovered / by a woman" astronomer who was "self-trained/because women were barred from universities" (16). This non-conventional portrait of the female pursuit of knowledge, gained out of hard work and outside male-governed education and scientific pursuit, asserts Shelley's own desires for her future. Judge casts Godwin as a hypocrite who, although his expectations "taught us independence is admirable, / and imagination indispensable" (19), falls in step with his second wife, Mrs. Clairmont, who convinces him to send Mary Shelley away because her inquiring mind presents a danger to the younger Clare.

Her dismissal by a potential mother figure makes Shelley unable "to stop thinking [...] / These are the limbs that ripped through my mother [...] But she no longer breathes, / Because I do" (32). The opposite page, in black and white like the entire graphic schema, shows Shelley in the foetal position, trying to feel the comfort of her spectral mother's arms, the woman whose omnipresence in the narrative's neo-Gothic counter-discourse of the feminine is continuous.[15] In turn, "Mother" delineates how she sees her mother; she knows that "Mary Wollstonecraft was mother to a rebellion / before she was mother to me" (43). Judge's consideration of the Marys reverses and extends the idea that "women writers have used Gothic historical fiction with its obsession with inheritance, lost heirs and illegitimate offspring, to explore the way in which the 'female line' has been erased in 'History'" (Wallace 2013, 5) by using the author, as character, to voice her own sense of inheritance as a literary heir and legitimate offspring to reinscribe her own, and her mother's, legacies through a neo-Gothic consideration of herstory, not history. Shelley understands that Wollstonecraft, in her moral strength, prevented "her father from beating his wife, / she rose from a childhood of abuse" and that "my mother challenged a world of angry men / with the soft feather of her pen" (43). Not only does Shelley recognise that even her mother's mother was victim to a patriarchal society without "laws / to prevent [him] from beating his wife" but that through her pen, her own mother garnered victories (43). Generations of remembered women come together as ghostly voices of encouragement for the authoress.

In these novels, the character of Shelley consistently rereads Wollstonecraft's words for advice, experience and warning so that her mother's "thoughts and ideas reach across the space of time" to give her a second birth where the dreams of the mother become her own (Judge 2018, 44). Here, the accompanying image shows how their symbiotic if spectral relationship gives her encouragement to continue; she reflects her own mother's image in the window of Skinner Street. Even though Percy Bysshe Shelley provides a bolt of lightning (74) that will change her life, they come together at her mother's grave in a kind of twinning of the two women with the revolutionary ardour of the poet. Problematically, but accurately, her stepmother senses and warns, here and in Antoinette May's *The Determined Heart*, "*He's in love with the idea of your mother* [...] *more than with you!*" (2015, 94; emphasis in original).

Finding nothing sublime in their first adventure, the already pregnant Shelley is haunted by children; she sees those whose "bones are bent, / their bodies deformed" as the outcome of male-waged wars; indeed, Judge intimates here that her horror lays the groundwork for *Frankenstein* because it is here Shelley sees it is man's unquenchable thirst for power / and violence that is truly ugly, / not these miserable children" (134) who covered in only rancid rags, one considered by society to be repulsive in their poverty. They, too, have been abandoned. Judge intuits how Shelley might have felt under her particular circumstances as the child who feels she is responsible for her own mother's death, cast out by her father and disdained by society: "I can't stop thinking how my birth / Caused my mother's death, / and I begin to fear what fate awaits me / upon the birth of my child" (153). With her daughter Clara's birth, Shelley believes she finally understands that she "didn't steal my mother's life" when she was born but that "she gave it, just as I have now given" (156) her daughter a life; sadly, it is brief and the repressed grief for her mother is now brought into connection with the depression brought with the death of her 10- day-old daughter. Shelley's real-life despair is laid bare in her dream where she wished she could waken her dead child.[16] Her sorrow covers Judge's pages where her unseeing eyes focus beyond the reader while the creature's eyes look upon her in pity; she is "daughter to a ghost / and mother to bones" (160–61).

A year later, she is pregnant again and gives birth to William, all before the fateful journey to Villa Diodati where the men speak of usurping women's nature to create life or to bring the dead back to life. Judge supplies Mary Shelley's possible reaction to such arrogance as a woman who has given birth to find sorrow and joy. In "What Do Men Know of Creating Life?" Shelley silently rages: "I am sickened they talk so easily of men, / not women, / creating life" and sees the terror of "what will happen if they assume the power / to create life?" (216) in what might be consider the "horrifying but pre-dictable consequences of an uncontrolled technological exploitation of nature and the female" (Mellor 2003, 9). Women suffer; Claire Clairmont (her stepmother's daughter) is cast out by Byron, whose child she carries; Harriet (Shelley's wife and mother of his heir) commits suicide by drowning; Fanny (her older half-sister by Imlay) commits sui-cide by laudanum because her future has been tainted by scandal. In self-preservation, he hides her suicide; her "Father lies. / And his lies condemn me / to silence" (245) over Fanny's death. Judge's neo-Gothic, postmodern mixture of one woman's variously positioned voices in the text allows for Shelley's defiant and angry thoughts to be given a voice to be heard.

The creature's voice reaches out to break her out of her depression; Shelley begins to write "until my pen scratches pain / as loud as screams" when "His voice calls out to me, / Now, Mary, / You begin to see" (255). The "I AM" becomes Mary Shelley, who "so rejected [...] must create a family from ghosts" which then blurs any distinction with "I AM THE WORDS torn from your mind / until they pulse like a BEATING HEART. / I am your Creature" (257; emphasis added). A striking image covers the next two pages; Shelley looks directly at the reader with the stitched together being behind her, watching, when she realises that "my Creature is me!" (258–59).[17] She finally sees that her self-creation and her fictional creation are born of a "bone crushing" birth, "Miserable / and beautiful, / like learning how to breathe again" (260). Her grief, later compounded and extended by more children lost to illness, causes her to embrace the creaturely, to become "Fearless" enough to "call up phantoms / from voiceless graves" so while her creature makes her wretched, she replies with strength; he gives her the right to be "vengeful" (265) and she returns love to him for his acceptance of her, a child to whom she can give strength to fight injustice (268). At nine months, *Frankenstein* is born but the death of William has her confess that she feels cursed (282). Now both characters—Mary and her companion creature—are outside the window, looking in, confronting the postmodern reader to be compassionate, but not nostalgic, where past history has been condemnatory.

Judge's "The Epilogue" provides us with a neo-Gothic return of voices from the past; "The Present" frame is a reminder from her creature that although she is 200 years dead, "her spirit whispers / eternally through me, / her creature" because it is he "who keep[s] her faith alive" (298). Judge has tried to give us "details [that] remain cloaked in mystery" (301) to fill in the historical record, particularly on Shelley's feelings on the joy and grief of mother(s), motherhood and mothering.

In David Punter's "Afterword: Meditation on the Monster, A Poem" he, too, has the monster speak on behalf of Shelley in his "polyphonic" narrative (2018, 15). She/her creature blend voices in a consideration over the "continuous self-pity of these men [...] absorbed in their grand schemes" (321) but unable to hear the solipsistic arrogance of their own desires; certainly, by "daring to compete with the male Romantics for literary fame, she oversteps the bounds of female propriety, neglects her authentic sphere of domestic nurturance, and so creates and becomes, a monster" (Ralston and Sondergard 1999, 205). Outsiders to society, both Shelley and her creature know it

> is hopeless,
> Men can never hear, they never hear, they will never hear,
> and so I forgive, I look upon
> my creatures with a kindly, a beneficent eye
> for they understand nothing, they know nothing,
> not even that from which they flee. (Punter 2018, 321)

The uniting of the voices of creator and creation—Shelley and her creature, not Frankenstein and his monster—have compassion for the maternal act of creation, that borrowed bit of the divine where

> The pages might be shredded, might turn into
> Floating leaves from which a new world might be born,
> Had it not been torn apart in its very inception
> As a woman is torn apart
> In the act of birth. (322)

In return for the pain of his creation, the now twenty-first century creature is aware that he is, in neo-Gothic contexts, "continuously reincarnated" and "appointed / as an avatar, as the emblem / of all those torn bodies" (322–23) of the female lineage that led to Shelley's right to write. He comes from another age, and Shelley speaks to us of female strength and warning from behind the creature's mask,

> authenticated, biographized, endlessly
> reincarnated, enjoined
> as the patroness of yet another struggle
> for a woman's voice.
> I salute you, of course, and am there with you;
> But how much have you understood of the torment
> Of creation, of reproduction?
> You women have, of course—but you men? (325)

Only Mary Shelley and her creature understand.

In one final narrative, Laurie Sheck's neo-Gothic *A Monster's Notes* (2009) uses fictional and biofictional characters, Gothic tropes, letters, documents and flash to create a complex neo-Gothic presentation of narratives to tell the story of Mary Shelley and her creature. Even in those existing documents that Moers has called Shelley's "workshop of her own creation" (1974, 26) there are still significant spaces of silence. The palimpsest of voices in these new narratives looking back adds the voice of the lost wisdom of Mary Wollstonecraft, one mother who understands her motherless but mothering daughter in a reflection of her own experience outside the realm of men; as her mother, she prophecies that her "daughter will feel how being tries to rise through words, how the mind mutinies against itself, violates each seeming certainty until each single thing is several things at once, decentered, precarious, unsolved—I stood in the visible world, a tree with tough roots and sturdy trunk, wind whipping around me—But I was also the shadow of that tree and the empty space beside it" (416), leaving both women hauntingly in and of two worlds.

Notes

1 The original 1818 version of Shelley's text is used throughout this chapter.
2 Judith Barbour argues vigorously that "a look at the intellectual background of her childhood explains that her early reading played a significant role in an unusual choice of subject" (2008, 33).

3 Elisabeth Bronfen focuses on literary lineage to make the case that "on a textual level Frankenstein's artificially re-generated body of dead component parts [...] refer back to writings of other members of her family" (1994, 29).

4 Another term that applies here is "biographical portraiture" (North 2010, 759) given it suggests differences in construction and shades of an historical person, or even for the purposes of a biofictional representation of characters and/or authors.

5 The irony is that it is discovered Elizabeth is of aristocratic lineage; in both *The Descent of Elizabeth Frankenstein* and Roszak's *The Memoirs of Elizabeth Frankenstein*, no direct lineage is acknowledged but it is traceable; in the first instance, it empowers her father-in-law, the Baron, to plot to regain his society respectability.

6 According to Judith Butler, "Gender reality is performative which means, quite simply, that it is real only to the extent that it is performed. It seems fair to say that certain kinds of acts are usually interpreted as expressive of a gender core or identity, and that these acts either conform to an expected gender identity or contest that expectation in some way [...] As performance which is performative, gender is an 'act,' broadly construed, which constructs the social fiction of its own psychological interiority" (1988, 527–28).

7 For a discussion of late eighteenth-century understandings of mental illness, see "The Monstrous Idea in Mary Shelley's *Frankenstein*" in which Kathleen Béres Rogers discusses how "the homosocial obsession with the creature, his filial obsession with his mother, or even his obsession with his father's lack of love" does "not square with the complex ways the Romantics conceived of the mind-brain" (2018, 356).

8 There are many other representations of this trope, neo-Gothic and otherwise, including Sarah Waters' *Fingersmith* (2002) and others that will be discussed in an upcoming collection of *Neo-Victorian Madness* by Maier and Ayres.

9 For comprehensive explanation of the term, see Eve Kosofsky Sedgwick's *Between Men: English Literature and Male Homosocial Desire* where she discusses, in particular, gender asymmetry and erotic triangles (1985, 21) relevant to *Frankenstein*.

10 While there are many discussions that should be had about the relation between Roszak's text and Shelley's novel that could be neo-Gothic revisionings of scientific experimentation, Enlightenment theory, patriarchal society and others, here the focus will be on the repainted portraits of women.

11 For a strong discussion of empirical method and "masculine scientific hubris," see van Leeuwen (2016).

12 Much like the implied violence in White's novel, the ongoing emotional, physical and potential sexual abuse perpetrated by Rosina's husband, Toma, makes it imperative that Elizabeth leave, if the opportunity presents itself, with Lady Caroline.

13 This move of the unconventional or potentially dangerous woman to the far reaches of the household goes forward into novels like *Jane Eyre* (1847) where Antoinette "Bertha" Mason is locked away in the higher floor of Thornfield Hall.

14 Excellent biographies abound; certainly Anne K. Mellor's *Mary Shelley: Her Life, Her Fiction, Her Monsters* (1988) makes clear the events of her life, the influences of her parents, her life with Shelley and the tragedies that befall her. The question to which biographies still seek an answer mirrors the initial question her reviewers asked—how does a young girl write such a master-piece? Charlotte Gordon casts mother and daughter in a dual biography as *Romantic Outlaws* (2015); another of significance is by Wollstonecraft and Charlotte Brontë biographer, Lyndall Gordon, who presents Shelley as one of the five great women writers in *Outsiders* (2019) along-side Emily Brontë, George Eliot, Olive Schreiner and Virginia Woolf. While a recent biog-raphy by Fiona Sampson literally admits the biographer is *In Search of Mary Shelley* (2018), there is a pattern to cast Shelley outside of the norm, to see her as one who stands apart from society but has a sisterhood across time with those women writers of whom there is a search for more.

15 Rita Felski uses this term in her excellent work (1991) on the late Victorian authors Oscar Wilde, J. K. Huysmans and Leopold von Sacher-Masoch.

16 Shelley wrote in her diary: "Dream that my little baby came to life again—that it had only been cold & that we rubbed it by the fire & it lived—I awake & find no baby" (J 70; quoted in Mellor 2003, 10).

17 Perhaps a pursuit for another day, when reading Judge's graphic poem, one is reminded of Emily Brontë's *Wuthering Heights* (1847), Heathcliff and the liminal figure of the spectral Cathy.

Bibliography

Arias, Rosario, and Patricia Pulham, eds. *Haunting and Spectrality in Neo-Victorian Fiction: Possessing the Past*. London: Palgrave, 2010.

Baldick, Chris. *In Frankenstein's Shadow*. Oxford: Clarendon Press, 1987.

Barbour, Judith. "The Professor and the Orang-Outang: Mary Shelley as a Child Reader." In *Frankenstein's Science: Experimentation and Discovery in Romantic Culture, 1780–1830*, edited by Jane Goodall, 33–48. London: Routledge, 2008.

Benton, Michael. *Literary Biography*. New York: John Wiley and Sons, 2009.

Bronfen, Elisabeth. "Rewriting the Family: Mary Shelley's 'Frankenstein' in Its Biographical/Textual Context." In *Frankenstein, Creation and Monstrosity*, edited by Stephen Bann, 16–38. London: Reaktion Books, 1994.

Brooks, Peter. "What Is a Monster? (According to *Frankenstein*)." In *New Casebooks: Frankenstein*, edited by Fred Botting, 81–106. New York: St. Martin's Press, 1995.

Butler, Judith. "Performative Acts and Gender Constitution: An Essay in Phenomenology and Feminist Theory." *Theatre Journal* 40, no. 4 (December 1988): 519–31.

Davison, Carol Margaret, and Marie Mulvey-Roberts. *Global Frankenstein*. London: Palgrave, 2018.

Felski, Rita. "The Counterdiscourse of the Feminine in Three Texts by Wilde, Huysmans, and Sacher-Masoch." *PMLA* 106, no. 5 (1991): 1094–105.

Gilbert, Sandra, and Susan Gubar. *The Madwoman in the Attic: The Woman Writer and the Nineteenth-Century Literary Imagination*. 1979. 2nd ed. New Haven, CT: Yale University Press, 2000.

Gordon, Charlotte. *Romantic Outlaws*. New York: Random House, 2015.

Gordon, Lyndall. *Outsiders*. Baltimore: Johns Hopkins University Press, 2019.

Hoeveler, Diane Long. *Gothic Feminism: The Professionalisation of Gender from Charlotte Smith to the Brontës*. Liverpool: Liverpool University Press, 1998.

Jacobus, Mary. "Is There a Woman in This Text?" *New Literary History* 14 (1982): 117–54.

Judge, Lita. *Mary's Monster: Love, Madness, and How Mary Shelley Created Frankenstein*. New York: Roaring Brook Press, 2018.

Kaplan, Cora. *Victoriana: Histories, Fictions, Criticism*. New York: Columbia University Press, 2007.

Lackey, Michael. "Locating and Defining the Bio in Biofiction." *a/b: Auto/Biography Studies* 31, no. 1 (2016): 3–10.

Lodge, David. *The Year of Henry James, or Timing Is All: The Story of a Novel*. London: Harvill Secker, 2006.

May, Antoinette. *The Determined Heart*. Seattle: Lake Union Publishing, 2015.

Mellor, Anne K. *Mary Shelley: Her Life, Her Fiction, Her Monsters*. New York: Methuen, 1988.

———. "Making a 'Monster': An Introduction to *Frankenstein*." In *Cambridge Companion to Mary Shelley*, edited by Esther Schor, 9–25. Cambridge: Cambridge University Press, 2003.

Moers, Ellen. "Female Gothic: The Monster's Mother." *New York Review of Books*, March 21, 1974, 24–28.

North, Julian. "Shelley Revitalized: Biography and the Reanimated Body." *European Romantic Review* 21, no. 6 (December 2010): 751–70.

Punter, David. "Afterword: Meditation on the Monster, A Poem." In *Global Frankenstein*, edited by Carol Margaret Davison and Marie Mulvey-Roberts, 319–28. London: Palgrave, 2018.

Punter, David, and Glennis Byron. *The Gothic*. Oxford: Blackwell Publishing, 2004.

Ralston, Ramona, and Sid Sondergard. "Biodepictions of Mary Shelley: The Romantic Woman Artist as Mother of Monsters." In *Biofictions*, edited by Martin Middeke and Werner Huber, 201–13. New York: Camden House, 1999.

Rich, Adrienne. "When We Dead Awaken: Writing as Re-vision." *College English* 34 (October 1972): 18–30.

Rogers, Kathleen Béres. "The Monstrous Idea in Mary Shelley's *Frankenstein.*" *Literature and Medicine* 36, no. 2 (Fall 2018): 356–71.

Roszak, Theodore. *The Memoirs of Elizabeth Frankenstein*. New York: Random House, 1995.

Sampson, Fiona. *In Search of Mary Shelley*. New York: Pegasus Books, 2018.

Sedgwick, Eve Kosofsky. *Between Men: English Literature and Male Homosocial Desire*. New York: Columbia University Press, 1985.

Sheck, Laurie. *A Monster's Notes*. New York: Alfred A. Knopf, 2009.

Shelley, Mary. Introduction to *Frankenstein, or The Modern Prometheus*, v–xii. London: Colburn and Bentley, 1831.

———. *Frankenstein; or, The Modern Prometheus*. In *Frankenstein by Mary Shelley, The Original 1818 Text*, 2nd ed., edited by D. L. MacDonald and Kathleen Scherf. Peterborough, ON: Broadview Press, 1999.

Van Leeuwen, Evert. "Theodore Roszak's *The Memoirs of Elizabeth Frankenstein:* A Countercultural Perspective on Alchemy, Gender and the Scientific Revolution." In *Restoring the Mystery of the Rainbow: Literature's Refraction of Science*, edited by Valeria Tinkler-Villani and C. C. Barfoot, 449–66. Boston: Brill, 2016.

Wallace, Diana. *Female Gothic Histories*. Cardiff: University of Wales Press, 2013.

White, Kiersten. *The Dark Descent of Elizabeth Frankenstein*. New York: Delacorte Press, 2018.

Chapter Three

THEORISING RACE, SLAVERY AND THE NEW IMPERIAL GOTHIC IN NEO-VICTORIAN RETURNS TO *WUTHERING HEIGHTS*

Carol Margaret Davison

The past few decades have seen numerous powerful creative revisions of Emily Brontë's Victorian Gothic novel *Wuthering Heights* (2003 [1847]) that racialise Heathcliff as black. This phenomenon, which began with Peter Forster's (1991) compelling and provocative wood engravings of *Wuthering Heights* for the Folio Society, was followed by Guadeloupean author Maryse Condé's *La migration des coeurs* (*Windward Heights*, 1995), Andrea Arnold's cinematic version of *Wuthering Heights* (2011), Caryl Phillips' *The Lost Child* (2015) and Michael Stewart's *Ill Will* (2018). These innovative reconceptions of Brontë's novel were borne, in large part, of the cultural and academic turn in the late twentieth century to postcolonial literature and theory. In tandem with the brilliant foundational philosophy and scholarship of the négritude and Pan-African movements, which included the writings of Aimé Césaire and Frantz Fanon and the theoretical work of critics such as Edward Said and Homi K. Bhabha that followed, postcolonial writers engaged in cultural resistance to established colonial/imperial narratives and ideologies. They took up, in particular, questions about nation and narration, subjectivity and Othering, voice, slavery, sovereignty, history, modernity and the relationship between culture and empire. That in dialoguing with British classics by developing narratives out of their textual gaps and silences they frequently employed Gothic tropes, themes and narrative dynamics makes artistic sense given that genre's efficacy for interrogating and undermining smug Enlightenment-based certainties. British imperialism, including the institutions at its heart, especially the triangular trade for which slavery served as the linchpin, was grounded in such certainties. While initially promoted and justified on rational and even Christian grounds, these imperial institutions, guilty of criminal brutalities and abuses of power, are frequently, and with specific intention, exposed in postcolonial works as quintessentially Gothic enterprises. Following from the popular Gothic dynamic relating to genealogical history, namely, that the sins of the fathers will be visited upon the sons, these systems and the worldviews that sustain them often prove impossible to exorcise or expunge—an idea in alignment with the postcolonial conception of empire.

In their attention to two crucial narrative gaps in *Wuthering Heights* relating to Heathcliff in the form, first, of his mysterious racial/ethnic origins and, second, the source of the fortune he gains over the course of his three-year absence from the Heights, these neo-Victorian revisions foreground the yoked personal and political, domestic and national, nature and impact of questions relating to race, economic relations and British imperialism that exist only at the margins of Brontë's Gothically insular narrative. It may be argued that, in some senses, these works minimise the masterful ability of their poetic mother-text to speak more broadly to the imperial question. As Terry Eagleton rightly notes about Brontë's deliberately obscure representation of Heathcliff that limns the boundary between race and class, "Possibly, but by no means certainly, Heathcliff may be a gipsy, or (like Bertha Mason in *Jane Eyre*) a Creole, or any kind of alien [including an impoverished Irish immigrant]. It is hard to know how black he is, or rather how much of the blackness is pigmentation and how much of it grime and bile" (1995, 3). Reading Heathcliff as a specifically racialised character shuts down his resonances for Britain's equally significant racial and imperial issues both at home, with the gipsy and Irish questions, and abroad, in such distant and distinct regions as India, Southeast Asia, the Caribbean and Africa. Such readings are signaled in Brontë's novel by way of repeated denigrating references to Heathcliff as a "gipsy," which appears six times,[1] and a "little Lascar" (Brontë 2003 [1847] 62), among others.

These neo-Victorian Gothic revisions portraying Heathcliff as black, possessing what Sally Shuttleworth characterises as a "self-reflexive consciousness about the problems of writing history in our postmodern age" (1998, 255), actually broaden the margins around Brontë's novel to widely divergent narrative ends. Bringing Britain's transatlantic Afro-Caribbean and African-American engagements into greater relief, literary and visual reimaginings of *Wuthering Heights* render more transparent and prominent the economic networks yoking Brontë's native Yorkshire, the slave trade and the Caribbean and American plantation economies, exposing the historical and cultural, conscious and unconscious, collisions and collusions between home and empire, self and Other. Often featuring uncanny, extreme encounters between the familiar/domestic and the foreign/imperial—what Homi K. Bhabha describes as "the *heimlich* pleasures of the hearth, [and] the *unheimlich* terror of the space or race of the Other" (1990, 2)—these neo-Victorian, postcolonial literary offspring serve as complementary narratives that both speak back and pay tribute to their mother-text, a work highly sensitive to issues of class-, gender- and race-based marginalisation.

Piggybacking on Brontë's intimate female Gothic recipe where love and its vulnerabilities exist at the crossroads of terror, these narratives figure love, to borrow a term from Mary Louise Pratt's work on imperial travel writing, as a type of fertile "contact zone" (1992, 6) where "disparate cultures meet, clash, and grapple with each other, often in highly asymmetrical relations of domination and subordination" (4). As with their meditations on the hauntings of history, both personal and political, the Gothic romance between Cathy and Heathcliff is richly revived and cunningly manipulated, often in association with the loaded theme of miscegenation, in these neo-Victorian, postcolonial texts to various ends—affective, aesthetic, poetic and political. In the mother-text, theirs is a dark romance doomed to failure because it cannot develop naturally beyond childhood.

In such an incisive and oppressive manner is the socio-economic system shown to affect the private sphere through an unnatural system of domestic slavery that grossly perverts human relationships. While commodifying and objectifying Cathy, and in the process denying her agency/choice as a desiring subject, patriarchal capitalism also dictates Heathcliff's wholesale dehumanisation followed, once he assumes the role of landowner, by his objectification of others.

Insofar as it sensitively exposes the traumatic impact of racial marginalisation and indicts capitalism, the engine of imperialism, as a dehumanising economic system commodifying individuals in a marketplace that inextricably binds the national and the domestic, and estranges them from their authentic selves, *Wuthering Heights* is an anti-imperial work. While Brontë develops a female Gothic narrative out of Cathy's experience in the marriage market where she becomes psychically divided in her decision to reject Heathcliff and marry Edgar Linton, she chronicles a similar narrative of psychic trauma with the racially indistinct Heathcliff who, in being outcast, abused and rejected by the only person who loves him, becomes Other—perhaps most damagingly—to himself, experiencing extreme self-division and self-loathing. Brontë's representations in this instance anticipate W. E. B. Du Bois' inspired psychoanalytic theory about double consciousness as advanced in *The Souls of Black Folk* (1965 [1903]), his incisive meditation on African American culture and experience in the Black Codes/Jim Crow era following the American Civil War. While Cathy's transition from a girl who is "half savage and hardy, and free" (Brontë 2003 [1847], 123) into a young woman tamed for the marriage market is class and gender based, Heathcliff's transformed self-conception is both class and race based, the latter of which fits Du Bois' theory more precisely. As Du Bois explains it, this psychological experience involves "always looking at one's self through the eyes" of a racist white society, and "measuring oneself by the means of a nation that looked back in contempt" (1965 [1903], 215). For Du Bois, this profound sense of self-estrangement was grounded in his upbringing as an African American in a European-dominated society, an experience paralleled by Heathcliff's racial background and his familial displacement.

In the face of Cathy's decision to marry Edgar Linton, Heathcliff tells Nelly, "If I knocked him down twenty times, that wouldn't make him less handsome or me more so. *I wish I had light hair and a fair skin*, and was dressed and behaved as well, and had a chance of being as rich as he will be!'" (Brontë 2003 [1847], 67; emphasis added). This experience of rejection on the basis of his inferior social status by the person he passionately loves and with whom he self-identifies destroys Heathcliff, who has experienced degradation and abuse at the hands of his adoptive brother, Hindley, after the death of their father. These traumas galvanise Heathcliff towards a double-edged revenge—a revolution of the established social order that nevertheless involves what Homi Bhabha (1984) will describe a century later as mimicry of the white coloniser who takes as his objectives domination and capitalist accumulation. Deprived of Cathy, who determines to marry the more socially acceptable Edgar Linton, Heathcliff single-mindedly and successfully strives towards capitalist gain, a venture he powerfully denounces as vacuous and detestable some 18 years later, just prior to his death. Brontë adeptly illustrates, in this instance, that this dehumanising force divorces one from family, human community and affection, serving as an unsuccessful mode of recovery from, and compensation for, traumatic emotional losses. The suicidal Heathcliff's articulation of the wish to destroy his property prior to his death (Brontë 2003 [1847], 283) dramatically brings Brontë's point home, a viewpoint notably in alignment with romanticised nineteenth-century views of gipsy culture. As B. C. Smart and H. T. Crofton claimed:

> Gypsies are the Arabs of pastoral England—the Bedouins of our commons and woodlands. In these days of material progress and much false refinement, they presented the singular spectacle of a race in our midst who regard with philosophical indifference the much-prized comforts of material civilization, and object to forego their simple life in close contact with Nature, in order to engage in their struggle after wealth and personal aggrandizement. These people, be it remembered, are not the outcasts of society; they voluntarily hold aloof from its crushing organization, and refuse to wear the bonds it imposes. (1875, xvi–xvii)

This idealisation of gipsies as anti-capitalist due to that economic system's deadly and enslaving nature speaks volumes when brought to bear on Heathcliff's bonding in childhood with Cathy and nature and his later, tragic life trajectory into a textbook case of erotic "monomania on the subject of his departed idol" (Brontë 2003 [1847], 277) that involves his willing enslavement to the love object and his rediscovery of her in other inanimate objects subsequent to her death (Esquirol 2003, 258). The devastating result is his physical and psychological deterioration over 18 years and premature death. Notably, however, their tragedies are more positively transmuted in the novel's utopian, Romantic, "comic" Gothic conclusion, which features Hareton's inheritance and marriage to the young Catherine, both of whom valorise love over money, and in Heathcliff's symbolic, liberating spiritual post-mortem release through the open window of his bedroom, into Catherine's ghostly, loving arms and the sublime moors beyond (Brontë 2003 [1847], 285).

In a novel whose primary message echoes Percy Bysshe Shelley's astute assessment of *Frankenstein*, "Treat a person ill, and he will become wicked" (1832, 730), Heathcliff's Gothic self is born of domestic rejection whereby he is cast out of the family and grossly mistreated by his tyrannical, alcoholic, adoptive brother, Hindley. Ironically and tragically, Hindley is engaged in enacting his own revenge for the favouritism his father exhibited towards Heathcliff, an orphan blasphemously renamed by Earnshaw for his son who died in childhood (Brontë 2003 [1847], 52). Heathcliff's subsequent return to the Heights where he goads this alcoholic gambler towards his own ruin and demise—a man who notably prefigures Heathcliff in his insurmountable grief for a beloved who dies in childbirth—acquires his property and then marries, torments and abuses Isabella Linton, the sister of his more socially respected rival, renders clear the essence of his monstrosity. In *Wuthering Heights*, to become a *monster* is to become the *master*, a tyrannical, abusive master who heartlessly, even sadistically, objectifies, dehumanises and controls those persons in his care. Considered in the light of his racial Otherness, Heathcliff's usurpation of this role would be deemed by Bhabha an example of colonial mimicry/mockery, an ambivalent act that both authorises and subverts the colonial power, authorises because the nature of the power remains intact, yet subverts because of the race of the person in whom it resides (1984, 126–27). Heathcliff proves that the figurative slave can rise and beat the master at his own game in a success that is, paradoxically, later revealed to involve his own dehumanisation.

Notably, the monster in *Wuthering Heights* is revealed to be a creature of nurture rather than nature. This standpoint strategically redefines monstrosity as an adherence to a perverse ideology rather than an inherent set of characteristics, which served as the basis for the essentialist foundations of racism that remained in place throughout the nineteenth century. This compelling and devastatingly tragic portrait is matched by an equally tragic depiction of a pure and profound love doomed to failure within a perverse social system that, along with the institutions that sustain it, valorises money over love, family and human community, a system that objectifies and commodifies people. *Wuthering Heights* lays bare the human and emotional costs of such a system/worldview while celebrating the triumphant power of love, which is heralded, in the second half of the novel, to be a sublime, virtually divine power that defies and surpasses secular traumas and death. Such a profound commentary on human nature and social systems, rendered in an innovative new style of Gothic fiction featuring such singular characters, has proven wonderfully amenable to postcolonial and feminist revision, as the works examined here evidence.

In response to the Folio Society's request that he create a fresh approach to illustrating *Wuthering Heights*, outspoken graphic satirist Peter Forster says in a letter that he "did rather hope that [his] concept of a Negro Heathcliff would vex the Tory gentry of Frinton-on-Sea" (quoted in Cooke 2006, 10). Although Forster makes clear in the same letter that he did not believe that Brontë's Heathcliff was actually black, he elected to depict him as such in his wood engravings as a contemporary equivalent to the idea of the gipsy in nineteenth-century England, a stigmatised cultural group with whom Heathcliff is associated throughout the novel. In his threatening and sublime nature, Forster's imposing, muscular and swarthy Heathcliff is reminiscent of Victor Frankenstein's creature. He may not summon up a supernatural sense of danger, as does Fritz Eichenberg's devilish and demonic Heathcliff in his famous woodcuts for Random House from 1943, but he is nevertheless sublimely menacing. Shown looming over his son in one image—the puny, vulnerable and pathetically submissive Linton—and looking as if he might crush him with his huge, sinewy arms and hands pressing down on his shoulders (174), Heathcliff's formidable nature and role as a usurper is underscored in a couple of Forster's linked images. The dark, empty entryway to the Heights that is featured in an early chapter, graced with Hareton Earnshaw's name engraved in the lintel above (11), is reconfigured several chapters later where a bemused, proprietary Heathcliff leans inside the doorway, blocking the entry (97).

Forster's depiction of a black Heathcliff, according to Simon Cooke, "uncovers a buried implication" in Brontë's novel relating to Mr. Earnshaw's discovery of Heathcliff in Liverpool where, as Cooke states, "slave-ships tied up on their way to America" (10). *Wuthering Heights* opens in "1801, the mid-point of the years of the Abolitionist debate (1779–1808) and a period of intense controversy," a historical backdrop that makes the implications of a black Heathcliff clear: He is "a 'dangerous other'—a man whose racial unacceptability makes him threatening and strange" (10). Notably, however, Forster does not reference this implication in his correspondence with Simon Cooke in July of 2004 or suggest that his representations of Heathcliff are in any way related to Britain's imperial engagements (22n15). Nevertheless, as Cooke likewise insightfully notes, a black Heathcliff "gives visual form, significantly, to Charlotte Brontë's suggestive description of him as a 'black gipsy'" (11).[2]

Forster's intention in racialising Heathcliff to accentuate his position as "a tragic outsider" and thereby elicit sympathy for him is, for the most part, successful, but it is Forster's manipulation of Heathcliff's blackness to forge deeper symbolic associations and emotional meaning that is especially compelling. Employed to accentuate his social marginalisation and Otherness, Heathcliff's blackness is also used to suggest a type of consanguinity between him and Cathy. This visible sign of difference sets them apart from other people while representing their shared passionate natures and powerful affinity. The most striking image conveying this idea is Forster's illustration of their anguished leave-taking prior to her death in childbirth. In it, an impassioned Cathy, her head dramatically thrown back, embraces Heathcliff who is seen only from behind. While she is represented wearing her own dress, she resembles Heathcliff in her black facial features and cropped, Afro-textured hair (136). This illustration renders dramatically visible the profound sense of identification between Heathcliff and Cathy, two marginalised figures, an idea consistently developed in the novel but best expressed in Cathy's compelling declaration to Nelly that she *is* Heathcliff (88). Forster's innovative depiction is further complemented by his incorporation towards the end of the novel of two racialised images of Emily Brontë. In the first, she is presented in a portrait over the mantle, which is suspended behind the embracing, racially indeterminate, Catherine and Hareton, who stand defiant in the face of the viewer, Heathcliff. Emily is notably portrayed as possessing black facial features in the form of thicker lips (263). This image nicely parallels an earlier one featuring two adjacent depictions of Emily Brontë and Heathcliff with strikingly similar, noticeably full lips (237). In such manner does Forster provocatively suggest that the characters of Heathcliff and Cathy serve, for their creator, Emily Brontë, as a type of self-portrait, their consanguinity residing in their shared childhood status as Romantic, untamed, nature-connected and loving outsiders. Thus do Peter Forster's wood engravings tell a fascinating story all their own, one that develops out of, while complementing, Brontë's tragic love story.

Maintaining that "there is a strong tradition of what is called literary cannibalism in the Caribbean" and that "there is something about the Brontë sisters that speaks to Caribbean women, regardless of their color, regardless of their age, regardless of the time they live in" (Wolff 1999), Maryse Condé expertly transplants *Wuthering Heights*, with noteworthy and profound implications, into a different, yet highly amenable time, place and culture in her novel *Windward Heights*. Notably, Condé never suggests in any interview that her sophisticated homage to *Wuthering Heights* was written in response to Brontë's implicit suggestions about a black Heathcliff. Instead, this exercise in narrative transplantation adeptly adapts the key Gothic ingredients of *Wuthering Heights* to the three locales of Cuba, (Roseau) Dominica and, primarily, Guadeloupe, told from the perspective of dozens of characters Condé calls "witnesses" (Wolff), and provides a sweeping overview of several centuries of Caribbean history while focusing especially on the nineteenth into the early twentieth century. In stark contrast to Brontë's implicitly political novel that only gestures outwards from a contained, claustrophobic private sphere to a larger, public sphere that dictates the terms of the private sphere's operation, *Windward Heights* is explicitly undergirded by historico-political commentary that firmly tethers the political and private spheres. By far the most significant factor at play determining Caribbean social hierarchies and power politics is the question of race. In Condé's blunt, unapologetic words during an interview, Guadeloupean society was, as a result of imperialism and the slave trade, an extremely segregated society "based on hate, contempt, […] [and] tension" where "the color of skin was a marker for everything […] your class, your condition, your culture" (Wolff). While Condé brilliantly and readily incorporates Brontë's Gothic strategies in this novel to suggest, as the mother-text does, the rich cultural nature of the supernatural in her social world and the coexistence of the supernatural and natural worlds, she also manipulates her mother-text's tropes and thematics to three particular ends: to indict the imperialist "sins of the fathers" and their irrevocable impact on the islands; to expose and condemn, by way of a female/feminist Gothic lens, the firmly entrenched misogyny that renders women the most brutalised slaves of all, the slaves of slaves; and to heighten, figuratively and symbolically, the devastating and long-term impact of patriarchy and imperialism, with their vast institutional apparatuses and perverting world views.

Condé's highly politically charged poetics suffuse her novel. In its polyphonic make-up that grants voice and subjectivity to dozens of characters from all races and walks of life, *Windward Heights* counters the silencing power of imperialism and its denial of individual subjectivity to its most abused and denigrated victims—former slaves. Strategically, Condé empowers her large cast of characters by chronicling their life stories in their own words, thus celebrating the richness and diversity of Guadeloupeans and their culture and society. As with Brontë's astute decision to recount her novel primarily through the questionable and biased lens of a servant, Nelly Dean, Condé's decision to employ multiple narrative viewpoints is both well considered and political. As she explains in an interview: "[The] slaves were always silent, forced to be silent. They knew they were the real masters of the island. It was a way of giving voice to my people, who were never given voices before. So it was an artistic and a political device" (Wolff). Condé's periodical use of untranslated French-based Creole also serves her agenda of disrupting traditional power structures by disorienting and disempowering the vast majority of her English-speaking readers who cannot understand the language. In this way, she signals her intended, primary readership—namely, Guadeloupeans. In her manipulation of this disarming and subversive strategy, she notably aligns herself with her neo-Gothic hero-villain, Razyé (her Heathcliff), who systematically works—ostensibly, at one point, with a Socialist agenda—to undermine the power of the white Creoles in Guadeloupe. This narrative strategy also disempowers and marginalises many readers, granting them a small taste of Razyé's experience as a social outcast, ostracised due to class and race.

While the obsessive yet doomed relationship between Cathy and Razyé remains the primary focus in *Windward Heights*, Condé incorporates dozens of other similar tales into her vast narrative tableau that render the Cathy–Razyé story emblematic of the innumerable Caribbean tragedies and atrocities produced by British imperialism. The grotesque distorting impact of imperialism on domestic relations is in evidence on every page. The skeleton of *Wuthering Heights* remains essentially intact, however, with racial/

class distinctions constituting the principal factor of social and domestic differentiations and hierarchies. In Condé's narrative, Cathy, the daughter of Hubert Gagneur, is a poor mulatto girl, while Razyé, a child of mixed native Indian and African racial heritage (1995, 8), the island's two most stigmatised races, is discovered among the heath (the *razyé*) where, in an act associating Razyé with Guadeloupe's supernatural *soukougnan*, he bites Hubert, who takes pity on him and brings him home.

Racial desire, denial and self-hatred are writ large in the events that follow. Ostracised, debased as a "monster" who is associated with the untameable forces of nature (80) and said to have been brought by "the evil spirits hidden in the wind of the hurricane" (23), Razyé wonders, occasionally and in keeping with the genealogical Gothic theme of its Brontëan precursor, if he is the child of rape paying for his father's crimes (42). For years following Mr. Gagneur's death, he is abused by Cathy's brother, Justin, who treats him as a field slave, disallowing him entry into the house (23). Cathy thereafter rejects him as a marriage prospect in favour of Aymeric de Linsseuil, a wealthy, white paternalist imperialist who, in many senses, idealises people of colour and works in earnest to educate them. Thus debased, the disaffected Razyé expresses his wish to be white and determines upon revenge (32).

Cathy's life trajectory is likewise incontrovertibly affected by race. Characterised as "a mulatto girl, torn […] between her two races" (42), it is said she elects to embrace her white side by marrying Aymeric, thereby killing and burying her African "wild girl" self (38). Things go from bad to worse as she is transformed into a suicidal zombie after Razyé's sudden departure from Guadeloupe (51), a state from which she is resurrected by a healer, Mama Victoire. In such a manner does Condé bring W. E. B. Du Bois' notion of double consciousness to bear on the psychic experiences of Cathy and Razyé, the former only gaining a peaceful reconciliation of her split self after her death in childbirth when her corpse is said to have grown blacker, a phenomenon that signals her return to greater authenticity (92). Unless his corpse, with its frightening "rictus" smile that makes him look like a bloodsucking *soukougnan* (289–90), suggests otherwise—a narrative element that adheres to the mother-text's depiction of Heathcliff as a type of undead vampire with "sharp white teeth" who, in his post-mortem state, wanders the moors at night with Cathy (Brontë 2003 [1847], 285–87)—Razyé seems to experience no such redemption on either side of the grave.

Given the historical and geographical setting, Razyé's Otherness—magnified as it is by his especially degraded racial hybridity—is brought into greater relief in Condé's narrative tableau where he becomes a far less sympathetic figure than Brontë's Heathcliff. His experiences, unlike Cathy's, fail to be transformative. Fleeing Guadeloupe and filled with *ressentiment* after Cathy's decision to marry Aymeric, Razyé, who is portrayed as a disaffected man, works for the Spanish in Cuba as a soldier for hire. Given a choice to slaughter others or rot and die in prison, he opts to kill innocent women and children, heartlessly and systematically, destroying their villages, turning at night to the self-medical distractions of alcohol, sex and gambling, where he amasses a small fortune. This tutelage in brutality and desensitisation sets the stage for his later personal vengeance as a Guadeloupean terrorist ostensibly in support of the Socialists. Despite his purportedly non-political engagement with violence and criminal activities, including the deliberate burning of sugar cane plantations of which Aymeric's family owns many along with the factory that processes the raw product, he severely undermines and destroys white Creole power—and that of his sworn enemies, the de Linsseuils—on the island (Condé 1995, 183). The tragic, quintessentially Gothic outcome, however, involves the repetition of history whereby new dominant powers emerge to govern the island—in this case, mulattos and blacks—while violence and brutality continue unabated. Thus does history fail to involve evolutionary change, a phenomenon also repeatedly referenced in the novel in relation to the peculiar institution. A disgruntled chorus of Condé's characters note, in passing, that while slavery has been abolished, nothing has essentially changed, socio-economically, politically or otherwise (21, 53). Everything remains, effectively, in a state of limbo, a position that notably plagues Razyé even beyond the grave. Condé gestures towards his eternal, tragic fate near novel's end when his ghost is spotted—as in the conclusion of Brontë's novel—on a tomb where he sits, tragically garbed in his funerary clothes, awaiting someone whose identity he says he has forgotten (308–10).

A key characteristic of Razyé's moral monstrosity is revealed by way of the female Gothic which is writ large in the form of Condé's consistent and trenchant feminist commentary. In his misogyny and brutal treatment of women, who are consistently figured throughout the novel as objects of exchange (44), Razyé is emblematic of all men regardless of race and class. The domestic sphere, whether a plantation/great house or a hovel, serves the role of monstrous prison and/or tomb for its female inhabitants (191). Condé very strategically portrays the traditional plantation/great house as a Gothic locale symbolising property, genealogy and a power and oppression seemingly undefeatable and immutable. Despite being repeatedly burned to the ground and then rebuilt, the de Linsseuils' Belles-Feuilles great house emblematises such power (56). Indeed, all of the novel's great houses are represented as accursed and haunted by the sins of the fathers who designed and built them (4–5, 162, 184), a situation that notably obtains in both *Wuthering Heights*, given the vast amount of Yorkshire wealth generated by the slave trade,[3] and Charlotte Brontë's *Jane Eyre*, where Rochester's fortune derives from Jamaican plantations.[4] The Brontës' novels likewise pay tribute to the objectified women sacrificed to the marriage market. While the child ghost of Cathy haunts the Heights, Bertha Rochester "haunts" Thornfield Hall.

In Condé's expert feminist hands, these edifices are revealed to function in both public and private/domestic capacities and represent the oppressive power of the master, especially in relation to women. Condé personifies the great house of Belles-Feuilles, groaning, shaking and resonating with "all the sounds of its secrets locked in its dressers and cupboards […] rapes, murders and theft of all sorts […] sometimes […] wail[ing] like a widow or a maman separated from her infants[, s]ometimes jabber[ing] like a madwoman" (64). She recounts how people expected the monstrous great house "to open its mouth and swallow everything up, the branches of the trees to change into whips and the rose bushes to grow giant thorns like crab claws" (204). Cathy's brother, Justin Gagneur, describes his sister's entry into her marital home in a manner consistent with the female

Gothic tradition and its indictment of sexual and familial relations, yet magnified by the race-based brutalities of the peculiar institution:

> The house of Belles-Feuilles was filled *with the sighs and sorrows of black, mulatto and white women united in the same subjection.* Slaves raped by sadistic planters. Mistresses poisoned by a rival and dying in unspeakable suffering at the banquet table. Virgins sold to old men for money and parcels of land. Sisters lusted after by their brothers. Mothers by their sons. A week after her marriage, one bride had thrown herself headfirst from the second-floor circular gallery, and the flagstones in the hallway were still stained with her blood. The servants covered it up with the pots of flamingo flowers and red ginger. After slavery was restored by the infamous Richepance, some Mandigo women strangled themselves rather than go back into irons. And discerning these wails and sighs amidst the echoes of the wedding feast, Cathy realized she was taking her place of her own accord in a long procession of victims. (85; emphasis added)

A similar situation obtains with Aymeric's upper-class sister Irmine, who marries Razyé and is characterised as being liberated from her tomb-like home of L'Engoulvent only after her brutalising husband's death (302). Condé suggests that Razyé acts like a slave-master towards Irmine, strategically seducing, marrying and impregnating her in order to sully her family line by way of miscegenation, the key weapon in his arsenal for revenge given his society's race-obsessed world view and hierarchy. Despite their knowledge of Irmine's abuse, her family and friends ignore her plight, likewise regarding her as an object of exchange, a woman who, in dishonouring the family name, merits her violent punishment and is now considered "dead" to her family (116).

Notably, the full extent of Razyé's revenge is not even known by him until novel's end when it is revealed that the children of the next generation who fall in love—Razyé II and Cathy II—are actually half-siblings. Both are Razyé's children. The mystery behind Cathy's peculiar, extremely difficult pregnancy, which is read as a sign that something is wrong with the baby and that her and her "husband's blood are not in agreement" (335), is subsequently resolved. Razyé II discovers, after Cathy's death, that she, who is notably very dark-skinned, is his half-sister, a fact that would have shocked and disgusted her given her hatred of Razyé whom she holds accountable for the death of Aymeric (379). Condé brings the Gothic theme of incest to bear on broader sociopolitical questions relating to Guadeloupe and the Caribbean when Father Bishop, a Catholic cleric in Roseau (Dominica), deems incest to be a regular phenomenon in the islands, due to imperial practises that resulted in a racially mixed people (339). On the basis of his two decades of island residency, Father Bishop surmises that "the tropical humus produced a society whose roots and branches were so intertwined, so twisted and interlocked, that falling in love and sharing a bed with a half-brother or an unknown first cousin was no surprise. What's more, African, European, and Indian blood had mixed in almost equal proportions in every inhabitant" (339). By way of rape, therefore, the sins of the colonising/imperial fathers are shown to be biologically and genetically written into the flesh for generations to come, the grotesque nature of slavery becoming, at once, incontrovertible and irreversible. As Father Bishop's statements also suggest, however, the miscegenation that Razyé wields as a source of Gothic terror is a natural phenomenon that exists across Guadeloupe, although not always readily visible to the naked eye.

In true Gothic fashion, miscegenation is represented as a highly ambivalent phenomenon. On one hand, it is described early in the novel as a source of terror with the extremely dark-skinned, Medusa-like Razyé (115–16), figured as a threatening sexualised monster who transgresses race, gender and class barriers (30, 41, 109), alongside the spectre being raised by white Creoles, of Guadeloupe becoming, by way of intermarriage, post-slavery, "one vast pig-swill where you couldn't tell one color or origin from the next" (54). On the other hand, democracy, which will transcend all racial distinctions and prejudices—a figurative form of miscegenation—heralds the future solution to Guadeloupe's race war (54). Such is the view of a young Aymeric, newly returned from France, after reading "much Montesquieu and other philosophers," with plans of "eradicating the very memory of slavery and transforming the Belles-Feuilles estate into a model plantation where there would be no white Creoles, no mulattos, no blacks, but free men, equal in the eyes of the law" (41). Until such time, and as the monologue of Cathy I's ghost makes clear (99–104), Condé suggests that only death may bring one to a place beyond race (108), freeing former slaves from pain while granting them the ability to become, truly, themselves (89). That this peace is withheld from Razyé after his death—when he is discovered with a fittingly sardonic "rictus" smile and resembling a bloodsucking *soukougnon* (289–90)—speaks to his grievous crimes against humanity, perpetrated to ensure his survival yet committed in collusion with the abusive imperial powers. In this, as in other instances, the cycles that make up the history of Guadeloupe are shown to be Gothic, with the overarching, resounding mantra captured in a popular French epigram—*plus ça change, plus c'est la même chose* (the more things change, the more they remain the same).

Where Condé rewrites *Wuthering Heights* as a commentary on the similar social worlds born of British imperialism that exists in distant corners of that empire, Andrea Arnold's controversial cinematic rendition of Brontë's novel introduces a black Heathcliff in order to connect exploitative British imperial practices and their capital gains at the margins with the centre. In such a manner does her neo-Victorian film aim to craft a fuller picture of how those practices, particularly its slave trade and plantation economies, serve as the source for Yorkshire wealth. Arnold's strategy in her aesthetically stunning, powerfully poetic film that works primarily through images as opposed to dialogue is to bring a series of carefully selected signs to bear on the insular environment of the Yorkshire moors in a manner that may be described as semiotic geopolitical superimposition. In sequences that comprise much of the film, Arnold figures the Heights as a plantation operating by way of plantation methods and a plantation economy. In her informative and provocative article "*Wuthering Heights* and the Liverpool Slave Trade," Maja-Lisa Von Sneidern argues, in relation to the Heights, that Brontë

> locates her plantation colony not on the margins of the empire, some exotic island half way around the world, but in the heart of Yorkshire. In the novel the Heights, corrupted by the introduction of the racially other, is the place where the figures of a system of bondage work out their relationships. These relationships are represented according to principles common to abolitionist, anti-abolitionist, and Anglo-Saxon racialist discourses available at the time the novel was composed. The Grange, like Mother England, is an estate isolated from a planter economy both by breeding and seeming cultural independence. At one point Isabella writes that the distance between the Heights and the Grange

is tantamount to "the Atlantic." Despite its insularity, the Grange becomes contaminated. (1995, 174)

The semiotics of Arnold's film advances a similar superimposition between the Heights and a slave plantation. Regarded by locals as a filthy heathen, Heathcliff experiences, from the outset, violence at the hands of Hindley, the hyper-Christian Mr. Earnshaw and the community, whose mission to baptise him at the local church is presented as an act of purification of a demonised Other and, from Heathcliff's perspective, an attempted execution by drowning. His quality of life is radically diminished when he is relegated to the moors where he is forced into gruelling farm labour and disallowed contact with Cathy. Regularly flogged, punished, chased and bitten by dogs (like a fugitive slave or black civil rights' activist) and segregated in a prison-like cell, Heathcliff is essentially reduced, on what seems like a plantation, to the status of a field slave. This suggestion is most powerfully made through the image of his horribly scarred back—a powerful emblem of the brutalities of slavery of which there exist extant photographs—following a vicious flogging from Hindley. Cathy's act of painstakingly licking Heathcliff's deep, oozing wounds with her tongue, like a young, wild animal for healing purposes, aligns with both Brontë's and Arnold's representations of their bonding in nature as children in an instinctual and tender way. Heathcliff may be portrayed throughout as a man of extremes—tender one minute and brutal the next—who is produced by his natural and social environments, but the violent and degrading system is shown to win out. With Heathcliff in full control of the Heights at the film's conclusion, his adopted son, Hareton, emulates his earlier act of hanging a puppy. Just as Heathcliff was beaten into submission and tutored in violence by his white paternal masters, Hareton follows suit, the cycle of violence remaining unbroken.

In stark contrast to Condé's novel yet in keeping with Arnold's film, Caryl Phillips' *The Lost Child* (2015) daringly forges a direct connection between the Earnshaws in *Wuthering Heights* and the slave trade by way, specifically, of plantations in Antigua. Comprised of sedimented, complementary narratives that shift between "real" and "fictional" worlds and histories to explore and meditate on racism, misogyny and the vulnerability of the oppressed, *The Lost Child* is bookended by Heathcliff's mother's tragic life story and incorporates an inset narrative devoted to the dying Emily Brontë's final days. Mr. Earnshaw's conflicted, hypocritical relationship with slavery is evidenced by his investments in Antigua and in Heathcliff's status as Earnshaw's bastard child born of his love affair with a former female slave in Liverpool. The concisely told tale of Heathcliff's mother, abandoned by Earnshaw after her pregnancy and forced to become a prostitute in order to survive, is followed by a brief reference to her vulnerable, terrified child—an emblem of Earnshaw's short-lived guilt—to whom he must do his "duty" (257) after the death of the child's mother.

Written on the heels of decades of race riots that transpired in the Brontës' beloved home region of Northern England—Leeds, Manchester and Birmingham—following the Bristol, London and Brixton riots of 1980–81, Phillips advances an incisive socio-historical commentary about the persistence of British racism and misogyny across a century and a half. The spectre of the Victorian world, with its regressive view of minorities, has cast a long and dark shadow. In such a critical manner is *The Lost Child* neo-Victorian. This critique is especially incorporated into the main narrative that chronicles the depressingly tragic life story of one Monica, a vivacious young Northerner who abandons her intellectual dreams and university degree, in adherence to social dictates, to get married. Her choice of an Afro-Caribbean husband, in defiance of social dictates, becomes especially plaguing for her two mixed-race children after the marriage fails and she relocates to the North. Although recounted in a prosaic manner, a chilling story follows: obtaining only sporadic employment, her children moving in and out of care, Monica is seduced and groomed by Derek Evans, a married man who sexually molests and then murders her youngest son, Tommy, on the moors, a horrific crime that happens off-page and conjures up the shocking moors murders of the mid-1960s perpetrated by Ian Brady and Myra Hindley. This child's mysterious social withdrawal and depression had become concerning to his older brother, Ben, from whose perspective this tragic section of the story is recounted as he subsequently and painfully uncovers the horrifying mystery.

The impact on Monica is severe. She suffers a breakdown and is thereafter institutionalised in a mental hospital where she commits suicide. An ironic statement voiced by a nurse urging Monica to "try to trust people a little" so she may be properly assessed and released (236) articulates one of Phillips' key commentaries. Trust and vulnerability lie at the heart of her tragedy given the paltry options open to women for validation and valorisation beyond sex, marriage and mothering in the mid-twentieth century when this novel is set, a world where predatory men who objectify women possess all of the respect, power and control. Phillips' inset narrative chronicling Emily Brontë's final days—although contentious given its portrayal of a dysfunctional family in which Emily exists as an outcast, "lost child"—is in keeping with his devastatingly bleak portrait and disturbing commentary about the challenges faced by visible minorities and women in realising their ambitions. The mind, Phillips suggests, offers a portal to one of two very distinct narrative outcomes—either self-realisation and freedom, or madness. While Emily Brontë's imagination provides her with a gateway to self-expression and freedom, Phillips suggests, Monica's turn inward has more devastating results in the form of her descent into madness. Possessing few options and even fewer survival strategies, vulnerable blacks, women and children find themselves at the mercy of their masters—masters often secured by random chance—an idea signalled in the novel's pathos-inducing closing lines where the young Heathcliff, having crossed the stormy moors with Earnshaw prior to entering Wuthering Heights for the first time, a child still yearning after his mother, entreats Earnshaw not to hurt him (260). Heathcliff's ultimate fate, where the sins of the fathers are shown to devolve upon the sons in a thwarted incestuous relationship and destructive property battle, is literary history as recounted in the mother-text.

As if piggybacking on Heathcliff's childhood history in Phillips' novel, Michael Stewart's clever and highly readable *Ill Will: The Untold Story of Heathcliff* (2018) is equally mother focused. Daringly told in the first person by its orphan narrator, Heathcliff, who is represented from the outset as a figurative slave dispossessed of his real name, language and family history, Stewart's hugely intertextual, generically hybrid story strives to fill in the mysterious gap in the mother-text around Heathcliff's three-year absence from the Heights. More in keeping with the female Gothic than the traditional Gothic in its detective-style maternal quest, this novel recounts Heathcliff's journey to find his mother and thus discover his origins and true identity. With a huge nod to the picaresque tradition, Heathcliff teams up, early on, with a resilient young female orphan named Emily, a survivor of childhood trauma and neglect, who subsists by her wits and her putative ability to speak to the dead. As memories of his childhood push increasingly to the fore, their road trip progresses through Manchester into Liverpool where it is ultimately revealed that Heathcliff's slave mother was transported from the Gambia to Liverpool where she was forced into prostitution in a neighbouring village on an estate owned by Jonas Bold, the city's richest man. After being impregnated by Mr. Earnshaw, a repeat customer who makes "a special agreement to use her exclusively" (309), and giving birth to Heathcliff, she commits suicide by starvation in a desperate act of liberation, defiance and revenge. Heathcliff thereafter proves his consanguinity by undertaking a series of vengeful bloody acts of his own: He castrates and kills the man, Pierce Hardwar, who bought her, and brutally and graphically slaughters the recently bereaved and putatively remorseful Jonas Bold, now a man of the cloth, before stealing some of his slave-based fortune and returning to the Heights.

Stewart's novel may be both historically inaccurate and anachronistic in its Victorian setting featuring workhouses and an industrial Manchester in full swing,[5] but this neo-Victorian revision cunningly and explicitly lays bare the source of vast amounts of British wealth in human trafficking and the exploitation of slave labour. Heathcliff's experience of Manchester likewise reveals the existence, on British soil, of another heartless exploitative system in the form of industrial capitalism that, as his encounters with labourers on his road trip reveal, galvanises the drive for workers' rights. Despite Heathcliff's self-righteous acts of brutal violence and the novel's role as a wish-fulfilment revenge fantasy where he regains his rightful maternal inheritance, the money's source, in true Gothic fashion, implicates this British gentleman-in-the-making in his own mother's exploitation. Stewart's inset narrative incisively identifies imperialism as the source of much Yorkshire wealth, persuasively accounting for Heathcliff's hardened, more vengeful character upon his return in the mother-text. It likewise and very cleverly explains the nature of Heathcliff's revenge in Brontë's novel—his drive towards acquiring the Earnshaws' treasured property, figuratively assuming the role of plantation owner, and assaulting, raping and degrading Isabella Linton in a manner consistent with his mother's objectification and brutalisation. As in Condé's novel, in view of Heathcliff's misogynistic actions to come, violence is shown to be genealogical and cyclical.

Extrapolating from repeated rhetorical and narrative suggestions in *Wuthering Heights* that present the hero-villain Heathcliff as a vampire, a demon, a ghost and a cannibal, the question of Heathcliff's monstrosity is also paramount in *Ill Will*. Drawing on one of the novel's primary themes of ventriloquising the dead, Stewart cunningly employs Mary Shelley's *Frankenstein* as an intertext equating the "blackamoor" (18) Heathcliff, a Gothic "half-man" and "half-monster" (23), with Victor Frankenstein's Creature. Like that wandering outcast, Heathcliff becomes literate, identifies with the fallen Lucifer he encounters in the Bible and finds his own voice as he tells his tale to the absent, haunting Cathy. The monster may be revealed to be a product of nurture rather than nature with the sins of the white fathers being visited on their interracial sons but, as Stewart shows in great graphic detail through the figure of Heathcliff, the sons may become their monstrous fathers, not only growing desensitised to violence but sadistically glorying in it.

While the Gothic heart of darkness in *Ill Will*, as in *Windward Heights* and *The Lost Child*, is shown to reside in Britain's imperial practices, and deep-seated racist and misogynistic violence—Heathcliff's mother, Lilith, whose name from the Jewish Apocrypha suggests she is the dark, independent Eve, is enslaved, displaced, raped, imprisoned and forced into prostitution—Stewart also cleverly reveals the Gothic self that lurks in the heart of Heathcliff. This young man, traumatised and abused in childhood, rejected in love and haunted by loss, who undertakes a journey to discover his mother, his history and himself, ultimately finds more than he bargained for. As Marxist poet and politician Aimé Césaire insightfully claims in his groundbreaking *Discourse on Colonialism* that exposes and indicts the colonial mission as "Gothic" (2000 [1955], 19) and regressive (63), "colonization works to *decivilize* the colonizer, to *brutalise* him in the true sense of the word, to degrade him, to awaken him to buried instincts, to covetousness, violence, race hatred, and moral relativism" (13; emphasis in original). As the neo-Victorian and postcolonial revisions of *Wuthering Heights* examined here render explicit, the pernicious mechanisms and ghosts of imperialism can never be entirely exorcised. Whether undertaken to indict "neo-Victorian" and benighted societies, enhance our vision of Victorian society based on recent cultural and/or historic findings or engage in the escapist pleasure of punishing the perpetrators of Victorian imperial ideologies, their Gothic lessons reveal that even the colonised are at risk, in their acts of colonial mimicry, of resurrecting them.

Notes

1 Heathcliff's very first description as "a dark-skinned gipsy" (Brontë 2003 [1847], 27) is followed by Nelly's characterisation of him as a "gipsy brat" (51). The young Earnshaw then addresses Heathcliff as "gipsy" when the latter bullies him into exchanging colts (54). Edgar Linton's mother expresses surprise when she realises it is Cathy who is "scouring the country with a gipsy" (62). Joseph informs Hindley that Cathy exhibits "bonny behaviour, lurking amang t' fields, after twelve o' t' night, wi' that fahl, flaysome divil of a gipsy, Heathcliff!" (92). After Heathcliff returns following several years of absence, Edgar Linton remembers him as "the gipsy—the ploughboy," a categorisation that Nelly says would upset Cathy (98).

2 In this instance, Cooke misquotes Charlotte Brontë who describes Heathcliff in that letter as being a "black gipsy-cub," a representation that underscores his initial role as a young child, a qualification Brontë employs to make her point in that sentence that Heathcliff "might possibly have been reared into a human being, but tyranny and ignorance made of him a mere demon" (Wise and Symington, 1933, 2:245).

3 Von Sneidern provides this information: "The English city with the most spirited commerce in slaves was Liverpool. At mid-century Liverpool ranked third behind London and Bristol, but by the interbellum period (1763–1776) she had eclipsed her competitors and was the premier slaving port in Britain [...] By 1764 Liverpool boasted more than twice the number of vessels engaged in the triangular trade than Bristol, and by 1804 Liverpool merchants were responsible for more than eighty-four percent of the British transatlantic slave trade" (1995, 170–71).

4 See my essay, "Burning Down the Master's (Prison)-house: Revolution and Revelation in Colonial and Postcolonial Female Gothic," about *Jane Eyre*'s abolitionist message, particularly as regards the sources of Rochester's and Jane's inheritances.

5 Curiously and problematically, Stewart provides an actual birth year for Heathcliff in this novel—1764 (2018, 316)—a year that would be in keeping with Brontë's novel but not with the Victorian setting Stewart describes. The workhouses referenced by the young Emily (81) were instituted after the New Poor Law of 1834, which would put Heathcliff in his seventies at the time of their journey.

Bibliography

Ashcroft, Bill, Gareth Griffiths and Helen Tiffin. *The Empire Writes Back: Theory and Practice in Post-colonial Literatures*. London: Routledge, 1989.

Bhabha, Homi K. "Of Mimicry and Man: The Ambivalence of Colonial Discourse." *October* 28 (1984): 125–33.

———, ed. "Introduction: Narrating the Nation." In *Nation and Narration*, 1–7. London: Routledge, 1990.

Brontë, Emily. *Wuthering Heights*. 1847. Boston: Bedford/St. Martin's, 2003.

Césaire, Aimé. *Discourse on Colonialism*. 1955. Translated by Joan Pinkham. In *Discourse on Colonialism*, edited by Robin D. G. Kelley, 29–78. New York: Monthly Review Press, 2000.

Condé, Maryse. *Windward Heights*. Translated by Richard Philcox. New York: Soho Press, 1995.

Cooke, Simon. "'The Ever-Shifting Kaleidoscope of the Imagination': Modern Illustrations to the Brontës." *Brontë Studies* 31 (2006): 7–22.

Davison, Carol Margaret. "Burning down the Master's (Prison)-House: Revolution and Revelation in Colonial and Postcolonial Female Gothic." In *Empire and the Gothic: The Politics of Genre*, edited by Andrew Smith and William Hughes, 136–54. London: Palgrave, 2003.

Du Bois, W. E. B. *The Souls of Black Folk*. 1903. In *Three Negro Classics*, 207–389. New York: Avon Books, 1965.

Eagleton, Terry. *Heathcliff and the Great Hunger*. London: Verso, 1995.

Eichenberg, Fritz, ill. *Wuthering Heights* by Emily Brontë. New York: Random House, 1943.

Esquirol, Jean Étienne. "Monomania." In *Embodied Selves: An Anthology of Psychological Texts, 1830–1890*, edited by Jenny Bourne Taylor and Sally Shuttleworth, 256–62. Oxford: Clarendon Press, 2003.

Forster, Peter, ill. *Wuthering Heights* by Emily Brontë. London: Folio Society, 1991.

Phillips, Caryl. *The Lost Child*. New York: Farrar, Strauss, and Giroux, 2015.

Pratt, Mary Louise. *Imperial Eyes: Travel Writing and Transculturation*. London: Routledge, 1992.

Shelley, Percy Bysshe. "On *Frankenstein*." *Athenaeum*, November 10, 1832, 730.

Shuttleworth, Sally. "Natural History: The Retro-Victorian Novel." In *The Third Culture: Literature and Science*, edited by E. S. Shaffer, 253–68. Berlin: de Gruyter, 1998.

Smart, B. C., and H. T. Crofton. *The Dialect of the English Gypsies*, 2nd ed. London: Ascher, 1875.

Stewart, Michael. *Ill Will: The Untold Story of Heathcliff*. London: HQ, 2018.

Von Sneidern, Maja-Lisa. "*Wuthering Heights* and the Liverpool Slave Trade." *ELH* 62 (1995): 171–96.

Wise, T. J., and J. A. Symington, eds. *The Brontes: Their Lives, Friendships and Correspondence*. Vol. 2. Oxford: Blackwell, 1933.

Wolff, Rebecca. Interview with Maryse Condé. *Bomb*, July 1, 1999. https://bombmagazine.org/articles/maryse-cond%C3%A9/.

Wuthering Heights. Directed by Andrea Arnold. Curzon Artificial Eye. 2011. DVD.

Chapter Four

TOXIC NEO-GOTHIC MASCULINITY: MR. HYDE, TYLER DURDEN AND DONALD J. TRUMP AS ANGRY WHITE MEN

Martin Danahay

Michael Kimmel's analysis of the causes of white male violence in his book *Angry White Men* (2013) paints a portrait of aggrieved white American masculinity that highlights the continuities and divergences between two fictional examples: Mr. Hyde from Robert Louis Stevenson's *Strange Case of Dr. Jekyll and Mr. Hyde* (2015 [1886]) and Tyler Durden from Chuck Palahniuk's novel *Fight Club* (1996) and David Fincher's film adaptation (1999). The cultural and historical forces that elicited aggressive responses from white males differ in each case, but they are united by an ideology that assumes anger and violence to be integral traits of masculine identity. The commonality between these texts lies in a combination of class, race and gender identifications, particularly that of angry, white, conventional male masculinity. This neo-Gothic genealogy of toxic masculinity can be traced from Mr. Hyde to the election of Donald J. Trump through the link of Tyler Durden and the term "snowflake" which has become the insult of choice for angry white men in the twenty-first century.

The Gothic as a popular literary genre taps into the fears and anxieties of its time, and both *Jekyll and Hyde* as a late Victorian "shilling shocker" and *Fight Club* as a neo-Gothic text explore the threat of male violence. In both texts the fear of the loss of male hegemony leads to outbursts of violence against perceived threats from other social groups.[1] Both Mr. Hyde and Tyler Durden (especially when played by Brad Pitt in the film version) are attractive figures for men in that they present violent solutions to a loss of male hegemony and present violence as a response to loss of status.[2] For Dr. Jekyll, Mr. Hyde represents a change of class status as he loses his professional designation as a doctor and becomes a mere "Mister," while for Durden and members of his club, violence functions as a compensation for the loss of "manly" occupations and their replacement by work in the service sector.

These angry white men also illustrate the differences between two terms that are widely used in masculinities studies, namely, "hegemonic masculinity" and "toxic masculinity."[3] White, upper-class men are hegemonic in *Jekyll and Hyde* while women are marginalised. The text thus exemplifies R. W. Connell and James W. Messerschmidt's definition of hegemonic masculinity in that Dr. Jekyll represents "the currently most honored way of being a man" which "legitimated the global subordination of women to

men" (2005, 832). While Connell and Messerschmidt do not locate their model in a specific historical period, their hypothesis elucidates attitudes that undergird assumptions of
masculine power. Applying their theoretical model to *Jekyll and Hyde*, the most honoured
social status in the Victorian Era was to be male, English, upper class and white.
Dr. Jekyll faces a crisis of masculinity because the prevailing mage of Victorian upper-
class manliness does not correspond to his "lived experience" (838), so that a contradiction arises between his gender and class position and his "undignified" (Stevenson 2015
[1886], 78) desires.

While hegemonic masculinity primarily describes male dominance, "toxic masculinity" includes not only practices that enable men to hold power but also how they can
actively damage others through aggression. Hegemonic masculinity includes behaviours
that are indirectly harmful to men themselves and oppressive to others, but the label
"toxic masculinity," which Connell and Messerschmidt would reject as focusing too much
on "toxic practices" (2005, 840),[4] includes outbursts of male anger and violence that
lead to verbal and physical attacks on other social groups. "Toxic masculinity" therefore
includes deliberate hostility and violence, not just privilege. The term "toxic masculinity"
applies to both Durden and Trump in that being male for them is the basis for active hostility and the threat of violence. Where the threat of violence is largely contained within
the male-dominated society of *Jekyll and Hyde*, Durden's aggression presents a threat on a
larger scale. Durden's "space monkeys" of Project Mayhem (Palahniuk 1976, 78) express
white male anger through small-scale provocations that, in the film version at least, ultimately lead to blowing up buildings. Donald J. Trump, as President of the United States,
can threaten "fire and fury" (Myers and Sang-Hun 2017) on a global scale that includes
nuclear weaponry.

Jekyll and Hyde has long provided a heuristic with which to explore the dynamics
of masculine anger. Nineteenth-century Gothic monsters like Hyde are "meaning
machines" (Halberstam 1995, 825) that can become the vehicles for a wide array of cultural anxieties; however, Mr. Hyde embodies a particular form of masculinity in which
a "surface respectability" is assumed to be the antithesis of violence (26), but this polite
exterior masks the anger and resentment bubbling beneath the surface. Dr. Jekyll could
not express a range of emotions because of the valorisation of repression in Victorian
culture, but even in the context of contemporary America there are strictures on male
behaviour, especially in personal relationships with other men. Homosexuality "haunts"
Jekyll and Hyde (66), but it also causes anxiety for contemporary heterosexual men whose
identity is predicated on the rejection of same-sex desire (Kimmel and Mahler 2004,
118). American male behaviour is restrained in different ways than that of a Victorian
gentleman, but certain desires are anathematised just as much, if for different reasons.

While adaptations of *Jekyll and Hyde*—such as the famous Richard Mansfield stage
version in 1887 (Danahay and Chisholm 2005, 47–78)—immediately introduced
female characters and made sexual violence against women the problematic in the text,
Stevenson's original has far more to say about the veneer of civilization that overlay
what he saw as more primordial and violent desires, emphasising the contradiction
between Dr. Jekyll's gentlemanly exterior and the repressed aggressive emotions that lay
beneath the polished surface. The tale's emphasis on secrets and silence underlines how

in Victorian society unacknowledged desires were known to exist but were repressed from expression lest they unleash violence. Mr. Hyde is described as a troglodyte and a throwback who exhibits his degenerate status through his actions in trampling a child as well as killing a member of Parliament (Stevenson 2015 [1886], 35 and 48); Stevenson thus sees him as the expression of a primordial masculine violence that is held in check only through severe repression. Dr. Jekyll's rebellion against this repression leads to his death.

The most immediate effect of Dr. Jekyll indulging his desires is to provide him with an alternative working-class body in which to conceal his illicit activities.[5] In the Victorian context working-class men (especially young men) were viewed as innately criminal and violent.[6] Working-class masculinity is a threat to upper-class men in Dr. Jekyll's social circle due to class resentment because Mr. Hyde bears signs of manual labour in his body and encodes a fear of working-class violence erupting within the social circle of upper-class white men. When Mr. Hyde confronts Dr. Lanyon, he notes that Mr. Hyde was too small for the gentleman's clothes he was wearing (74) signaling Dr. Jekyll's literal loss of stature. The revelation of Dr. Jekyll's dual identity, which Hyde warns him will be a "prodigy to stagger the unbelief of Satan" (74), leads eventually to his death.

The contrast between the upper-class and working-class body is represented most overtly in the bedroom scene in which Dr. Jekyll wakes up in his house and finds to his horror that he is inhabiting the body of Mr. Hyde:

> I smiled to myself, and, in my psychological way began lazily to inquire into the elements of this illusion, occasionally, even as I did so, dropping back into a comfortable morning doze. I was still so engaged when, in one of my more wakeful moments, my eyes fell upon my hand. Now the hand of Henry Jekyll (as you have often remarked) was professional in shape and size: it was large, firm, white and comely. But the hand which I now saw, clearly enough, in the yellow light of a mid-London morning, lying half shut on the bed-clothes, was lean, corded, knuckly, of a dusky pallor and thickly shaded with a swart growth of hair. It was the hand of Edward Hyde. (84)

Others have noted the markers of degeneration in this passage, particularly the "swart growth of hair" (82).[7] The majority of adjectives, however, point to this hand being working class: It is muscled as if from manual labour, tanned from being outside and shows signs of inadequate nutrition. The scene represents a disruption of class boundaries as the working-class male body is out of place in Dr. Jekyll's upscale bedroom with its "decent" furniture (84). The working-class body is an insurrection within the respectable household. The horror of the moment lies in Dr. Jekyll's involuntary transformation into a working-class man and his subsequent plunge down the social hierarchy.

In *Fight Club*, by contrast, the insurrection led by Tyler Durden is an effort to reinstate male hegemony rather than the eruption of an anathematised working-class body. Violence is represented as a way of reasserting male power in the face of consumerism and the erosion of job prospects. The narrator follows a trajectory from white- to blue-collar occupations and the founding of Fight Club as a way to express a general feeling of loss of social status based on occupation.[8] Where Mr. Hyde threatens social cohesion, in *Fight Club* violence between men creates bonds based on damaged male bodies.[9] Fight

Club is like a soccer club or bowling league in that it creates community, but the bonds between the members are asserted through the marks of violence rather than a uniform or shared hobby.

The common denominator linking Stevenson's original 1886 tale to subsequent remakes of his story and *Fight Club* is the portrayal of a divided masculinity that underscores contradictions in gender ideology. Dr. Jekyll is a handsome man and Richard Mansfield, who turned the story into the first hit play, was a lead in many romantic comedies; Fredric March, who played the role in the Paramount version directed by Rouben Mamoulian (1931), was a matinée idol and Brad Pitt is a famous Hollywood star in Fincher's adaptation. In both cases the handsome lead actors accentuated the division between the charming male surface and the violence that lay beneath the appealing exterior. The posters for the 1931 film featuring March and for the 1991 film featuring Pitt and Edward Norton are similar in that they use a split screen of an attractive figure on one side and the threatening character on the other.[10] These split screen images recall the trick photograph of Richard Mansfield as both Dr. Jekyll and Mr. Hyde that the actor used to promote his performances (Danahay and Chisholm 2005, 46). The actors combine attractiveness with danger when playing their roles, portraying masculinity as both appealing and innately violent. In this they exemplify the Gothic as a mixture of desire and fear defined by that which undermines conventional Victorian gender ideology and betrays the contradiction in masculine identity (Day 1985, 84).

These contradictions in masculine identity are not confined to the Victorian Era but can also be found in later neo-Gothic texts. Masculinity is not a static or stable category and contemporary theorists use the term "masculinities" to acknowledge the variety of often contradictory styles of being a man in any historical moment (Kimmel 2010). What acting "like a man" means changes according to historical context, class position and ethnicity. Rather than outline a historical trajectory for toxic masculinity, the ambition here is to trace echoes across three distinct cultural moments where masculinity, class and violence coalesced in two fictional texts and a real political figure. The commonality between all three is the central role of an angry white man; the major differences between the three can best be summarised in comparing and contrasting hegemonic and toxic versions of masculinity.

Dr. Jekyll's failure as a gentleman

Kimmel, drawing on remarks by Alexis de Tocqueville about American masculinity in the nineteenth century, uses the phrase "lucky men restless in the midst of abundance" (2013, 19), which is an apt description of Dr. Jekyll at the beginning of Stevenson's text. Whereas in the American context this restlessness was based on seeking new frontiers and the accumulation of ever more wealth, in the British Victorian context of *Jekyll and Hyde* the dissatisfaction arose not from abundance but from the strictures of propriety. Dr. Jekyll's self-division arises from a conflict between his desires and the behaviour expected of him as a professional and as a gentleman. As his "Statement of the Case" explains, he was born into a privileged position and respected for his public persona: "I was born in the year 18—to a large fortune, endowed besides with excellent parts, inclined by nature to industry, fond of the respect of the wise and good among my fellow-men, and thus, as might have been supposed, with every guarantee of an honourable and distinguished future" (Stevenson 2015 [1886], 75).

Dr. Jekyll's class status means he must follow norms of behaviour that led him to repress yearnings incompatible with the standards of his social circle. These behaviours were associated with the term "gentleman" which was a highly valued class marker for men in the period. Samuel Smiles in his chapter titled "Character—The True Gentleman" in *Self-Help* underlined the importance of the designation, writing that "every man is bound to aim at the possession of a good character as one of the highest objects of life." "Gentleman" is a term that was connected to masculinity and metaphorical "possession" as if it were land or a material object that validated the owner's class status (1897).[11] The amount of discourse on the definition of the term attests to its importance as a sign of class position as well as to the difficulty in defining the term if it was disconnected from material signs such as ownership of land or capital; all writers uniformly linked it to behaviour rather than any material measurement (Ruskin 1909, 343). Smiles cites character traits rather than wealth or social status as essential to being a man and a gentleman: "Truthfulness, integrity, and goodness—qualities that hang not on any man's breath—form the essence of manly character [...] He is strong to do good, strong to resist evil, and strong to bear up under difficulty and misfortune" (1897).

Smiles' formulation here underlines the connection between the qualities that he extols and masculinity, reinforcing the point later by writing that "a man must really be what he seems or purposes to be." This definition contrasts with Dr. Jekyll's description of his divided consciousness in which he "concealed [his] pleasures," leading a "profound duplicity of life" (Stevenson 2015 [1886], 75–76). Dr. Jekyll hides his deviance becoming both double when he should integrate and lying when he should be truthful rather than "being what he seems to be" in a failure of what Smiles would term "manly character." He is not behaving like a gentleman within the parameters laid out by Smiles and others and thus loses class status when he becomes Mr. Hyde to indulge prohibited desires. Dr. Jekyll's "full statement of the case" does not reveal what "pleasures" he sought that led him to this double existence; rather, their exact nature is not as important as the fact that he has failed the test of gentlemanly character. While on the surface Dr. Jekyll appears respectable and a member of his social class, there is a disjuncture between appearance and aspects of his identity that he is concealing. Eventually this side of him will be bodied forth in the persona of Mr. Hyde (whose name implies the hidden), but at this point the text underlines a situation in which Dr. Jekyll is in danger of losing his class position and his status as a gentleman.

Mr. Hyde is the antithesis of a gentleman. In the first scene involving Hyde, he tramples a child and then shows no remorse, thus directly contravening a trait of the gentleman that is so important for Smiles that he puts it in capital letters: "There are many tests by which a gentleman may be known; but there is one that never fails—How does he EXERCISE POWER over those subordinate to him? How does he conduct himself towards women and children?" (1897). We do not directly observe Hyde's behaviour towards women, but he certainly shows cruelty towards a child. Indeed, Hyde is shown as angry and violent to the point of committing murder, suggesting the seething rage beneath Dr. Jekyll's polite surface. The fact that he is *Mr.* Hyde in contrast to *Dr.* Jekyll shows that he has a lower-class status, and this is reinforced by his choice of lodging in the disreputable area of Soho and in the description of his hand. Where Dr. Jekyll has a "professional" hand, Hyde's by contrast shows signs of bad nutrition in being "lean" and of having worked at manual labour in being "corded" and muscular (Stevenson 2015 [1886], 81).

Dr. Jekyll's crisis of masculinity leads therefore to him inhabiting the body of a violent, working-class man. In John Ruskin's terms "self-command is often thought a characteristic of high-breeding" (1909, 385), but Hyde has no self-control at all and in killing Sir Danvers Carew "broke out of all bounds" and clubbed him to death (48). Along with Mr. Hyde's physical characteristics his behaviour links him to Victorian stereotypes of the working classes as innately violent and in evolutionary terms less advanced than the upper classes according to Cesare Lombroso's degeneration theory (57–63). Dr. Jekyll's statement alludes to this when he refers to the "primitive duality of man"; Mr. Hyde's degenerate status is also inferred by Hyde's "swart growth of hair" (82), which positions him as a simian throwback in comparison to Dr. Jekyll. The description echoes Darwin writing about anger and ascribing human canines to a primitive ancestor (155–57). The chain of association here is that for Dr. Jekyll to express violence he must drop "lower"; he must lose class status and revert to a more primitive version of *Homo sapiens* in order to become violent. Mr. Hyde is described as "like a monkey" (64) by Poole, cementing the connection between him and Dr. Jekyll's primitive ancestor, thus explaining his innate violence.

Masculine bonds are under pressure in *Jekyll and Hyde* from the Labouchère Amendment (1885) as part of the legal and cultural drive to criminalise homosexuality; as Richard Dury notes, "Veiled allusions to homosexuality are particularly frequent" in the text (2004, xxx). Mr. Hyde as a working-class younger man is possibly a "rent boy" or male prostitute. Mr. Utterson refers to him as a "young man" (Stevenson 2015 [1886], 47) and worries that he represents some youthful indiscretion by his client, presumably of a sexual nature (39). Although Stevenson himself rejected reading the text in terms of sexuality, writing in a letter to John Paul Bocock that Jekyll was not "Great Gods! a mere voluptuary," but rather "the harm was in Jekyll, because he was a hypocrite" (quoted in Maixner 1995, 231). Kimmel and Mahler describe hegemonic masculinity as dependent on the rejection of homosexuality, and the eventual killing of Hyde enacts a ritual expulsion of the threat of homoeroticism from the band of professional men that constitute Dr. Jekyll's social circle (2004, 114–15). Dr. Jekyll's social circle is "exclusive" in that it is not only open solely to white men of a certain social class, but it is actively policed by its members like Utterson who are not officials but rather turned into amateur sleuths by the challenge of Mr. Hyde; Utterson says, "If he be Mr. Hyde [...] I shall be Mr. Seek" (Stevenson 2015 [1886], 41). Like Sherlock Holmes, Mr. Utterson is not a detective for an agency but a self-nominated guardian of propriety who functions to support a particular social order (Jann 1990, 687), especially class distinctions (695). Dury notes that the text "has been seen as a protest against how the dominant professional classes [...] defend their own social position" (2004, xxxix), which is borne out by Mr. Hyde's fate. He is treated like a virus that must be expelled from the male social body, and his fate suggests that upper-class masculine hegemony is protected by his demise. Hyde dies not only because he expresses violence that threatens the social status of a gentleman but also because he expresses the anathematised potential of sexual desire among men that undermines the homosocial bonds of the male clique in *Jekyll and Hyde*.[12]

Fight Club: Violence as male bonding

In *Fight Club* violence is a form of homoeroticism and a way to exorcise homosexual desire; the text manages to be both homoerotic and homophobic simultaneously. There are similarities in the portrayal of hegemonic masculinity in *Jekyll and Hyde* and *Fight Club* in that there are codes of silence that inhibit relationships among men and prevent intimacy. In *Jekyll and Hyde* Mr. Utterson and Mr. Enfield were in the habit of taking Sunday walks together in which "they said nothing" (Stevenson 2015 [1886], 33) to each other, and Mr. Enfield expresses an aversion to asking questions about other men because "it partakes too much of the style of the day of judgment" (37). In *Fight Club* the first and second rules are that you do not talk about fight club (Palahniuk 1997, 48) so that a code of silence is also enshrined as its defining aspect: fight club "isn't about words" but is about not talking (151); male relationships in the novel and the film version are primarily expressed through violence rather than words. In contrast to *Jekyll and Hyde* however, where violence is a threat to social cohesion, in the book and film versions of *Fight Club*, fighting becomes a non-verbal form of communication between men and a substitute for intimacy. Where Dr. Jekyll wanted to escape restrictions on how he could behave, the narrator is a "lucky man amid abundance" at the opening of *Fight Club* who nonetheless feels stifled by consumer culture. He is a "slave to [his] nesting instincts" (43), "trapped" in a "lovely nest" in which his only activity is to buy more products (44). Contemporary American consumer culture is represented in the narrator's view as both unsatisfying and emasculating. Rather than look at pornography, which presumably was a previously manly behaviour, the narrator scans catalogues and furnishes his apartment (43). His work assessing insurance claims for damage and death is also represented as stultifying. As Robert Schulz argues, what lies at the heart of this text, as it does in Herman Melville's "Bartleby, the Scrivener" (1853), is "an increasingly suffocating, mundane existence devoid of fulfilling, meaningful work and other social practices" (2011, 587). Similarly, Matt Jordan sees Project Mayhem as comprised of men who "have failed to achieve the degree of success that shores up masculine identity" (2002, 375). Jordan is right about the failure, but this failure of masculinity is not because of a lack of success but because he has been feminised by consumer culture and is more interested in buying things than fighting with other men which Durden corrects by destroying his apartment and founding Fight Club. As with Dr. Jekyll, the narrator in *Fight Club* feels oppressed by his social position and creates a violent alter ego to act out desires that he cannot acknowledge overtly and to compensate for his failure to achieve a successful masculine identity. He has at the outset failed to act in a manly way, just as Dr. Jekyll was a failure as gentleman.

Like Dr. Jekyll, the narrator in *Fight Club* moves down the class hierarchy when he assumes the persona of Durden. At the beginning of the narrative he has a white-collar job in a corporate structure that pays for him to fly throughout the United States, although he experiences this apparently privileged occupation as a form of oppression. The narrator finds that his constant traveling subverts his sense of individuality as "the mobile nature of his job reinforces his feeling that he is no more than one interchangeable component among many" (373), but it is a mark of his class status that he is able to travel in this way. Durden, by contrast, has a part-time job as a projectionist (25) and another in the food service industry (9), during which he urinates in the food being served. These are blue-collar jobs that are lower in social status than the narrator's original career and are the vehicle to express class conflict. Whereas Mr. Hyde erupted in violence on the streets of London, the narrator and Durden are "guerilla terrorists of the food service industry" (81), covertly expressing class resentment through acts of food sabotage. Mr. Hyde was a vehicle through which to embody fears of working-class violence erupting from the East End of London, whereas Durden expresses the resentment of blue-collar workers who see their incomes and job prospects eroding and enacts symbolic revenge on the upper classes. In both cases male bodies are the vehicles through which class resentments are expressed.

This sense of resentment is also directed towards women as scapegoats. The narrator says that "what you see at fight club is a generation of men raised by women" (Palahniuk 1997, 50) and "I'm a thirty-year-old boy, and I'm wondering if another woman is really the answer I need" (51), which express a fear of women as emasculating while violence between men is represented as the antidote and a way to create a "hard" masculine identity to counter this threat. The punishment for revealing the existence of Fight Club is to have your testicles removed, showing that emasculation is the most feared consequence for its members. The threat to the narrator's maleness that Fight Club counters is represented in the opening pages as he participates in the "Remaining Men Together" testicular cancer support group; he cries into Bob's "bitch tits" which were a result of his taking hormones to build up his muscles. Bob's feminine characteristics are seen as subverting his masculinity and a marker that at this point in the narrative neither he nor Bob are really "men." The threat to the narrator's masculinity is reinforced by Marla Singer coming to the "Remaining Men Together" group and interfering with the narrator's weekly emotional release. The narrator exorcises the threat to male hegemony posed by a female presence by deciding that "maybe self-destruction is the answer" (49), thus using self-directed violence to restore male power. The masochistic logic expressed here is that damaging the body restores male autonomy and obviates dependency on others. The recourse to self-destruction aligns with the pervasive nihilism of the book and, like Trump's promotion of violence (Jacobson and Tobias 2017), is based on anger at other social groups such as women and immigrants.

Class resentment and misogyny are expressed through soap in *Fight Club*. In the text, making soap is linked to human sacrifice in a monologue by Durden about people finding that their clothes were made cleaner in a spot in the river because of burned bodies producing lye and fat and, ultimately, soap (Palahniuk 1997, 76–77). Soap, like Fight Club, is linked to violence. The Paper Street Soap Company that Durden runs collects collagen and turns it into soap, and the primary source for collagen is Marla Singer's mother. When Marla finds out what Durden is doing with her mother's collagen she starts screaming "you boiled my mother!" (93); in the film this theme is amplified by showing a raid on a liposuction clinic and the narrator in a voiceover saying that they were making money by "selling rich women their own fat asses back to them" (Fincher 1:04:30–1:04:45). Men's bodies are not made into soap, and women are portrayed as naïve consumers in buying the Paper Street Company products derived from their own fat. Women's bodies are thus liquefied and turned into commodities in an expression of combined misogyny and class antagonism, but the hostility is expressed indirectly through soap, whereas between men violence is overt and registered visibly on their bodies.

Fight Club contains vivid images of damage to men's bodies, and these wounds become the basis for recognition between the club's members (Palahniuk 1997, 48). Damage to the body is the ultimate sign of manhood in the text. Some of the most disturbing descriptions in *Fight Club* occur when the narrator beats himself up to force the manager of the Pressman Hotel to pay him for not coming to work (116), which in the film version is turned into him beating himself up in his boss' office (Fincher 1:17:09–1:18:43). The narrator destroys his own body in such incidents, enacting the self-destruction that takes the place of support groups, in a narcissistic rage. Since Durden is in fact the narrator's alternate identity in the same body, not two different bodies as in *Jekyll and Hyde*, the pain inflicted on the narrator by his double is in fact self-torture. The scene in which Durden gives him a lye "kiss" that leaves a scar on his hand is particularly disturbing and auto-erotic because the narrator is inflicting this pain on himself (Palahniuk 1997, 72). This autoeroticism sets up a closed loop of self-inflicted pain and scarring that symbolises the wounded and self-destructive narcissism driving the narrator to create an alter ego and found fight club. Self-inflicted damage is taken to an extreme in the film version of *Fight Club* when toggling between the "fight" between the narrator and Durden and a surveillance camera shows him throwing himself downstairs and through plate glass (Fincher 2:08:04–2:09:37). The kiss and this scene in the film underscore the violent narcissism that enables the creation of the double.

The use of the double in *Fight Club* recalls not only *Jekyll and Hyde* but other Gothic classics such as Mary Shelley's *Frankenstein* (1823), in which Dr. Frankenstein's creature enacts his unacknowledged violence, making him an early example of toxic masculinity. The connection with doubles is one of several connections between Fight Club and the neo-Gothic. The decaying Paper Street house in *Fight Club* with its leaking roof and rusting nails (Palahniuk 1997, 56–57) is reminiscent of the "mould'ring caverns dark and damp" analysed by Richard Davenport-Hines in *Gothic* (2000, 3–4). The Paper Street house is the site of a monstrous masculinity that, like Mr. Hyde, threatens the social order and will eventually erupt in organised violence in Project Mayhem (Palahniuk 1997, 119). In another parallel, Mr. Hyde is referred to with simian references when he erupts in "ape-like" fury (Stevenson 2015 [1886], 48) to murder Sir Danvers Carew in an attack on institutional authority, as when the "space monkeys" carry out Durden's Project Mayhem to create chaos by attacking upscale targets (Palahniuk 1997, 131–33).

Like *Jekyll and Hyde*, *Fight Club* also exorcises what it views as the threat of homosexuality. Violence is an acceptable form of male bonding while sexuality is not, although the narrator states that after fight club anything else is "watching pornography when you could be having great sex" (50), which describes men fighting other men as displaced intercourse and eroticises male-on-male violence. The most graphic and disturbing representation of the purging of homosexuality as a threat comes with the beating of the man referred to as "angel face," who is described as too beautiful to be a man: "Put him in a dress and make him smile, and he'd be a woman" (128). The narrator "wanted to destroy everything beautiful I'd never have" (123) in fighting angel face, combining class resentment with misogyny and homophobia.[13] In *Jekyll and Hyde* Dr. Jekyll's hand is described as "comely" (Stevenson 2015 [1886], 81), which implicitly feminises him, whereas Mr. Hyde's hand is muscular, so that his alter ego is more manly and violent than his creator. In both cases violence exorcises the feminine. In *Fight Club* male violence is also explicitly aimed at men who are too close to the female, such as Bob with his "bitch tits" (Palahniuk 1997, 17), and is part of the general misogyny expressed in the text. This misogyny is echoed by Trump in his many denigrating remarks about women (Filipovic 2017).

Snowflakes and white male supremacy

Fight Club was an influential film among the right wing in the United States, particularly in helping to introduce the term "snowflake" into American political discourse. The word comes up in one of Durden's speeches to fight club: "You are not a beautiful and unique snowflake. You are the same decaying organic matter as everyone else, and we are all part of the same compost pile" (Palahniuk 1997, 34). In the context of the book, this speech criticises self-help movements and expresses white male resentment at their aspirations not being realised; the speech as delivered by Brad Pitt as Durden in the film was interpreted differently by male audiences who felt their economic future was in jeopardy. Kimmel notes that "the movie resonated powerfully with young men who faced such an uncertain future. Immediately after the film as released, real-life fight clubs sprang up all over America" (2013, 220). These fight clubs were "the province of young white men, searching for something that feels real" (222) who shared the anomie of the narrator in the book and the movie and felt that male-on-male violence would give them what they lacked in their lives. Dr. Jekyll created Mr. Hyde and released his violent instincts and, for young American males, Tyler Durden and Fight Club became their vehicle to express their anger and frustration at their diminished prospects.

The film was popular on social media (205) and introduced an insult to level against left-wing opponents. The term "snowflake" originally referred to somebody with an exaggerated sense of their own importance, but by 2016 had become "an overly sensitive person, incapable of dealing with any opinions that differ from their own. These people can often be seen congregating in 'safe zones' on college campuses," and then "an entitled millennial SJW-tard [Social Justice Warrior] who runs to her 'safe space' to play with stress toys and coloring books when she gets 'triggered' by various innocuous 'microaggressions' [*sic*]" (Goldstein 2017). Goldstein conveys that people protesting the election of Donald Trump were labeled "snowflakes" as a political insult. The attraction of "snowflake" for right-wing commentators is that it implicitly identifies them as supposedly manly and tough in contrast with the imputed effeminacy of their political opponents; however, this "tough-guy posturing seems rooted, paradoxically, in threat and fear: fear of defeat, fear of lost status and fear that society is growing increasingly ill-suited to tough-guy posturing in the first place" (Hess 2017). "Snowflake" compensates in its hypermasculinity for an underlying sense of threat to traditional "manliness." As with the narrator in *Fight Club*, men wielding this insult feel that their masculinity needs to be reasserted.

The film version of *Fight Club* radically changed the message of Palahniuk's book and it is the film rather than the book that provides the model of aggressive masculinity that is popular among right-wing groups. At the end of Palahniuk's *Fight Club* the narrator is in a mental asylum, and his creation of Durden as an alter ego is clearly the result of psychosis. The words "liar" and faker" appear in his narrative, and the narrator calls the asylum "heaven" and his therapist "God" (Palahniuk 1997, 206–7). The references to surveillance evoke the Panopticon and neo-Gothic films such as Terry Gilliam's *12 Monkeys* (1995) with its Gothic architecture and its "panopticism" (Del Rio 2001, 384). The sets in *12 Monkeys* were meant to suggest a mouse maze and prison cells (Calhoun 1996, 34), and the film begins where *Fight Club* ends with a similar protagonist waking from a recurring dream incarcerated and unsure of reality.

The film *Fight Club* by contrast with the novel ends with explosions bringing down financial institutions housed in skyscrapers while the narrator holds hands with Marla Singer, who has been delivered to him by his followers, making the ending a romance and the beginning of a real Project Mayhem designed to destroy the contemporary social order. Far from being insane, at the end of David Fincher's film version of the story the narrator is the leader of an insurrection against oppressive financial institutions and the government. This ending fits in very well with the ideology of right-wing extremist groups in the United States that see the government, the United Nations and globalisation as threats that need to be met with violent resistance (Andersen 2018). Their anger at what they see as conspiracies to rob them of their autonomy and manhood was echoed in Fincher's version of the story.

Neo-Gothic toxic American masculinity

The term "snowflake" links Mr. Hyde, Tyler Durden and the election of Donald J. Trump as President of the United States. In Trump's toxic masculinity anger is turned into nihilism and a general desire to destroy. Mr. Hyde exhibited some of this tendency in the murder of Sir Danvers Carew, which was an attack on the established power structure in killing a member of Parliament. A maid servant looking out of an upper window witnesses an "aged and beautiful gentleman with white hair" meet "a very small gentleman" (Stevenson 2015 [1886], 47), who she recognises as Hyde, and ask him something, perhaps directions. Hyde listens, at first with "an ill-contained impatience," and then suddenly clubs him to death (48); the scene is reminiscent of the destruction of "angel face" in *Fight Club* in that the narrative emphasises that the man is "beautiful" and that he also exuded an "innocent and old-world kindness" that in itself was a provocation for a display of violence. In *Jekyll and Hyde*, however, Mr. Hyde's attack is a random piece of urban violence that in many ways defies rational explanation whereas in *Fight Club* the beating of "angel face" is an expression of misogyny. Any hint of femininity threatens masculine identity must be exorcised through violence.

In *Fight Club* the violence, especially in Project Mayhem, is linked to an agenda that attacks any sign of the feminine but also all attempts at conservation and preservation. The beating of angel face leads directly into a passage by Durden advocating destroying the environment as a rejection of conservation measures: "Burn the Amazon rain forests. Pump chlorofluorocarbons straight up to gobble the ozone. Open the dump valves on supertankers and uncap offshore oil wells" (Palahniuk 1997, 123). Conservation measures such as recycling are derided as "like someone who quits smoking on his deathbed" (125). In parallel to Durden, Trump has called climate change a "hoax" (Matthews 2017) and presided over the rollback of environmental protections in moves that resonate with his base. Government regulation is seen as oppressive and the attempts to curb emissions and control oil spills as weak-minded attempts to curb American masculine industry.

For Trump's supporters pollution and masculinity are related, as shown most obviously in "rolling coal" cars that are modified to emit large amounts of black smoke.[14] A series of symbols of masculine potency and a nostalgia for vanishing forms of working-class labour are combined in "rolling coal." The trucks are modified by adding phallic stacks that enhance the masculine emissions. This form of modification is closely identified with right-wing politics and class-based values that see cars like the Prius as pretentious symbols of left-wing politics (Walker 2014). The modification was also seen as resisting President Obama's environmental policies that were characterised as an attack on the coal industry. Trump echoed this association with pollution, coal and work in his claims that Obama had been waging a "war on coal," which tapped into the class and racial resentments of people who voted for him (Grunwald 2017). Coal, pollution and masculinity are thus linked closely in Trump's rhetoric, and he appeals to people who see jobs such as coal mining as manly labour that is threatened by government regulations limiting emissions. The "war on coal" in this context is read as an assault on working-class jobs. Carol Wolkowitz argues that photos of working-class labour are marked by a nostalgia that seems to have been "occasioned by awareness of the rapid disappearance of labouring communities" (2000, 87). Trump's coal references allude to this sense of loss and the desire to restore lost versions of masculine physical power embodied in certain occupations.

Trump's campaign slogan "make America great again" was read by many of his supporters as "make white men great again" and thus as a promise to restore white male hegemony. Trump's misogyny was expressed in his references to "nasty" women and his persistent denigration of women in terms of their appearance (Filipovic 2017). Trump in this echoes the misogyny of *Fight Club* and a general hostility towards women interfering with men's hegemony; Marla Singer in the plot disrupts the camaraderie of "Remaining Men Together" because she makes him feel like a "liar and a fake" (Palahniuk 1997, 23). Similarly, Trump seems threatened by women with any power who presumably make him feel like a "liar and a fake" too.

Trump taps into the resentments of white male Americans who felt what Kevin Alexander Boon has termed a "nostalgia" for male violence because men have had to restrain aggressive impulses after critiques by "the rhetoric of anti-aggression" that prevented them from expressing antisocial slurs (2003, 267).[15] Trump gives voice to "aggrieved entitlement" in which social superiority as a group is combined with a feeling of loss of power at an individual level (Rosin 2013).[16] Trump's angry, aggressive style results in his notorious Twitter insults and encouragement of violence at his rallies, as Salena Zito documents in "Trump's Voters" (2016). *PolitiFact*, a respected fact-checking source in the United States, followed up on a claim by his spokesperson Sarah Huckabee Sanders that Trump had never "promoted or encouraged violence" (Jacobson 2017). The result of the *PolitiFact* survey was a list of the many times that he had in fact encouraged his audience to act violently; *The New York Times* also compiled a video review of such incidents (Tiefenthäler 2016). Just as Mr. Hyde unleashed Dr. Jekyll's repressed violence, Trump elicits angry responses from his supporters through such incitements to violence.

Conclusion

While *Jekyll and Hyde* represents hegemonic masculinity and the fate of a gentleman who tried to maintain the veneer of civility while enacting violence as Mr. Hyde, both the film version of *Fight Club* and Trump's fueling of white male rage represent a toxic masculinity that is actively malevolent towards other social groups. This toxicity is made literal in that it identifies with destroying the environment and pollution as forms of aggression. Trump is from a privileged background and has considerable personal wealth, but his discourse aligns him with white working-class masculinity and appeals to their values: "Trump leaned heavily on shared working-class values in his campaign speeches, often in the context of a threatened America. For example, he often portrayed immigrants, Muslims, and refugees as direct threats to the safety and well-being of women and children" (Lamont et al. 2017). His language both emphasises the core values of the white working class and directs their animosity towards certain groups as the supposed cause of their economic difficulties.

The United States likes to think of itself as a classless society in which anybody can succeed through individual initiative, but this ideology is contradicted by the lived experience of its white working-class citizens. Alan Abramowitz and Ruy Teixiera describe the declining economic fortunes of the American white working class, which they argue has lasted decades and has led to growing resentment (2009, 391–92). Such people are rightly feeling aggrieved, but their resentment has been exploited and channeled by Trump. He has succeeded in unleashing the Mr. Hyde in his supporters and made expressions of misogyny and racism acceptable, all the while assuring them that they are "good" people in contrast to "bad" people such as illegal immigrants. Dr. Jekyll disavowed Mr. Hyde's violence claiming "He, I say—I cannot say, I" (Stevenson 2015 [1886], 87), and Trump notoriously would not acknowledge the violence by racists in Charlottesville, Virginia, by asserting that there were some "very fine people on both sides" (Rosie Gray 2017). Where unleashing Mr. Hyde in *Jekyll and Hyde* and Tyler Durden in *Fight Club* led to acts of violence against individuals, Trump has the capacity to mobilise large-scale actions against targeted groups while portraying himself and his supporters as aggrieved victims. Trump is a modern-day Dr. Jekyll who disavows violence overtly but encourages it covertly through rhetoric aimed at his supporters. He is hypocritical in a way that Stevenson would readily have recognised in that, like Dr. Jekyll, he is trying to maintain his own social position, and further his own ends, whilst disavowing the violence that he has unleashed.

Notes

1 Kirsten Stirling has examined the commonalities between *Jekyll and Hyde* and *Fight Club* in terms of the "urban Gothic" but doesn't address anger and class (2004).
2 My own copy of the film *Fight Club* was given to me by a female undergraduate; her boyfriend had given it to her as a birthday present, and she hated it so much that she wanted to give it away, showing its gendered appeal (or lack of appeal).
3 For a genealogy of the term "toxic" and the relationship to violence, see Syed Haider (2016, 557–58).
4 See also the discussion of labeling masculinity a "risk factor" in Tim Lomas et al. (2016, 291).
5 On Dr. Jekyll's "two bodies," see Martin Danahay (2013).
6 See Drew Gray (2013) on the Victorian media representation of working-class young men as innately violent. A fictional counterpart to Gray's analysis is Arthur Morrison's *A Child of the Jago* (2014 [1896]).
7 Grace Moore in claims that the hairiness marks the hand as that of a masturbator (2004, 155). Richard Dury in "The Hand of Hyde" places this quotation in a rich context of allusions to hands in other texts, noting how this scene registers anxiety about class, the nonhuman and the coherence of identity (2003, 101–16).
8 Alex Tuss reads this loss of status as a critique of American ideologies of "success" (2004, 93); this misses the idealization of blue-collar occupations as more "manly" than white-collar jobs like the narrator's at the beginning of the novel.
9 While I read the damage to male bodies as signs of homosocial bonding, Olivia Burgess (2012) reads male bodies as "revolutionary" and utopian.
10 For the 1931 *Jekyll and Hyde* film poster, see https://en.wikipedia.org/wiki/Dr._Jekyll_and_Mr._Hyde_(1931_film); and for the Fincher 1991 *Fight Club* poster, see https://www.imdb.com/title/tt0137523/mediaviewer/rm590641920.
11 The confusion in terminology resulted in part from a shift in social status from a basis in landed property to accumulated capital; see Robin Gilmour (1981, 3–6).
12 In my use of "homosocial," I am drawing Sedgwick's *Between Men* (1985) and its analysis of male social and erotic bonds.
13 On homophobia, masculinity and violence, see Michael Kimmel and Matthew Mahler (2004).
14 For a definition of "Rolling Coal," see https://en.wikipedia.org/wiki/Rolling_coal. For an image of a vehicle, see https://en.wikipedia.org/wiki/Rolling_coal#/media/File:F-450_coal_rolling_Monster.jpg.
15 Oddly, although "nostalgia" is in Kevin Alexander Boon's title "Men and Nostalgia for Violence: Culture and Culpability in Chuck Palahniuk's *Fight Club*," the word does not appear in the body of his article.
16 See also Christopher Vito (2018) on "aggrieved entitlement."

Bibliography

Abramowitz, Alan, and Ruy Teixera. "The Decline of the White Working Class and the Rise of a Mass Upper-Middle Class." *Political Science Quarterly* 124, no. 3 (Fall 2009): 391–422.
Andersen, Kurt. "How the GOP Went Crazy." *Slate*, February 2, 2018. https://slate.com/news-and-politics/2018/02/right-wing-conspiracy-theories-from-the-1960s-to-today.html.

Boon, Kevin Alexander. "Men and Nostalgia for Violence: Culture and Culpability in Chuck Palahniuk's *Fight Club*." *Journal of Men's Studies* 11, no. 3 (June 1, 2003): 267–76.

Burgess, Olivia. "Revolutionary Bodies in Chuck Palahniuk's *Fight Club*." *Utopian Studies* 23, no. 1 (January 2012): 263–80.

Calhoun, John. "'12 Monkeys': Jeffrey Beecroft Builds a Maze through Time for Terry Gilliam's Bizarre New Film." *TCI* 30, no. 3 (March 1996): 34. http://link.galegroup.com/apps/doc/A18072466/AONE?u=st46245&sid=AONE&xid=e6e6e994.

Connell, R. W., and James W. Messerschmidt. "Hegemonic Masculinity: Rethinking the Concept." *Gender & Society* 19, no. 6 (December 2005): 829–59.

Danahay, Martin. "Dr. Jekyll's Two Bodies." *Nineteenth Century Contexts* 35, no. 1 (March 2013): 23–40.

Danahay, Martin, and Alex Chisholm, eds. *Jekyll and Hyde Dramatized*. Jefferson, NC: McFarland, 2005.

Darwin, Charles. "'Anger' from *The Expression of Emotions in Men and Animals*." In Stevenson 155–57.

Davenport-Hines, Richard. *Gothic: Four Hundred Years of Excess, Horror, Evil and Ruin*. New York: North Point Press, 2000.

Day, William Patrick. *In the Circles of Fear and Desire: A Study of Gothic Fantasy*. Chicago: University of Chicago Press, 1985.

Del Rio, Elena. "The Remaking of 'La Jetée's' Time-Travel Narrative: *Twelve Monkeys* and the Rhetoric of Absolute Visibility." *Science Fiction Studies* 28, no. 3 (November 2001): 383–98.

Dury, Richard. "The Hand of Hyde." In *Robert Louis Stevenson Reconsidered: New Critical Perspectives*, edited by William B. Jones, Jr., 101–16. Jefferson, NC: McFarland, 2003.

———. Introduction to *Strange Case of Dr Jekyll and Mr Hyde*, xix–lxii. Edinburgh: Edinburgh, 2004.

Filipovic, Jill. "Our President Has Always Degraded Women—and We've Always Let Him." *Time*, December 5, 2017.

Fincher, David, dir. *Fight Club*. Los Angeles: 20th Century Fox, 1999.

Gilliam, Terry, dir. *12 Monkeys*. Los Angeles: Universal Pictures, 1995.

Gilmour, Robin. *The Idea of the Gentleman in the Victorian Novel*. London: George Allen and Unwin, 1981.

Goldstein, Jessica M. "The Surprising History of 'Snowflake' as a Political Insult." *thinkprogress.org*, January 9, 2017. https://thinkprogress.org/all-the-special-snowflakes-aaf1a922f37b/.

Gray, Drew. "Gang Crime and the Media in Late Nineteenth-Century London." *The Journal of the Social History Society* 10, no. 4 (2013): 559–75.

Gray, Rosie. "Trump Defends White-Nationalist Protesters: 'Some Very Fine People on Both Sides.'" *The Atlantic*, August 15, 2017. https://www.theatlantic.com/politics/archive/2017/08/trump-defends-white-nationalist-protesters-some-very-fine-people-on-both-sides/537012.

Grunwald, Michael. "Trump's Love Affair with Coal." *Politico*, October 15, 2017. https://www.politico.com/magazine/story/2017/10/15/trumps-love-affair-with-coal-215710.

Haider, Syed. "The Shooting in Orlando, Terrorism or Toxic Masculinity (or Both?)." *Men and Masculinities* 19, no. 5 (2016): 555–65.

Halberstam, J. *Skin Shows: Gothic Horror and the Technology of Monsters*. Durham: Duke University Press, 1995.

Hess, Amanda. "How 'Snowflake' Became America's Inescapable Tough-Guy Taunt." *New York Times Magazine*, June 13, 2017. https://www.nytimes.com/2017/06/13/magazine/how-snowflake-became-americas-inescapable-tough-guy-taunt.html.

Jacobson, Louis, and Manuela Tobias. "Has Donald Trump Never 'Promoted or Encouraged Violence,' as Sarah Huckabee Sanders Said?" *PolitiFact*, July 5, 2017. http://www.politifact.com/truth-o-meter/statements/2017/jul/05/sarah-huckabee-sanders/has-donald-trump-never-promoted-or-encouraged-viol.

Jann, Rosemary. "Sherlock Holmes Codes the Social Body." *ELH* 57, no. 3 (Autumn 1990): 685–708.

Jordan, Matt. "Marxism, Not Manhood: Accommodation and Impasse in Seamus Heaney's *Beowulf* and Chuck Palahniuk's *Fight Club*." *Men and Masculinities* 4, no. 4 (April 2002): 368–79.

Kimmel, Michael. *Misframing Men: The Politics of Contemporary Masculinities*. New Brunswick: Rutgers University Press, 2010.

———. *Angry White Men: American Masculinity at the End of an Era*. New York: Nation Books, 2013.

Kimmel, Michael, and Matthew Mahler. "Adolescent Masculinity, Homophobia, and Violence: Random School Shootings." In *Off White: Readings on Power, Privilege, and Resistance*, edited by Michelle Fine, Lois Weis, Linda Powell Pruitt and April Burns, 114–27. New York: Routledge, 2004.

Lamont, Michèle, Bo Yun Park and Elena Ayala-Hurtado. "What Trump's Campaign Speeches Show about His Lasting Appeal to the White Working Class." *Harvard Business Review*, November 8, 2017. https://hbr.org/2017/11/what-trumps-campaign-speeches-show-about-his-lasting-appeal-to-the-white-working-class.

Lomas, Tim, Tina Cartwright, Trudi Edginton and Damien Ridge. "New Ways of Being a Man: 'Positive' Hegemonic Masculinity in Meditation-based Communities of Practice." *Men and Masculinities* 19, no. 3 (2016): 289–310.

Maixner, Paul. *Robert Louis Stevenson: The Critical Heritage*. London: Psychology Press, 1995.

Mansfield, Richard. *Dr. Jekyll and Mr. Hyde*. 1887. Unpublished ms. Washington, DC: Smithsonian Institution.

Matthews, Dylan. "Donald Trump Has Tweeted Climate Change Skepticism 115 Times. Here's All of It." *Vox.com*, June 1, 2017. https://www.vox.com/policy-and-politics/2017/6/1/15726472/trump-tweets-global-warming-paris-climate-agreement.

Moore, Grace. "Something to Hyde: The 'Strange Preference' of Henry Jekyll." In *Victorian Crime, Madness and Sensation*, edited by Andrew Maunder and Grace Moore, 147–62. Aldershot: Ashgate Publishing, 2004.

Morrison, Arthur. *A Child of the Jago*. 1896. Edited by Diana Maltz. Peterborough, ON: Broadview Press, 2014.

Multz, Diana C. "Status Threat, Not Economic Hardship, Explains the 2016 Presidential Vote." *PNAS: Proceedings of the National Academy of Sciences of the United States of America*, April 23, 2018. http://www.pnas.org/content/early/2018/04/18/1718155115.

Myers, Steven Lee and Choe Sang-Hun. "Trump's 'Fire and Fury' Threat Raises Alarm in Asia." *New York Times*, August 9, 2017. https://www.nytimes.com/2017/08/09/world/asia/north-korea-trump-threat-fire-and-fury.html.

Palahniuk, Chuck. *Fight Club*. New York: Henry Holt, 1996.

Rosin, Hanna. "Even Madder Men: 'Angry White Men,' by Michael Kimmel." *New York Times Sunday Book Review*, November 22, 2013. https://www.nytimes.com/2013/11/24/books/review/angry-white-men-by-michael-kimmel.html.

Ruskin, John. "Of Vulgarity." 1909. In *The Complete Works of John Ruskin*, edited by Edward T. Cook and Alexander Wedderburn, 37: 343–45. London: George Allen and Unwin, 1903–12.

Schulz, Robert. "White Guys Who Prefer Not To: From Passive Resistance ('Bartleby') to Terrorist Acts (*Fight Club*)." *Journal of Popular Culture* 44, no. 3 (June 2011): 583–605.

Sedgwick, Eve Kosofsky. *Between Men: English Literature and Male Homosocial Desire*. New York: Columbia University Press, 1985.

Shelley, Mary. *Frankenstein or, The Modern Prometheus*. Edited with introduction and notes by M. K. Joseph. Oxford: Oxford University Press, 2008.

Smiles, Samuel. *Self-Help, with Illustrations of Conduct and Perseverance*. 1897. *Project Gutenberg*. http://www.gutenberg.org/files/935/935-h/935-h.htm.

Stevenson, Robert Louis. *Strange Case of Dr. Jekyll and Mr. Hyde*. 1886. 3rd ed. Edited by Martin A. Danahay. Peterborough, ON: Broadview Press, 2015.

Stirling, Kirsten. "Dr Jekyll and Mr Jackass: *Fight Club* as a Refraction of Hogg's Justified Sinner and Stevenson's *Dr Jekyll and Mr Hyde*." *Postmodern Studies* 35, no. 1 (August 2004): 83–94.

Tiefenthäler, Ainara. "Trump's History of Encouraging Violence." *New York Times: Times Video*, March 14, 2016. https://www.nytimes.com/video/us/100000004269364/trump-and-violence.html.

Tuss, Alex. "Masculine Identity and Success: A Critical Analysis of Patricia Highsmith's *The Talented Mr. Ripley* and Chuck Palahniuk's *Fight Club*." *Journal of Men's Studies* 12, no. 2 (Winter 2004): 93–103.

Vito, Christopher. "Masculinity, Aggrieved Entitlement, and Violence: Considering the Isla Vista Mass Shooting." *International Journal for Masculinity Studies* 13, no. 2 (April 2018): 86–102.

Walker, Hunter. "Conservatives Are Purposely Making Their Cars Spew Black Smoke to Protest Obama and Environmentalists." *businessinsider.com*, July 5, 2014. http://www.businessinsider.com/conservatives-purposely-making-cars-spew-black-smoke-2014–7.

Wolkowitz, Carol. "The Working Body as Sign: Historical Snapshots." In *Constructing Gendered Bodies*, edited by Kathryn Backett-Milburn and Linda McKie, 85–103. Basingstoke: Palgrave, 2000.

Zito, Salena. "Trump's Voters Love His Twitter Rants against Popular Culture." *New York Post*, November 1, 2016. https://nypost.com/2016/11/21/trumps-voters-love-his-twitter-rants-against-popular-culture.

Chapter Five

SHADOWS OF THE VAMPIRE: NEO-GOTHICISM IN *DRACULA*, *RIPPER STREET* AND *WHAT WE DO IN THE SHADOWS*

Jamil Mustafa

Neo-Gothicism, like vampirism, is an afterlife; or, more precisely, an un-death in which, as William Faulkner's Temple Drake famously observes, "The past is never dead. It's not even past" (2011, 69). Both neo-Gothicism and vampirism elide past and present, life and death, and shadow and substance—which last conflation is especially striking in neo-Gothic films and television series about vampires. Like the recorded image of a vampire, the neo-Gothic is a shadow of a shadow. Neo-Gothicism differs significantly from neo-Victorianism, because the latter's relationship to history and culture is more direct than the former's. *Victorian* denotes a specific historical period, whereas *Gothic* connotes not only the Medieval period, but also adaptations, interpretations and fantasies of it—which original *neo*-Gothic expressions in art, literature and architecture emerged in the eighteenth century and flourished during the Victorian period. The Gothic and the neo-Gothic thus tend to merge, rendering the contemporary neo-Gothic work a simulacrum of a simulacrum, positioning its interpreters in a textual *mise en abyme* and greatly enhancing its metatextual and intertextual characteristics. Given the compelling parallels between neo-Gothicism and vampirism, neo-Gothic narratives featuring vampires are arguably the richest of all such texts. The shadowy relationship between vampirism and neo-Gothicism is illustrated, with considerable complexity and nuance, by two exemplary neo-Gothic vampire narratives: "A White World Made Red" (2016; hereafter "White World"), an episode of the BBC series *Ripper Street* (2013–16); and *What We Do in the Shadows* (2014; hereafter *Shadows*), the faux documentary written and directed by Jemaine Clement and Taika Waititi.

These works are themselves shadows of the original neo-Gothic vampire story, Bram Stoker's *Dracula* (1897), whose neo-Gothicism is far more than a function of its adapting the traits of its eighteenth-century forebears. The most noteworthy neo-Gothic feature of *Dracula* is Stoker's decision to bring what he conceives of as a Medieval monster into his own late-Victorian world, thereby blurring the lines between past and present, fact and fiction, and superstition and science. Stoker's long-standing engagement with these categories—and their amalgamation—is evident in his 1897 interview for the

British Weekly, in which he accounts for his long-time interest in "the vampire legend" by characterising vampirism as "a very fascinating theme, since it touches both on mystery and fact." He explains, "In the Middle Ages the terror of the vampire depopulated whole villages," for when someone fell "into a death-like trance" and was "buried before the time," later to be "dug up and found alive," naïve villagers "imagined a vampire was about" and fled (Stoddard 2000 [1897], 486). In Stoker's account, and in his novel, the vampirism of the Medieval past (fore)shadows the catalepsy of the Victorian present: superstition at once antedates and coexists with science, serving as its double. Indeed, as Van Helsing reminds Seward, superstition and science are sometimes difficult to disentangle. "Ah, it is the fault of our science that it wants to explain all; and if it explain not, then it says there is nothing to explain," the professor tells his protégé. Echoing Stoker himself, Van Helsing then observes, "There are always mysteries in life" (Stoker 2000 [1897], 229). Harker likewise acknowledges the coexistence of past and present. While noting that his contemporaneous diary is "nineteenth century up-to-date with a vengeance," he accepts that the "old centuries had, and have, powers of their own which mere 'modernity' cannot kill" (67).

The dynamic nexus of past, present, fact and fiction both informs and shapes Stoker's neo-Gothic project of terrorising Victorians with a vampiric version of the fifteenth-century Wallachian warlord Vlad III (1431–1476). The narrative frame of *Dracula* likewise highlights neo-Gothic juxtapositions and convergences. Taking its cue from the preface to the second edition of Horace Walpole's *The Castle of Otranto* (1765), the preface to Harker's diary concerns itself with authenticity/falsity, fact/fiction and present/past. "All needless matters have been eliminated, so that a history almost at variance with the possibilities of later-day belief may stand forth as simple fact," it begins and continues: "There is throughout no statement of past things wherein memory may err, for all the records chosen are exactly contemporary" (Stoker 2000 [1897], 29). This statement of past fact is, of course, present fiction. However streamlined and contemporary, the materials of *Dracula* consist almost exclusively of highly subjective first-person accounts. The "Note" concluding the novel does recognise that those who wrote these accounts "could hardly ask anyone [...] to accept these as proofs of so wild a story"—not because they are inherently unreliable, but because "in all the mass of material of which the record is composed, there is hardly one authentic document; nothing but a mass of typewriting" (419), as if "so wild a story" were reliable when handwritten, but improbable when typewritten. That *Dracula* was itself typewritten (by both Stoker and Mina)[1] and that late-Victorian readers found fault with its innovative approach to a traditional demon further complicate the novel's already multifaceted neo-Gothicism.[2]

Just as *Dracula* is framed by its preface and "Note," so too is "White World" framed by *Dracula*. Set in 1897, the year of the novel's publication, the episode begins with close-ups of its pages and original yellow cover. These shots establish verisimilitude even as they remind viewers that both the novel and the episode are works of fiction with shared themes. They also suggest that the novel's *outré* plot will somehow be replicated in the episode—though, given that until this point *Ripper Street* has been a detective drama in which supernatural elements are entirely absent, this suggestion is alluring but improbable. The opening *mise en scène* is conventionally Gothic: sitting in the dark at a parlour table with her hair undone, clad in a white nightdress and reading *Dracula* by flickering candlelight is the enthralled Mathilda Reid (Anna Burnett), the daughter of Edmund Reid (Matthew Macfadyen), the inspector of the Metropolitan Police's H Division in Whitechapel, who is based on Detective Inspector Edmund John James Reid (1846–1917), the one-time head of the district's Criminal Investigation Department. The scene shifts to a foggy, moonlit London street, where a pale young girl in a white dress, holding a lamp, beckons an anxious woman to follow her. Subsequent crosscuts between these locales reinforce links between the events occurring in each. A door creaks, and Mathilda hurriedly extinguishes her candle; meanwhile, the girl opens an ominous blood-red door and disappears behind it. Mathilda hears footsteps approaching and holds her breath—only to see her father pass by. She returns to *Dracula*, while the woman follows the girl into a room filled with the hanging carcasses of slaughtered animals—and a man hanging upside down. The woman's scream, and the series credits, follow. In the next scene, Reid finds that Mathilda has passed the entire night in the parlour, reading, and reprimands her: "What is this robs you of your rest? Vampires? Really? Go. Ready yourself" (Watson 2016, 04:00–04:01). During the course of the episode, Reid, alongside Head Inspector Bennet Drake (Jerome Flynn), the American forensics expert Homer Jackson (Adam Rothenberg) and Detective Sergeant Frank Thatcher (Benjamin O'Mahony), discovers that the hanging man is the executed convict Percival Monks; he had been exsanguinated via a puncture wound to the neck before his corpse was hung in a refrigerated meat locker. They then find the corpse of the woman, a Polish seamstress named Agniezka (Janice Byrne), with her throat likewise punctured, lying in an alley. Their investigation reveals that, aided by the Newgate Prison doctor Carlyle Probyn (Ed Hughes), the renegade French surgeon Tristram Blanchard (Dylan Smith) has been transfusing refrigerated blood drawn from newly hanged prisoners, together with fresh blood from working-class women, into his daughter Camille (Emelia Devlin) in an attempt to save her from porphyria. After Blanchard's arrest, Mathilda and her father recommence their discussion of *Dracula*.

Like all episodes of *Ripper Street*, "White World" is grounded in history and takes artistic license mostly in terms of its plot—which, in another form of historical grounding, resembles that of a Victorian melodrama or Grand Guignol. The episode approaches outright Gothicism but appears to retreat from it, only ultimately to adopt the mode by adapting it. The text's sophisticated neo-Victorianism and neo-Gothicism are amply demonstrated by how skilfully it employs *Dracula* to align the diegetic and extra-diegetic late-Victorian worlds it depicts and references, even as it explores the gaps between these worlds, and examines both alignments and gaps between these worlds and our own. "White World" joins *Dracula* in paying homage to its Gothic forebears, celebrating contemporary technology and thoughtfully comparing science with superstition. It departs from Stoker's novel, however, by exposing the Gothic horrors of late-Victorian technological advancement, laissez-faire capitalism and xenophobia.

Both "White World" and *Dracula* showcase cutting-edge technology as a means of defeating their respective antagonists, sacrificing a degree of verisimilitude in order to do so. The headquarters of H Division features recently installed telephones, a telegraph, a microform reader and a state-of-the art autopsy room that includes cold chambers for corpses. Drake uses the telephones throughout the episode to communicate with his officers; the telegraph sends crucial information about Blanchard from Paris to London, and the cold chambers serve both forensic and symbolic functions. While this technology is appropriate for 1897, the episode takes liberties—as does *Dracula*, to a much lesser extent—in terms of how accurately it represents late-Victorian scientific experimentation and advancement. That both Abraham Van Helsing and Homer Jackson conduct blood transfusions is unremarkable: the first transfusion was performed in 1818 by the Scottish obstetrician James Blundell (1790–1877), and in 1870 Robert McDonnell (1828–1889) transfused his own filtered blood into a 14-year-old girl (McCann 2016, 19). That Van Helsing and Jackson's transfusions *succeed*, however, is far less likely. Not until 1901 did Karl Landsteiner (1868–1943) discover the major blood groups, and "[recognise] the possibility of a fatal reaction if different blood types were mixed in a patient" (19). In 1907, Ludvig Hekoten (1863–1951) "recommended testing the blood groups of [the] recipient and prospective donor and crossmatching them before transfusion" (19). In 1913 Reuben Ottenberg (1882–1959) "conclusively proved the necessity for crossmatching before transfusion by showing that antibodies in patients' blood could be harmful to donors' red cells" (19).

Years before these discoveries, without any apparent knowledge of blood types, and certainly without conducting any cross-matching, Van Helsing transfuses blood from Arthur, Seward, himself and Quincey into the repeatedly exsanguinated Lucy. His potentially deadly ineptitude is exemplified by his assurance to Seward that Arthur is "of blood so pure that [they] need not defibrinate it" (Stoker 2000 [1897], 158). Given Van Helsing's dubious medical practices, Lucy's surviving four transfusions at his hands are nearly as remarkable as her transformation into a vampire. Showing a great deal more scientific acumen than Van Helsing, Jackson discovers a "blood match" (Watson 2016, 29:30) four years before Landsteiner's breakthrough and concludes that his adversary and scientific doppelgänger Blanchard has done the same. When Blanchard tears a transfusion needle from the throat of Magdalena (Julia Rosnowska) in an effort to escape the police, Jackson saves her life by transfusing Thatcher's blood (which he has already determined is a match for her own) into her body.

Science appears to vanquish the supernatural in "White World," as it does in *Dracula*, but both texts demonstrate that appearances deceive. When the detectives begin their investigation by discovering the bodies of Percival Monks and Agniezka, the situation could be interpreted either supernaturally or scientifically. Ice-cold and deadly pale, Monks is found hanging upside down, drained of blood via a puncture in his throat. Agniezka is located in the street, her throat likewise pierced with blood having poured from her wound. Both appear to be victims of a vampire, and the man's hanging upside down like a bat suggests that he has begun to change into a vampire himself. In the realistic world of *Ripper Street*, of course, this reading is untenable. In fact, both are victims not of a vampire, but of a renegade surgeon conducting illicit experiments. The triumph of scientific fact over Gothic fantasy appears complete when Drake asks Jackson, who has just finished his examination of Monks, "What more?" "What do you think this is, a crystal ball?" Jackson retorts, holding up his magnifying glass (Watson 2016, 10:31–10:33). Yet Jackson recognises that there is indeed more to life—and blood, for "blood is life" (26:27–26:28)—than what he sees through a magnifying glass or a micro-scope. Jackson's appreciation for the mysteries in life—and science's inability to cope with them—is expressed in a story he tells of a friend stabbed to death by a "Comanche brave" in a Wyoming mountain pass "full of virgin snow" while he was helpless to intervene. "My friend died," he explains. "And I'm a doctor, understand? So, well, the impotence of it. All I could do was watch as blood spread through the eyes. A white world made red" (20:30–21:50). This story illustrates Jackson's contention that the fear of blood is an "instinctive phobia, as inescapable a part of any man as, well, his blood itself" (20:01–20:12). As Jackson tells his gruesome tale, he prepares a slide of blood and examines it under a microscope. A subjective camera shot shows the blood cells moving, while a diegetic heartbeat pulses and portentous music plays. The focus first blurs and then sharpens, as Jackson adjusts the microscope. During the momentary distortion, we see, through his eyes, both a slide of blood in the microscope's aperture and what resembles a bloody eyeball. The white tiles of the autopsy room—whose whiteness, designed in part to highlight the presence of blood, emphasises the interplay of white and red—echo the "virgin snow" stained by the stabbed man's blood, as do the white dresses of the virginal Mathilda and Camille, the white gauze applied to bleeding wounds throughout the episode and Blanchard's immaculate white lab coat. The white world of science—suggesting at once pure reason and cold objectivity—is thus balanced by the red world of horror.

A white world is made red when we recognise that science and the supernatural are not complementary but identical and that scientists are not opposed to vampires—they *are* vampires. This conflation is both literal and figurative. Drawing a firm line between the normal and the paranormal is difficult, as Van Helsing teaches Seward, because this boundary is always shifting with the (re)discovery of knowledge—"the growth of new beliefs" that "are yet but the old, which pretend to be young" (Stoker 2000 [1897], 228). Van Helsing's metaphor is more ominous than he realises; after arriving in London the centuries old Dracula likewise appears "young" (210). In life, Dracula was an "alchemist—which […] was the highest development of the science-knowledge of his time" (342); thus, it makes sense that this rejuvenated vampire-scientist is "experimenting, and doing it well" (343). His coffins are inventoried by the Whitby solicitor Billington as "cases of common earth, to be used for experimental purposes" (265) as indeed they are, for "this monster has been creeping into knowledge experimentally" by testing "whether he might not himself move the box[es]" (343).

Renfield, another (would-be) vampire-scientist, imitates Dracula by conducting his own experiments in vampirism and mimics Seward by recording their results in "a little notebook in which he is always jotting down something" (102). "He gave many flies to one spider and many spiders to one bird, and then wanted a cat to eat the many birds," Seward writes in his own notebook, and wonders, "What would have been his later steps? It would almost be worth while to complete the experiment" (103–4). Seward's completing Renfield's experiment—which would logically culminate in the doctor's observing his patient drink human blood—would itself be vampiric: not only because it would foster Renfield's vampirism, but also because Seward would figuratively vampirise Renfield in order to "advance [his] own branch of science" (104). Seward himself recognises a parallel between his experiment and Renfield's: "I must not think too much of this, or I may be tempted; a good cause might turn the scale with me, for may not I too be of an exceptional brain, congenitally?" (104). Ironically, Seward does enable Renfield to complete his experiment in vampirism. After Renfield cuts him, Seward observes the aspiring vampire "licking up, like a dog, the blood which had fallen from [his] wounded wrist" (177–78). His simile reinforces the connection between vampire and scientist, for Renfield is a dog with two masters: Dracula, whom he calls "Master" (135, 137, 138, 193, 320), and in whose presence he "sniff[s] about as a dog does" (135), and Seward, who views Renfield as his "pet lunatic" (272–73) and seeks to become "master of the facts of his hallucination" (93). This conflation of vampire and scientist extends to their respective instruments: Lucy's body is punctured repeatedly by both Dracula's fangs and Van Helsing's needle. Vampires and vampire-hunters are likewise connected by their use of pointed blood-draining and blood-letting tools. After being bitten and needled, Lucy is staked by Arthur while "the blood from [her] pierced heart [wells] and [spurts]" (254); Dracula uses his "long sharp nails" to "[open] a vein in his breast" before forcing Mina to drink "the blood [that begins] to spurt out" (328); and, as hunter becomes hunted, Dracula's body is slashed and pierced by Jonathan's and Quincey's knives.

Dracula's conflation of scientists, vampires and vampire-hunters is thoroughly incorporated into "White World." The surgeon-scientist Blanchard, whose name, according to the *Oxford English Dictionary*, means "whitish," blanches Monks, Agnieszka and Magdalena by piercing their throats with a needle and draining their blood, in a vampiric attempt to give his porphyria-stricken daughter Camille unnaturally renewed life. "She will recover. She will transform. She will live" (Watson 2016, 47:01–47:05), he declares while transfusing Magdalena's blood into her body. Like Dracula, who vampirised the women in his castle and whom Jonathan believes "seeks to create a new and ever-widening circle of semi-demons to batten on the helpless" (Stoker 2000 [1897], 84), Blanchard has sired another vampire. Jackson underscores the tie between Camille's malady and vampirism when he diagnoses her as suffering from "porphyria," involving "discolouration of the teeth, anaemia [and] photosensitivity" (42:56–43:01), while tapping a copy of *Dracula*. Fittingly, Camille—whose skin is pale, whose teeth are disturbingly stained and whose own name evokes Dracula's precursor and inspiration, the vampire Carmilla[3]—lures Agniezka to her death and consumes a good deal of Magdalena's blood. Though the vampire-hunter Jackson stops the vampire Blanchard, the two men— who, as Reid observes, can communicate "surgeon to surgeon" (45:04–45:05)—closely resemble each other. Most obvious are their blood ties: both draw, refrigerate, study and transfuse blood. Other links are more subtle but equally significant. Jackson menaces Probyn with a scalpel, just as Blanchard later holds a scalpel to Magdalena's throat shortly before swapping it for the needle he presses against Camille's throat, thereby demonstrating not only the literal and figurative interchangeability of these penetrative scientific instruments, but also their association with a vampire's fangs. When Drake, Reid and Thatcher enter Blanchard's operating theatre after he has fled from it, they find Jackson hovering over Magdalena's body, her blood literally on his hands.

Both Blanchard and Jackson, moreover, employ cutting-edge technology to preserve corpses. Jackson places bodies in the refrigerators of his newly renovated morgue at the headquarters of H Division, while Blanchard disposes of Monks' corpse in the innovative cold-storage room of a slaughterhouse. Although cold storage was introduced to Smithfield, London's principal meat market, in 1889, it spread so gradually that "in 1897, vessels with refrigeration were repurposed solely for cold storage because London's land-based cold storage capacity had not grown fast enough" (Rees 2013, 113). The sober-minded Drake and the forward-thinking Reid respond in character to "the new cold stores" (Watson 2016, 07:06–07:07). "They may keep meat for six months before it spoils," Reid remarks admiringly, while Drake retorts, "Who wants mutton that's half a year old?" (07:10–07:17). His question echoes Reid's own query about Monks' being placed in cold storage: "Why preserve a dead thing?" (15:10–15:12). That meat, (exsanguinated) corpses and blood are all artificially preserved underscores the relation between state-of-the-art technology and vampirism; this link is reinforced by the fog-like condensation produced in the cold stores, together with the coffin-like shape of the morgue refrigerators. Cold storage also illustrates how both animals and people can be (pre)served as food, and how vampires can "batten on the helpless"—a phrase that calls to mind both Monks' hanging upside down like a vampire bat, and Van Helsing's tale of vampire bats that feed not only on "cattle and horses" but also on "sailors" (Stoker 2000 [1897], 229). Finally, though somewhat anachronistically, the slaughterhouse tableau evokes *The Blood Drinkers* (1898) by Joseph Ferdinand Gueldry (1858–1945). The editor of *The Magazine of Art* describes this extraordinary painting as depicting "a group of consumptive invalids, congregated in a shambles, [who] are drinking the blood fresh from the newly-slain ox lying in the foreground—blood that oozes out over the floor— while the slaughterers, themselves steeped in gore, hand out the glasses like the women at the wells" (Dijkstra 1986, 338). Among these anaemic women is "one young girl, pale and trembling" (338) who resembles Camille. The visual reference to Gueldry's painting reinforces the interchangeability of human and animal blood: the invalids drink the ox's blood in an attempt to supplement and revivify their own. It also underscores the horror and peril of late-Victorian science as practiced by Blanchard.

Blanchard and Jackson are not the only vampiric scientists in "White World." Dr. Carlyle Probyn—whose surname denotes the nature of his transgressions—draws blood from the prisoners of Newgate in an effort to assist Blanchard's illicit experiments. Like Blanchard and Jackson, he brandishes needles. When Drake, Reid and Jackson raid Probyn's office, Reid demands, "Where is it you keep your needles, Doctor?" (Watson 2016, 31:37–31:39), and upon examining them notes, "Your instruments are much used, sir" (32:08–32:10). When Probyn is dismissed from his post, in another vampiric crime he attempts to extort money from Jackson's estranged wife Long Susan (MyAnna Buring)—who, in condign punishment for his wrongdoing, stabs him through the heart. Even Reid, who hunts the vampiric Blanchard and Probyn, and who disapproves of *Dracula*'s Gothicism, is linked by his daughter Mathilda with the infamous vampire. After he reprimands her for spending all night reading Stoker's novel, she tells him, "When the Count comes to London, he makes his lair in Whitechapel—like you" (04:10–04:15). Her remark, though spiteful, is accurate: Dracula does indeed deposit six of his boxes in "Mile End New Town" (Stoker 2000 [1897], 300), a squalid area of Whitechapel. The seediness of the neighbourhood is remarked upon by Quincey, who is to accompany

Arthur there in a raid: "Look here, old fellow, [...] don't you think that one of your snappy carriages with its heraldic adornments in a byway of Walworth or Mile End would attract too much attention for our purposes?" (334). That Dracula would establish one of his dens in Whitechapel—where, presumably, he also finds victims—aligns him with both Jack the Ripper and Reid, who spends most of his time working there as a homicide detective and thus, in a sense, also lives upon the blood spilled in the district.

The latter association is bolstered by the fact that both Blanchard and Reid are attempting to protect their (virginal, white-clad) daughters—the former from disease, the latter from exploitation and disgrace. Musing over Blanchard's actions, Reid says, "A child. His child. No sin too great to save her, I imagine." Jackson responds, "Perhaps you know how he feels, Reid" (Watson 2016, 40:53–41:01). Reid's connection with Blanchard (and Dracula) is made stronger yet by his counselling her to take a scientific approach to her budding relationship with Sergeant Samuel Drummond (Matthew Lewis). "You would prefer I created experiments to test what matter he is made of," Mathilda tells him. "I might, yes," he responds with enthusiasm. Holding up the copy of *Dracula* that she has loaned Drummond to discern whether he enjoys it as much as she does, Mathilda asks, "But do you not see this is that experiment?" (53:02–53:13). Reid then advises her to "make [her] test" (54:24–54:26). That a novel focused on experimentation itself becomes the means of an experiment illustrates how well Justin Young and Richard Warlow, the writers of "White World," understand their source text. Their willingness to critique both that text and its sociocultural context is demonstrated when Mathilda calls attention to the fact that Dracula has a lair in Whitechapel and refers to him as "the Count," thereby stressing his role as an aristocrat who literally feeds on the lower classes.

Mathilda's portrayal of the aristocrat-as-parasite is classically Gothic. The neo-Gothic "White World" updates this familiar critique for the late-Victorian period—and for our own neoliberal era of socioeconomic disparity—by revealing that the ultimate vampire is not Reid, Jackson, Probyn or even Blanchard: it is the laissez-faire economic system, which exploits and imperils foreign sweatshop workers. The episode thereby reinscribes the link between vampirism and economics drawn by Karl Marx in the first volume of *Capital*: "Capital is dead labour, that, vampire-like, only lives by sucking living labour, and lives the more, the more labour it sucks" (2007 [1867], 257). Marx continues to describe how capital vampirises the working class, not only by draining their vitality but also by making them unnaturally nocturnal: "The prolongation of the working-day beyond the limits of the natural day, into the night, only acts as a palliative. It quenches only in a slight degree the vampire thirst for the living blood of labour" (282). In "White World," Blanchard, a bourgeois surgeon, literally drains "the living blood of labour" by exsanguinating Agnieszka, a Polish seamstress working in a sweatshop, and by attempting to suck dry her coworker Magdalena. The fungibility of these two women within a capitalist economic framework becomes evident when Magdalena, detained only briefly in the headquarters of H Division, begs to return to work, lest another desperate woman quickly replace her: "Now, please, I must leave. Or there will be no work when I return" (Watson 2016, 18:01–18:05). Likewise, when Magdalena decides to sell her blood to Blanchard and leaves work voluntarily, a nearly identical worker, whom Thatcher seizes by mistake after barging into the sweatshop, soon replaces her. Finally, when Agnieszka fails to meet his needs, Blanchard lures Magdalena, as he did her coworker, by promising her "a thousand times over what she would make with a needle in her hand" (18:02–18:06).

Blanchard's promise underscores how the episode contrasts the needles men hold with those women hold. The former are phallic symbols of science's potency, whereas the latter signify exploitation and powerlessness. Both sorts pierce women's bodies. Inspecting Agniezka's corpse, Jackson points out the "scarring of seamstress needles," and Drake concludes, "She's been sweated" (14:02–14:03). The allied vampires of laissez-faire capitalism and pseudoscience use not fangs but needles to draw sweat and blood from their victims.[4] Like the sweatshop seamstresses, Blanchard's other victim, the Newgate prisoner Monks, is disempowered and needled. Probyn haughtily proclaims, "So what if I took blood from inmates? Is there a law that says I cannot? I am a public servant" (35:12–35:21). His remark illustrates how both individual members of the bourgeoisie and the corrupt system as a whole function as vampires—and his being driven primarily by the money Blanchard pays him underscores this point. "What did he give you?" Jackson asks. "Money," Probyn responds. "A promise of more." Jackson retorts, "Now we know how motivated you are by that currency, don't we?" (37:00–37:11). The cold-storage room in which Monks' body hangs alongside the carcasses of food animals thus becomes a synecdoche for all of Whitechapel: a vast, cold meat market for both animals and human beings.

In thoroughly neo-Gothic fashion, "White World" at once captures and condemns the laissez-faire capitalism that informs *Dracula*. It takes the same approach to the novel's xenophobia. Reid ridicules *Dracula*'s portrayal of "the evil Transylvanian Count" who must be destroyed "because all foreigners are dangerous predators set on the parasitic cannibalism of our young women" (41.49–41:59). His curt critique reinforces an observation made by Dr. Frederick Treves (Paul Ready) as he lectures on the physiology of Joseph Merrick, the Elephant Man: "We are keen […] to attribute animal, primal qualities to that which we do not understand. Here, deformity. Elsewhere, perhaps, foreignness" (23:00–23:18). Both Reid and Treves anticipate our contemporary understanding that "xenophobia and racism may certainly be traced in *Dracula*" (Hindle 2003, xx), which is likewise conveyed in the episode's plot. In "White World," the threats come from within Britain, not outside it. Indeed, in an elegantly ironic twist, the very features that have defined the nation during the Victorian era—revolutionary scientific advancement and rapid economic growth—now menace it. Yet Blanchard, the episode's proximate antagonist and stand-in for these hegemonic forces, is not British but French. That Probyn is unaware of the man's name but identifies him as "French" (37:36) underscores how his nationality delimits and obscures his identity. The same dynamic is at work in Reid and Drake's conversations with Thatcher about the staff of the French embassy whom the latter awakens in the middle of the night to demand information about Blanchard. Reid instructs Thatcher to "simply shout louder" (43:16–43:17) if they fail to comprehend his bad French. "They moaned a good deal, sir," Thatcher later tells Drake, who responds, "This is because they are French." The sergeant continues, "But as Mr. Reid suggested, I shouted. And they soon packed up their moaning." "That is also down to their being French," his superior concludes (44:36–44:48). While these exchanges comically illustrate long-standing British antipathy towards the French, they also disclose how, on the diegetic level, "White World" replicates the xenophobia of *Dracula* even while repudiating it. On the extra-diegetic level, their impact is weakened considerably—not only by our sympathy for Blanchard, who is desperately trying to save his daughter's life, but also by our recognition that a foreigner may be either a victim or a villain; and, in Blanchard's case, both.

This interplay between the diegetic and extra-diegetic levels, though important in "White World," is crucial to *Shadows*, whose neo-Gothicism depends upon it. The opening and closing sequences, like the narrative frames of *Dracula* and the *Ripper Street* episode, update the classical Gothic frame while eliding past/present and fact/fiction. The movie begins with contemporary credits for its distribution and production companies, which are followed by what seems to be a much older credit for the fictional New Zealand Documentary Board. When this logo appears, dated music plays and the film becomes scratched and faded. These credits imply that twenty-first century film companies are presenting a twentieth-century documentary; thus, the present frames the past, and fiction frames fact. After the credits, we read, "Every few years a secret society in New Zealand gathers for a special event: THE UNHOLY MASQUERADE[.] In the months leading up to the ball, a documentary crew was granted full access to a small group of this society" (Clement and Waititi 2014, 01:00–01:08). We then read, after a pause and in a new intertitle, "Each crew member wore a crucifix and was granted protection by the subjects of the film" (01:36–01:42). This unexpected information unsettles the fact-fiction frame, and the destabilising move repeats when another intertitle, "Viago," introduces one of the main characters (Taika Waititi) and is followed in a moment by the revelation that he is "379 years old" (02:01–02:04).

By this point, however, the fragile boundary between fact and fiction has already been obliterated: Viago has arisen, bolt upright, from his coffin. The allusion to Count Orlok's iconic rise from his own coffin in *Nosferatu* (1922), the first of many references to other films featuring vampires, introduces the intertextuality that permeates the movie and enhances its neo-Gothicism, even as it heightens tension between the "factual" documentary format and the *outré* subject matter. In yet another formal and generic complication, humour joins horror as Viago has trouble getting (it) up while being watched by the cameraman (and us). His performance anxiety, which often reveals itself in nervous, fang-disclosing smiles to the camera, renders him a sympathetic monster. Our sympathy for him is both tested and reinforced when we watch him seduce and murder victims in spectacularly bloody tableaux that are at once shocking and funny. He twice haplessly "hit[s] the main artery" (20:47–20:48) when biting women, and then frantically tries (and fails) to drink the blood spouting from their necks. The most remarkable feature of these and similar scenes is not how they deftly combine Grand Guignol with comedy, but how they draw performers and viewers into a highly complex relationship.

This bond is established when characters break the fourth wall, thereby highlighting the film's neo-Gothic self-awareness—and making both documentarians and viewers complicit in murder. As Viago entertains a victim, he describes his genteel approach to killing in a voiceover: "It's their last moment alive, so why not make it a nice experience?" (19:41–19:45). He then looks into the camera, smiles and raises his eyebrows impishly.

The woman seems unaware that a cameraman is in the room—perhaps because he is standing behind heavy drapes. We watch through a gap in these drapes, which emphasise our voyeuristic position and frame the scene as if it were occurring on stage. The contrast between the woman's unawareness and our own understanding generates dramatic irony, exacerbates our complicity (and the cameraman's) and underscores the ongoing tension between the diegetic and extra-diegetic. (That the film's title uses the pronoun *We*, not *They*, further implicates both filmmakers and viewers: all of us are involved.) A similar dynamic is at work in the dinner-party scene. After being hypnotised by Deacon (Jonathan Brugh) into seeing his spaghetti as worms and his penis as a snake, Nick (Cori Gonzalez-Macuer) attempts to flee. Unlike Viago's earlier victim, Nick acknowledges the cameraman, and even talks to him: "You don't think this is weird?" (26:09–26:10). He then begins talking to himself, and the cameraman disappears. In this frenetic scene, Nick is pursued by the vampires and the cameraman alike; thus, vampirism and filmmaking are aligned. Their connection is elucidated by the interpolated interview in which Deacon explains his hypnotic trick: "We stole that idea from *The Lost Boys*. But I put a nice twist on it" (25:28–25:32). This remarkable statement further complicates the already intricate relations among fact, fiction and (vampire) films. We recognise that *Shadows* has "put a nice twist"—indeed, many twists—on not only *The Lost Boys* (1987), which likewise features a prank-prone, all-male vampire coven, but also *Nosferatu, Bram Stoker's Dracula* (1992) and—more subtly and significantly—*Shadow of the Vampire* (2000), in which Max Schreck (Willem Dafoe) is an actual vampire playing a fictional one, and Friedrich Wilhelm Murnau (John Malkovich) is making *Nosferatu* as a snuff film. In *Shadow of the Vampire* and *Shadows*, both directors and stars are vampires who drain life in order to sustain or create something immortal. This point is neatly underscored by the fact that the directors of the latter film, Jemaine Clement and Taika Waititi, play the vampires Vladislav and Viago in it.

The titles of the two films likewise call attention to the shadowy and vampiric essence of cinematic representation, together with the paradoxes of depicting vampires on film. In *Shadows*, one such paradox involves the vampires' motive for participating in a documentary that will prove fatal to them. "Vampires have had a really bad rap," Viago explains. "We're not these mopey old creatures who live in castles. And, well, some of us are, a lot of us are. But there are also those of us who like to flat together in really small countries like New Zealand" (Clement and Waititi 2014, 10:34–10:50). His motive, then, appears to be dispelling stereotypes. As Vladislav points out, however, "If the humans found out what we were, they would destroy us" (16:34–16:38). The documentary's release will usher the vampires out of the shadows and into the light—which transition will presumably kill them, even as sunlight kills the ancient Petyr (Ben Fransham). "Petyr, get away from the sunlight! Get in the shadows, Petyr!" Viago screams as the vampire burns (48:02–48:04). Even a little publicity can be fatal: Petyr's death results from the newly turned vampire Nick's having widely shared the news of his transformation, thereby alerting a vampire hunter. Oblivious to consequences, Nick revels in performing his new role as vampire, and in casting himself in the lead of the documentary. "You know the main guy [in] *Twilight*?" he asks a man. "That's me. There's cameras following me around" (41:32–41:360). This moment is among a significant few in which characters explicitly acknowledge the presence of cameras (as opposed to merely looking knowingly into them).

These moments promise but never deliver a justification for the film, or a resolution of its paradoxes. When Deacon castigates Nick for "flying around [the] house" and "draw[ing] attention to [it]" from the neighbours, the new vampire responds, logically enough, "You've got a whole documentary crew following you around" (30:36–30:41). Deacon offers no response. When the police enter the vampires' home to investigate the disturbance caused by Petyr's demise, Constable O'Leary (Karen O'Leary) asks, "What's with the fellow? What's with the camera?" (51:39–51:41). A cut follows, after which, oddly and amusingly, she begins explaining the situation to the cameraman. Presumably, during the time gap, Viago has offered some sort of phony rationale for the cameraman's being there, which the gullible officer has accepted—but we never hear it. Later, Phillip (Frank Habicht), the leader of a werewolf pack the vampires encounter, asks, "What are you filming?" (34:06–34:07). No one answers. Finally, during the Unholy Masquerade, Pauline (Elena Stejko) demands in broken English, "What is cameras doing here?" Vladislav begins, "They're making a documentary on—" before Julian (Jason Hoyte) cuts him off: "This is a private, secret society, mate! You don't go bringing your bloody cameras into everything!" (1:09:09–17). The paradox thus remains unresolved, though we do learn how dangerous the documentary is—not only to its subjects, but also to its creators.

Seeking to placate Julian and the other vampires while protecting his human friend Stu, Vladislav offers one documentarian as a human sacrifice. "You will not eat Stu, and you will not eat the camera guy," he states, before relenting and gesturing towards the camera filming him: "Maybe one camera guy" (1:09:18–22). One cameraman is indeed killed, by a werewolf rather than a vampire, at the climax of a sequence that, by this innovative film's standards, is fairly conventional. The cameraman flees through the woods as shaky subjective shots show the ground at his feet. Suddenly a werewolf appears in the frame, and the camera is knocked from his hands. After a moment of digital distortion, the camera captures its operator, screaming, being mauled by the werewolf before it drags him out of the frame. The point of view then shifts to the second cameraman. If we accept the film's *donnée*, then we can only imagine what occurred during the editing process. Such acceptance is challenging, for it requires considerable willing suspension of disbelief—not only in the vampires and werewolves, but also in the paradoxical documentary structure framing their narratives. Whatever rationale exists for this project—which destroys those on both sides of the camera—is available only offstage.

Our suspension of disbelief is made yet more challenging by the paradoxical (meta) physics of representing vampires: They can be captured by cameras, but they do not appear in mirrors. This inconsistency is arguably a function of the film's conceit: if the vampires could not appear on film, then there would be no film. That said, a good deal more than expediency is at issue. The representational paradox is featured when Viago is filmed standing in front of a mirror, holding a teacup that appears to hover. "A ghost cup! Floating all by itself!" he exclaims (14:43–14:50). Viago's characterisation of the cup as spectral evokes Jean Cocteau's observation in *Orphée*: "You only have to watch yourself all your life in a mirror, and you'll see Death at work like bees in a glass hive" (1933, 24). Because Viago cannot die, the ghost is not himself but the cup. Similarly inapplicable to Viago is Susan Sontag's insight, in *On Photography*, that photographs depict "the vulnerability of lives heading towards their destruction, and this link between photography and death haunts all photographs of people" (1978 [1977], 70). Because Viago and his fellow vampires are no longer people, in the photographs of them taken through the decades that constitute part of the film's opening sequence, their clothing and surroundings change but they remain eternally the same—both within and outside their pictures. Likewise, when Vladislav poses for a photograph in front of a portrait of himself, the only difference between the photo and the painting is his outfit. Unlike Dorian Gray, whose soul is transferred into an undead picture, the vampires are themselves soulless, undead pictures. Accordingly, the key to the cup-and-mirror scene is its duality, and lack thereof: one material cup appears in Viago's hand; another, its ghost, materialises in the mirror. Viago himself is not doubled, because he is already a ghost.

Spectral duality of this sort is at the core of *Shadows*. Jacques Derrida explains that "cinema can stage phantomality almost head-on, to be sure, as in a tradition of fantasy film, vampire or ghost films," but this approach "must be distinguished from the thoroughly spectral structure of the cinematic image" itself (2015, 26). A film about vampires preoccupied with films about vampires, and with film and photography more generally, is profoundly neo-Gothic—not only because it takes a meta approach, or involves itself in a *mise en abyme* of intertextuality, but because it uncannily doubles the spectrality of its own medium and creates multiple "levels of phantomality" (27). As Sigmund Freud notes in "The Uncanny," for many the uncanny manifests itself "in the highest degree in relation to death and dead bodies, to the return of the dead, and to spirits and ghosts" (1955 [1919], 241). An "extraordinarily strong feeling of something uncanny" also results from "the figure of a 'double'" (236)—which figure may itself be doubled as both "an assurance of immortality" and a "harbinger of death" (235). An intensely uncanny spectrality is on display when the dance Deacon performs for his flatmates—a dance of the (un)dead—doubles one earlier in the film, which appears to have been recorded in the earliest days of cinema. This weirdly erotic-comedic *danse macabre* is, moreover, one of many examples of the film's campiness, which in turn is bound up with its (uncanny) intertextuality and performative self-awareness. That much of its humour could be considered camp makes perfect sense, given Sontag's definition, in "Notes on 'Camp,'" of camp as "Being-as-Playing-a-Role," and "the farthest extension, in sensibility, of the metaphor of life as theater" (1999 [1964], 56). This campiness is also arguably a form of aesthetic vampirism: the film feeds upon other films—many of which could themselves be considered campy.

The question of how camp in general and queerness in particular function in neo-Gothic narratives involving vampires is well worth answering, and Tim Burton's *Dark Shadows* (2012) engages it with panache. A good deal more work might also be done to explicate how spectrality and the uncanny relate to both the vampiric and the neo-Gothic, especially given the leading role played by duality in all of these areas. *What We Do in the Shadows* (2019), the television show that shadows its namesake, is arguably even more neo-Gothic than its inspiration and merits careful analysis. *Dracula*, "White

World" and *Shadows*, while remarkable and sophisticated texts, are only starting points for exploring the shadowy realm where vampirism and neo-Gothicism intersect.

Notes

1   For the significance of typewriting in *Dracula*, see Wicke (1992).
2   In her introduction to *Dracula*, Glennis Byron notes that "the modernity of *Dracula* in its emphasis on technology and data accumulation [...] did not seem particularly to impress the Victorians themselves," who "did not generally seem to consider Stoker's documentation and display of the inventiveness of the age appropriate to this particular tale of terror" (2000, 12). For example, the reviewer for *The Spectator* believes Stoker's "story would have been all the more effective if he had chosen an earlier period. The up-to-dateness of the book—the phonograph diaries, typewriters and so on—hardly fits in with the mediaeval methods which ultimately secure the victory for Count Dracula's foes." See Appendix H to *Dracula* (2000 [1897], 483).
3   Both Camille and Carmilla have unusual teeth, wander by night in search of victims and vampirise young women. See Le Fanu (2013 [1832], 3–98).
4   The association of sweat and blood calls to mind the "great drops of sweat" that "[spring] from [Arthur's] forehead" as he stakes Lucy and blood spurts from her body (Stoker 2000 [1897], 254), together with the psychoanalytic claim that bodily fluids are interchangeable to the unconscious. See Freud (2010 [1900], 413n1) and Jones (1931, 119).

Bibliography

"Blanchard, adj." OED Online. December 2019. Oxford University Press. https://www-oed-com.ezproxy.liberty.edu/view/Entry/19848?redirectedFrom=blanchard.

Byron, Glennis, ed. *Dracula* by Bram Stoker. 1897. Peterborough, ON: Broadview, 2000.

Clement, Jemaine, and Taika Waititi, dirs. *What We Do in the Shadows*. New York: Unison Films, 2014. Blu-ray Disc, 1080p HD.

Cocteau, Jean. *Orphée: A Tragedy in One Act and an Interval*. Oxford: Oxford University Press, 1933.

Derrida, Jacques. "Cinema and Its Ghosts: An Interview with Jacques Derrida." By Antoine de Baecque and Thierry Jousse. Translated by Peggy Kamuf. *Discourse* nos 1–2 (Winter/Spring 2015): 22–39.

Dijkstra, Bram. *Idols of Perversity: Fantasies of Feminine Evil in Fin-de-siècle Culture*. Oxford: Oxford University Press, 1986.

Faulkner, William. *Requiem for a Nun*. New York: Random House, 2011.

Freud, Sigmund. "The Uncanny." In *The Standard Edition of the Complete Psychological Works of Sigmund Freud*. 1919. Vol. 17, translated and edited by James Strachey, 217–56. London: Hogarth Press and the Institute of Psycho-Analysis, 1955.

———. *The Interpretation of Dreams: The Complete and Definitive Text*. 1900. Translated and edited by James Strachey. New York: Basic Books, 2010.

Hindle, Maurice, ed. *Dracula*. By Bram Stoker. Rev. ed. London: Penguin Books, 2003.

Jones, Ernest. *On the Nightmare*. London: Hogarth Press, 1931.

Le Fanu, Sheridan. *Carmilla: A Critical Edition*. 1872. Edited by Kathleen Costello-Sullivan. Syracuse: Syracuse University Press, 2013.

Marx, Karl. 1867. *Capital: A Critique of Political Economy*. Vol. 1. *The Process of Capitalist Production*. Edited by Friedrich Engels. New York: Cosimo, 2007.

McCann, Shaun R. *A History of Haematology: From Herodotus to HIV*. Oxford: Oxford University Press, 2016.

Rees, Jonathan. *Refrigeration Nation: A History of Ice, Appliances, and Enterprise in America*. Baltimore: Johns Hopkins University Press, 2013.

Sontag, Susan. *On Photography*. 1977. New York: Farrar, Straus & Giroux, 1978.

———. "Notes on 'Camp.'" 1964. In *Camp: Queer Aesthetics and the Performing Subject: A Reader*, edited by Fabio Cleto, 53–65. Ann Arbor: University of Michigan Press, 1999.

Stoddard, Jane. "Appendix H: Mr. Bram Stoker: A Chat with the Author of *Dracula*." 1897. In *Dracula* by Bram Stoker, edited by Glennis Byron, 484–88. Peterborough, ON: Broadview, 2000.

Stoker, Bram. *Dracula*. 1897. Edited by Glennis Byron. Peterborough, ON: Broadview, 2000.

Watson, Luke, dir. *Ripper Street*. "A White World Made Red." Season 4, episode 3. Aired January 29, 2016, BBC One.

Wicke, Jennifer. "Vampiric Typewriting: *Dracula* and Its Media." *ELH* 59, no. 2 (1992): 467–93.

Chapter Six

"HERE WE ARE, *AGAIN!*": NEO-GOTHIC NARRATIVES OF TEXTUAL HAUNTING, FROM PETER ACKROYD'S *DAN LENO AND THE LIMEHOUSE GOLEM* TO *THE LIMEHOUSE GOLEM*

Ashleigh Prosser

For over forty years contemporary English author, biographer and popular historian Peter Ackroyd, CBE FRSL, has produced a vast collection of writing that can be broadly classified as neo-historical because of his insistent return to the past and its texts within his own, but it is worth noting that many of his works are concerned with or clearly influenced by the nineteenth century in particular and often referenced in neo-Victorian scholarship. For instance, Dana Shiller employs Ackroyd's *Chatterton* (1987) alongside A. S. Byatt's *Possession* (1990) to exemplify one of the earliest definitions of the neo-Victorian as "texts that revise specific Victorian precursors, texts that imagine new adventures for familiar Victorian characters, and 'new' Victorian fictions that imitate nineteenth-century literary conventions" (1997, 558). Shiller argues that in *Chatterton*, Ackroyd created "a postmodern novel that plays on (and with) our certainties about history while simultaneously delighting in what *can* be retrieved of the past" (540; emphasis in original), which is the quintessence of a neo-Victorian text as Shiller proceeds to then define it. In addition to Ackroyd's neo-Victorian Gothic novel *Dan Leno and the Limehouse Golem* (2007 [1994])—the focus of this chapter's analysis—and *The Casebook of Victor Frankenstein* (2008), which is also set in nineteenth-century London, other works by Ackroyd such as *The Great Fire of London* (1993a [1982]), *The Last Testament of Oscar Wilde* (1993b [1983]) and *English Music* (1992) have similarly attracted the attention of neo-Victorian scholars for they, too, seem to channel the famous voices of the age in the ways Shiller describes. *The Great Fire of London*, for example, is set in 1980s London but the city Ackroyd portrays is heavily reminiscent of Dickens' own, as the lives of the characters are haunted by the world of Dickens' *Little Dorrit* (1857), none more so than Audrey Skelton who actually believes she has been possessed by the spirit of Dickens' character Amy Dorrit. Ackroyd takes the neo-Victorian metaphor of providing the Victorians with a new voice even further in *The Last Testament of Oscar Wilde* by creating a conscious pastiche of the voice of Oscar Wilde through the first-person reflections and confessions of his (fictional) deathbed diary, thus raising the postmodernist concern with the (in)authenticity of our attempts to recapture the past in a playfully self-reflexive way. Such literary ventriloquism is perhaps at its most excessive in *English Music*, wherein Timothy Harcombe recounts his upbringing between the World Wars in the style of a Dickensian bildungsroman in the odd-numbered chapters, while the even-numbered chapters are a series of textual pastiches that narrate young Timothy's visionary experiences as he is transported inside canonical English works, interacting with the characters and their worlds alongside the writers, artists and composers that created them.

Hence, as Ackroydian scholar Barry Lewis suggests, "the language of possession comes readily to mind when considering the indefinable process of influence" (2007, 168) that underlies much of Ackroyd's neo-historical writings. Ackroyd's recurrent recourse to such acts of literary possession throughout his oeuvre reveals his textual impersonations to be a kind of mimetic performance, one that frequently serves to communicate the relationship he believes to exist between the past and present in London and its literature as one of haunting by the city's "Gothic *genius loci*" (2001 [2000], 580), as I have previously argued.[1] Throughout Ackroyd's fictional and nonfictional works, this "spirit of London place" (580) continually returns with uncanny effect, often described through the language of the Gothic mode as an experience of haunting, and it is frequently attributed to be the source of patterns of coincidence and continuity that Ackroyd finds to be repeated throughout the city's 2,000 years of historical life. It is an aesthetic approach that is thus inherently underscored by the concept of textual haunting, one that has been persuasively explored in relation to the neo-Victorian by Julian Wolfreys (2002), and most recently with specific reference to Ackroyd who through such means "ventriloquises or otherwise acts as our spirit medium to the haunting alterity of the nineteenth-century" (Wolfreys 2013, 165). The key to Wolfreys' conceptualisation of textual haunting, then, is that a text "partakes in its own haunting, it is traced by its own phantoms, and it is this condition which reading must confront" (2002, xii). Tracing the metatextual presence of these literary phantoms is thus what informs this chapter's reading of the neo-Gothic narrative form as one of textual haunting, since for over 250 years the Gothic mode has partaken in its own haunting for it has returned again and again in various guises, its ghosts refusing to be laid to rest, instead finding new ways to haunt our homes once more.

The prevalence with which neo-Victorian texts involve spectres or spiritualist practices (the theatrical séances that gained widespread popularity during the nineteenth century),[2] and current scholarship's repeated highlighting of these as master tropes of the mode as Margaret D. Stetz has justly noted, reveals "the 'haunting' presence of the Victorians in (post)modern life" (2012, 343).[3] While the spectral metaphor in the neo-Victorian text is thus often equated with (post)modernity's wrestle with the uncanny's return of the repressed, in this chapter I wish to focus on how such specifically neo-Gothic repetitions evoke an experience of the uncanny as a "sense of déjà vu" wherein, Rosario Arias and Patricia Pulham argue, we are haunted by the "pervasive presence of the Victorians through their textual/spectral traces in popular culture" (2009, xv–xvi). Moreover, this déjà vu-like reading experience relies on the fact that the neo-Victorian text is quite literally defined by the haunted and haunting connection that it has with its Victorian predecessors, for the prefix "neo-" serves to remind us that it is always already an uncanny double, a counterfeit ghost of the long-dead original. I am here invoking

Jerrold E. Hogle's well-known theorisation of the Gothic as counterfeit in which the "Gothic ghost of the counterfeit" (2012) functions as a conceptual metaphor for the mode's reinventions of its past forms with each new period of literary revival. The textual haunting by such ghosts and the uncanny feelings of déjà vu they generate that are so inherent to the creation and consumption of the neo-Victorian text, I propose, further facilitates a kind of metatextual séance within such neo-Gothic narratives set in the nineteenth century. The contemporary author thus acts as the séance's medium conjuring up these counterfeit ghosts, since it is through the mimetic performance of such spectral possession that the literary phantoms of the Victorians are summoned to haunt a strangely (un)familiar (meta)fictional world.

This chapter will pursue the possible implications of such a reading, for I argue it is this mimetic performance of the neo-Gothic that creates the metatextual séance within *Dan Leno and the Limehouse Golem,* and the metatextual *mise-en-séance* of its recent adaption by screenwriter Jane Goldman as *The Limehouse Golem* (2017), a neo-Victorian horror film directed by Juan Carlos Medina. Underlying the plot of both the novel and the film is the suggestion that Victorian London's East End is haunted by a malevolent spirit of place that appears to have manifested itself in the monstrous acts of the Limehouse Golem serial killer. In what follows, I propose that this malevolent spirit of place is an inheritance of the area's real history of violence combined with its literary history in the Late-Victorian Gothic, for Ackroyd's narrative is textually haunted by those "shadows, spectres and written ghosts" of the neo-Victorian city that Ann Heilmann and Mark Llewellyn suggest "never quite materialize into substantive presences but instead maintain simulations of the 'real'" (2010, 145). Yet it is of significance that the real which is invoked here is by necessity an *imagined* reality, one that is informed by a vision of the world that the Victorians left behind in their own texts, which is furthered by neo-Victorian adaptations of those texts, and of their forms and styles, characters and tropes. Heilmann and Llewellyn's definition of the neo-Victorian is particularly apt then, for they argue that it is "*more than* historical fiction set in the nineteenth century […], texts (literary, filmic, audio/visual) must in some respect be *self-consciously engaged with the act of (re)interpretation, (re)discovery and (re)vision concerning the Victorians*" (4; emphasis in original). This chapter will thus examine precisely how such a neo-Victorian (re)vision is at play within *Dan Leno and the Limehouse Golem* and its adaption in *The Limehouse Golem.* For, it will argue that both are textually haunted works of historiographic metafiction that envision the imagined realities of Victorian literary phantoms in an evocation of the neo-Victorian Urban Gothic in popular culture.

First published in 1994, Ackroyd's eighth novel *Dan Leno and the Limehouse Golem* is an intricately assembled palimpsest of plots and perspectives, framed as a collection of authentic historical materials compiled and narrated by an unnamed contemporary historian. It recounts two fictitious Victorian murder cases that occurred within the Limehouse area of London in the autumn of 1880. The first case is an account of the trial of Elizabeth Cree, and her early life as the Victorian music hall performer "Lambeth Marsh Lizzie," who is found guilty for the murder of her wealthy husband John Cree, and whose execution begins the novel. The second case concerns the gruesome unsolved murders committed by a serial killer nicknamed by the press the "Limehouse Golem."

The Golem's killing spree consisted of the strangely ritualistic dismemberment of two prostitutes (Jane Quig and Alice Stanton) on the Limehouse streets, and of the elderly scholar Solomon Weil in his home in the Jewish quarter of Limehouse, and mysteriously culminated in the slaughter of the Gerrard family in a grisly recreation of the Ratcliffe Highway murders in the very same house where the original massacre of the Marr family by John Williams took place.[4] The way in which the novel is constructed is thus exemplary of Linda Hutcheon's proposition that historiographic metafiction privileges "modes of narration" which work to "problematize the entire notion of subjectivity" through the use of "multiple points of view [...] or an overtly controlling narrator" (1987, 297). Ackroyd simultaneously employs both of these modes of narration to achieve this destabilising effect, for the chapters alternate between the contemporary narrator's omniscient perspective on the crimes and the lives of the people who are coincidentally connected to them, such as the titular music hall star Dan Leno, the young writer George Gissing and the elderly philosopher Karl Marx, alongside a selection of excerpts from the various archival documents of each case. Ackroyd's fake historical primary sources include: the court transcripts taken from the *"Illustrated Police News Law Courts and Weekly Records"* of Elizabeth Cree's trial (2007 [1994], 9), and the first-person autobiographical testimony of her life and career; the personal journal of "John Cree" which exposes him as the Limehouse Golem (revealed in the novel's conclusion to be forged by the real murderer, his wife) *"now preserved in the Manuscript Department of the British Museum, with the call-mark Add. Ms. 1624/566"* (24; emphasis in original); and articles from Victorian newspapers such as the *Morning Advertiser* detailing the crimes committed by the Limehouse Golem.[5]

Billed as "a gothic murder mystery set in the darkest alleys of Victorian London," the cinematic adaptation of *Dan Leno and the Limehouse Golem* by screenwriter Jane Goldman, directed by Juan Carlos Medina and produced by Stephen Woolley and Elizabeth Karlsen, was released globally in 2017 under the title *The Limehouse Golem*.[6] Goldman's script commendably attempts to follow closely the complex multilayered plots of Ackroyd's novel, but as is the nature of adaption from page to screen, a few necessary changes are made to the crux of the highly textual narrative to enable its translation to the visual medium of film. In lieu of the contemporary historian-narrator who constructs the narrative retrospectively for the reader of the novel and collates the archival documents included therein, the film shifts the viewer's perspective to follow the investigation into the Limehouse Golem serial killings led by Inspector Kildare (Bill Nighy) of Scotland Yard by beginning with the Golem's last crime, the brutal massacre of the Gerrard family in their home on Ratcliffe Highway. Parallel to the investigation is the ongoing trial of Elizabeth Cree (Olivia Cooke) for the murder of her husband John (Sam Reid), which Kildare and his assistant Constable Flood (Daniel Mays) soon find converge in mysterious ways. A new addition to the narrative is the Latin phrase *"non minus cruore profunditor qui spectat, quam ille qui facit"* (meaning "he who observes spills no less blood than he who inflicts the blow") found written in blood at the Ratcliffe Highway crime scene, and it is the clue that leads Kildare's investigation to the British Museum's Reading Room and to their copy of Thomas De Quincey's 1827 satirical essay "On Murder Considered as one of the Fine Arts." Within its margins they find scrawled the Golem's diary of their crimes, and so Kildare suspects one of the essay's readers to be the potential author: Dan Leno (Douglas Booth), Karl Marx (Henry Goodman), George Gissing (Morgan Watkins) or Elizabeth's husband John Cree. Elizabeth's first-person autobiographical narrative is conveyed in flashback sequence from her prison cell as she tells Kildare of her troubled childhood, her life as a performer in Leno's company and her unhappy marriage. As they grow closer with each visit, Kildare hopes to exonerate Elizabeth by proving her late husband was the Limehouse Golem through a process of elimination. Kildare and Flood proceed to take each of the suspects' handwriting samples in interviews during which Kildare reads an extract of the Golem's diary, each time recounting a different murder, and the gruesome scene is played out for the viewer featuring the suspect as the Golem narrating the diary extract through their own demonically distorted voice as they gleefully commit the gory crime.

The film's dramatic cinematography (by Simon Dennis), evoked in atmospheric hazy visual tones and shadowy lighting contrasted with partly desaturated colouring, historically accurate props, elaborate sets and period costume design, along with the theatrical release's promotional tagline—"Before the Ripper, fear had another name"—clearly signal an aesthetic embrace of the neo-Victorian Urban Gothic, tropes that have shaped many neo-Victorian depictions of London on the big and small screens in recent years. As the work of this chapter endeavours to show, they are also the tropes that help to define the novel's metatextual séance, and thus its cinematic adaption presents an excellent opportunity to consider how they could be comparatively read to further form a kind of metatextual *mise-en-séance* through the medium of film.

Before we proceed, it is worth noting that *Dan Leno and the Limehouse Golem* has also been published under an alternative title, *The Trial of Elizabeth Cree: A Novel of the Limehouse Murders* (originally used for the North American edition [1995]). While both titles emphasise the area of London's East End where the narrative takes place, they differ in their positioning of the two main characters. Little about the narrative is revealed by the first title, which suggests only that the real Victorian music hall performer Dan Leno (with whom readers may or may not be familiar) is somehow linked to a mythical creature of Jewish folklore, the Golem, in London's infamous Limehouse district. The second title offers the reader much more since it suggestively evokes the popular true-crime historical genre by focusing solely on the person whose trial the novel retells and the crimes committed (which one assumes are connected), but whether or not it is inspired by real events appears purposefully ambiguous.

An interesting parallel can be drawn, then, between the doubling of the title of the novel and its duplicitous characters and fraudulent plots, as well as with the composite way in which the narrative is retold from various (unreliable) perspectives and through deceptively realistic Victorian court transcripts, newspaper extracts and diary entries. When considered together, and indeed in conjunction with the film's simplified retitling as *The Limehouse Golem*, what these titles subtly suggest is the narrative's own metatextual identity as a representation of neo-Gothic Victorian London "being composed and asserting its identities as a resonant configuration of textual grafts" (Gibson and Wolfreys 2000, 200). Previous scholarship has predominantly explored how themes of performativity and theatricality permeate the text of *Dan Leno and the Limehouse Golem* in this fashion[7]; however, in this chapter I propose that the metatextuality of Ackroyd's neo-Gothic narrative, when considered alongside its cinematic adaptation, can be better understood as an example of textual haunting, for it is even the means through which Ackroyd emulates the real Dan Leno's own uncanny practice of monopolylinguism.

Famously known as "the funniest man on earth" during the late Victorian era, Dan Leno (the stage name of George Galvin) was renowned for his exceptional talents as one of London's greatest monopolylinguists, a centuries-old tradition Ackroyd describes in his 1993 lecture "London Luminaries and Cockney Visionaries" (2002 [2001], 341). Monopolylinguists are "comedians or actors who play a number of quick-change parts in the course of one performance" (344), but to break down Ackroyd's definition according to the word's oxymoronic etymology, the skill of the mono-poly-linguist lies in his or her ability to use one (mono) voice to speak as if they are many (poly) different voices (linguist). It was through Leno's spectacular, effortless ability to manipulate his whole persona into that of another, rapidly transforming from familiar pantomime characters into his own inimitable caricatures of everyday Londoners in Victorian street scenes that Ackroyd explains "the great pantomime dame, comic and music hall star [...] came to symbolize all the life and energy and variety of the city itself" (341). For such talents, Ackroyd considers Dan Leno to be a Cockney visionary, one of a collection of Londoners throughout history who "in their art have expressed the true nature and spirit of this place" (342) because they understood "the pity and mystery of existence just as surely as they understood its noise and its bustle" (346). Ackroyd suggests Leno inherited his particular visionary understanding of London's spirit of place from Samuel Foote and Charles Mathews, and believes Leno's tradition lives on in the contemporary routines of the city's street performers, stand-up comics and impersonators in which the same sense of "pathos and comedy, high tragedy and low farce, are effortlessly combined" into a singular voice that speaks for and as many others (344–45). Ackroyd's fictionalised Leno is similarly positioned within this line of inheritance and is shown to be the successor of the tradition from Joseph Grimaldi in a characteristically Ackroydian example of the power of coincidence and continuity in the city. In chapter 34 of the novel, it is specifically because of Leno's study of Grimaldi, the history of pantomime and "the conditions, which had, in a sense, created him" (2007 [1994], 193) that he is then led to save the unborn life of his own heir, Charlie Chaplin, in the very same house where Grimaldi had once lived.

Ackroyd's approach to much of his own neo-historical writing is certainly exemplary of this monopolylinguistic practice as he explains: "I presume my interest in lifting or adopting various styles, various traces, various languages, is part of my imaginative trend, and I suppose the use of historical fact as well as other people's writings is just an aspect of this" (Onega 1996, 213). Such aspects of Ackroyd's monopolylinguism are most prominently conveyed, rather fittingly I propose, through the polyphonic narratives of *Dan Leno and the Limehouse Golem*. In chapter 20, Lizzie offers a particularly apt description of Leno's talent for monopolylinguism, explaining "somehow, he was always himself. He was the Indian squaw, the waiter, the milkmaid, or the train driver, but it was always Dan conjuring people out of thin air" (108). Dan Leno is thus the consummate monopolylinguist because he can use his voice to speak as if he were many other people, yet his impersonations always remain uniquely his own. Lizzie's method, however, is unlike Leno's for she is a monopolylinguist; her mental instability from the trauma of her abusive past at the hands of her mother causes her fragile sense of self to be monopolised by the monomaniacal characters she creates, so much so that her own voice is eventually consumed by them. I propose that like Leno, Ackroyd as the author-cum-monopolylinguist of the narrative is similarly conjuring people out of thin air but in his own characteristic way, through his creation of the alternating cacophony of characters' voices who each narrate the story, and in the fusion of quotations within them from real historical figures or impersonations of their imagined perspectives alongside authentic citations and fabricated texts. Ackroyd's approach thus creates a neo-Gothic narrative that functions like a piece of monopolylinguism, for it is a textually haunted mimetic performance staged within the literary theatre of neo-Victorian London. In what follows, I argue that it is the literary phantoms of a characteristically neo-Victorian Urban Gothic London that Ackroyd conjures in these works, for the 1811 Ratcliffe Highway massacre and the unsolved Jack the Ripper murders of 1888 alongside the Gothic literature they inspired, such as Thomas De Quincey's 1827 essay "On Murder Considered as One of the Fine Arts," are reworked as textual ghosts that haunt Ackroyd's narrative in ways that are further uncannily doubled in its cinematic adaptation.

First published in *Blackwood's Magazine* in 1827, Thomas De Quincey's "On Murder Considered as One of the Fine Arts" (2006 [1827]) is a real satirical essay of a fictional lecture for the fake London Gentlemen's Club "The Society of Connoisseurs in Murder" (8). The essay enthusiastically argues for the aesthetic appreciation of the act of murder, irrespective of any moral or ethical qualms, and envisions John Williams' Ratcliffe Highway murders to have been the "sublimest and most entire in their excellence that ever were committed" (29). De Quincey returned to the subject 12 years later in "Second Paper on Murder Considered as One of the Fine Arts" (2006 [1839]), another darkly humorous artistic study of murder written, once again, under the guise of the same connoisseur recounting the events of a celebratory dinner party for fellow aesthetes. Twenty-seven years after the publication of the original essay, De Quincey wrote the lengthy "Postscript [To On Murder Considered as One of the Fine Arts]" (2006 [1854]), in which he vividly recounts the night of the Marr murders from the perspective of the only absent member of the household, the maid Mary who returned mere moments later to the horror of the crimes. In all three essays of De Quincey's "On Murder," he refers to the act as a "performance" and describes it in artistic terms as if it were designed for a theatrical stage (2006 [1827], 10), suggesting Williams' hair was dyed "bright yellow" to give his face a "ghostly pallor" (100), and that he wore a costume of the "very finest cloth" (102) to conduct his "stage spectacle" (96) on the Ratcliffe Highway. De Quincey's "On Murder" essays were considered such popular successes precisely because of the theatrics of his decadent approach in which he "aestheticized violence, transforming it into liberating and intellectual entertainment […] in a variety of fictive, impassioned, and satiric guises" (Morrison 2006 [1854], xxiv). Hence De Quincey's essays on the Ratcliffe Highway killings played a significant role in the rise of the modern Gothic form in detective fiction and in sensationalist literature in the nineteenth century (and beyond), rapidly popularised by "a reading public insatiably interested in palatable versions of murder that disturbed in order to excite and seduce" (xxiv).[8]

De Quincey and his works are self-referentially incorporated throughout *Dan Leno and the Limehouse Golem* by the contemporary narrator and the characters alike, with "On Murder Considered as One of the Fine Arts" acting as a kind of literary phantom that guides the characters' engagement with, and understanding of, this particularly Gothic vision of the city and its history of perpetuating violence.[9] The narrative's contemporary narrator explains, for example, that Gissing's first (fictitious) article for the *Pall Mall Review*, titled "Romanticism and Crime," was a reflection on the titular topics with reference to De Quincey and, in particular, this essay's transformation of the Ratcliffe Highway murderer into "a wonderful Romantic hero [...] of sublime impulse who rearranges (one might say, executes) the natural world in order to reflect his own preoccupations" (37). In chapter 9 of the novel, Gissing reads an extract from his article, in which he argues that the Ratcliffe Highway murders "reached their apotheosis in the prose of Thomas De Quincey, who with purple imagery and soaring cadence has succeeded in immortalising them" (36). Gissing further admires De Quincey's vision of "a sinister, crepuscular London" that came to dominate "the landscape of his imagination [...] in which suffering, poverty and loneliness are the most striking elements" (38–39), in a revealing reflection of Ackroyd's own views on the city's spirit of place. Moreover, when Dan Leno is briefly suspected of being the Golem's next victim, due to the "curious factors" (201) of the case connecting him with each death, a copy of De Quincey's essay is found open on his desk, which prompts Kildare to contemplate the resemblance between it and the overt theatricality of the Golem's slaughter of the Gerrard family since there are "too many resemblances for it to be entirely natural" (204). Leno's link to De Quincey's essay is revealed as another example of the city's strange capacity for coincidence; Leno had instead read the previous entry in the volume, De Quincey's (fabricated) essay on pantomime "Laugh, Scream and Speech," a work which the Golem confesses also inspired their own "little dramas on the streets of London" (191).

In both the novel and its cinematic adaptation, De Quincey's "On Murder" essay affects its most haunting presence in the Limehouse Golem's murderous effort to construct their own "immortal" Gothic narrative in the same macabre theatrical fashion.[10] In the novel, the author of the diary repeatedly and overtly implies that the Golem's murderous acts have been purposefully carried out as an homage to De Quincey's essay. "May I quote Thomas De Quincey?" begins the Golem's diary entry on their "first great work," which they view as a "rehearsal" for their greatest performance "upon the stage of the world" inspired by Williams' "glorious crime," since it was in De Quincey's essay they "first learned of the Ratcliffe Highway deaths, and ever since that time his work has been a source of perpetual delight and astonishment" (2007 [1994], 25–30). However, it is a form of textual haunting that the film instead makes implicit yet tangibly visually literal for the viewer since the Golem's diary is instead visibly shown to be inscribed over the actual text of De Quincey's essay.

The Golem, in both the novel and the film, is shown to enact their crimes with the same macabre theatricality that De Quincey employs in his essay to describe Williams' actions, for they view themselves as an "understudy" aspiring to emulate this "artist who used London as the 'studio' to display his works" (26) and "dressed for each murder as if he were going upon the stage" (30). It is, therefore, grotesquely appropriate that the

Golem's killing spree culminates in a carefully staged re-enactment of Williams' slaughter of the Marr family precisely as described in De Quincey's "On Murder" essays. The Golem's butchery of the Gerrard family is carried out silently within their own home under the cloak of darkness, with the same murder weapons of a mallet and a razor; like Williams, the Golem also unknowingly leaves a solitary survivor. The echoic spirit with which the Golem's massacre of the Gerrard family is thus performed is exemplary of the uncanny's return of the repressed as it is found in the Gothic, wherein dark events or horrible secrets from the past that were thought to have been buried return to haunt the present by being repeated. The Golem envisions the Gerrards' deaths as such, explaining that they are to represent the inevitability of these "patterns of eternity" in the city's violent past, and so by replicating Williams' actions as they are described in De Quincey's work, the family's "wounds reflect the inflictions of recurrent time" and act as a "testimony to the power of the city over men" (60). Hence, the uncanniness of the Golem's re-enactment of De Quincey's fictional recreation of the real Ratcliffe Highway murders self-reflexively performs the Gothic's return of the repressed by making it a part of the textual haunting that is at work in Ackroyd's neo-Gothic narratives of London's past, in which the repetition of the dark (literary) history of the city's East End comes to function as its guiding spirit of place.

The textual construction of the Golem's diary can be further read as a reflection of De Quincey's satirical notion of the murderer as an artist. As an extension of the Golem's persona, not only does the diary provide an insight into the murderer's perverse motivations for producing their art, but its fabrication is itself quite literally a work of fine art composed by Elizabeth to frame her husband for the Golem's crimes, which have been her own grotesque performance art played in the theatre of the city's streets. For example, when the Golem murders the prostitute Jane Quig, they explain their desire to create "such a spectacle that no eye seeing it could fail to be moved" and so positions the victim's decapitated head "upon the upper step, just as if it were the prompter's head seen from the pit of the theatre, and [...] applauded my own work" before exiting the murder scene because "there came a noise from the wings" (62). In the same manner, after cutting the throat of Mr. Gerrard the Golem whispers to the dying man that "the play has just begun," and mimics a theatrical stage entrance by "mounting the stairs, with the open razor in my hand [...] all bathed in blood and with my face besmeared in dirt" to kill his wife and children (161).

The staged dramatic pretence of such actions, made particularly evident in the film's theatrical reproduction of the murders carried out by each suspected Golem, clearly show Elizabeth is consciously playing the sensationalist De Quincian role of the murderer as artist through the Limehouse Golem persona. The diary entries thus become a way to affirm her artistic choice to perform the role of the Golem, supposedly satisfying the grotesque appetites of the London public since "Londoners love a good killing, on stage or off" (166), and to legitimise her actions: "I am invoking a legend, and anything will be forgiven me as long as I remain faithful to my role" (126). Elizabeth thus appears as if possessed by the literary phantom of Williams' legendary character as the murderer-artist of De Quincey's work; she is so haunted by the sensationalism of his construction, and the immortal fame it brought, that she believes rewriting it as her own Gothic play-text will afford her the same status as the murderer-artist the Limehouse Golem. As Kildare astutely notes, the Golem's crimes appear to have been performed in exactly such a manner, as if by "an actor playing a part […] in a blood tub off the Old Kent Road," to which Dan Leno perceptively adds that perhaps De Quincey's "On Murder" essay is "this terrible thing" that serves "as his prompt-book" (204–5). De Quincey's essay certainly is the "terrible thing" that provides "a script for the homicidal performance" (Robinson 2011, 157) of the Limehouse Golem's narrative in the novel, and particularly so through the film's depiction of the diary entries as literally written over the essay's text which then becomes the scripts for the imaginary re-enactments of each crime. De Quincey's essay can, therefore, be further understood to function as the theatrical prompt-book for Elizabeth's own textual attempt through the creation of the Golem's diary to achieve precisely the same form of literary immortalisation that De Quincey afforded Williams; by adopting a dramatic persona to re-enact a series of echoic killings, each sadistically staged as an artistic sacrifice resonant of those that came before, and will inevitably come to be performed again, on the cruel theatre of the city's violent streets.

The Golem's De Quincey-inspired recreation of the Ratcliffe Highway massacre is not the only murderous historical event from the city's violent past rewritten into the narrative's haunted textual palimpsest. Susana Onega has drawn attention to the resemblances between Elizabeth's "undetected 'secret' poisonings of several family members and music-hall comedians" subtly alluded to throughout her testimony, and real Victorian cases of domestic homicide by middle-class murderesses, which shattered the idealised image of the Angel in the House and were "decisive in the appearance of sensation novels" that portrayed such shocking violations of the private sphere (2011, 276–77).[11] As Onega further notes, there is an interesting similitude between Elizabeth's case and that of Florence Maybrick, who was convicted in 1889 for poisoning her husband James, a wealthy Liverpool cotton broker like John Cree's father, with a lethal dose of arsenic, the same method used to kill John Cree (277). The similarities between the Crees and the Maybricks continue when, in 1992, a diary that was allegedly written by James Maybrick was found in which he claimed to be Jack the Ripper by vividly detailing the crimes, but it was later proven to be a forgery by Michael Barrett who had discovered it.[12] The incorporation of the mythology of Jack the Ripper into the characterisation of the Limehouse Golem is of significance for the uncanny déjà-vu-like effects that are achieved by allusions to the infamous history of the Ripper within a narrative that is set eight years before their crimes were actually committed. While a chronological line of spatio-temporal influence can be logically drawn between the Ratcliffe Highway killings committed by Williams and the Golem's replication of them decades later, the Golem's sexual mutilations of the murdered prostitutes distorts this logic for they replicate the distinctive infamous modus operandi of the Ripper's patterns of crimes that the reader knows will not occur for another eight years. This line of influence appears to extend even further into the future since, as Onega has suggested, the Golem's crimes can be associated with those of the "Yorkshire Ripper," a serial killer who murdered 13 women between 1975 and 1981 and who the British press "represented as the son of Jack the Ripper" (293).[13] The novel's adaptation as a neo-Victorian horror film explicitly signals such associations with Ripper mythology through its marketing—"Before the Ripper, fear had another name"—and through the costuming of the Golem in the Ripper's mythical attire of a gentleman's suit, long black cloak and top hat that bathes them in shadows often partially obscuring their appearance. In both the novel and the film, then, the uncanniness of the Golem's apparently prescient actions comes from our strange familiarity with such recognisable influences even when they appear out of time. Positioning the novel's reader, and indeed the viewer of the film, to view events concurrently both forwards and backwards through time, echoing the experience of déjà vu, thus reveals "an ever-growing cyclical pattern of horror materialising out of the suffering of the inhabitants of that deprived and degenerate area of Victorian London" (Onega 1999, 144). It is a pattern that has endured into the contemporary through the perpetuation of precisely such kinds of self-referential representations of the East End during the Victorian era in literature and popular culture, and one that the mythology of the Ripper has certainly come to symbolise for the neo-Gothic.

Moreover, the historical responses of Victorian society to the Ripper murders are mimicked in the novel's depiction of the public's reactions to the Golem's killings, which the unnamed contemporary narrator retrospectively recounts throughout the narrative. In chapter 28, for instance, the narrator relates the impact that the Golem murders had on attitudes towards public social reform in the city's East End, mirroring events that historically occurred because of the Ripper murders (162–64).[14] At various points in the story, usually after the Golem's latest murder, the narrator emphasises the responsibility that the Victorian press carried for provoking public mass-hysteria in response to the crimes, as they did with the Ripper murders:

> The daily newspapers reported every practice in which "The Golem" or "The Golem of Limehouse" engaged, while certain details were embellished, or on occasions invented, in order to ensure more notoriety for what were already gruesome accounts. Could it have been the journalist on the *Morning Advertiser*, for example, who decided that the "Golem" had been chased by an "irate crowd" only to be seen "fading away" into the wall of a bakery by Hayley Street? But perhaps that was not an instance of editorial licence since, as soon as the report was published, several residents of Limehouse confirmed that they had been among the mob which had pursued the create and watched it disappear. [...] So the legend of the Golem was born, even before the final and most shocking act of murder. (6–7)

Therefore, the "lurid melodrama of the popular press" (35) depicted in the novel, and the sensationalism which saturates their representation of the Golem's crimes, thus not only replicates the New Journalism movement of the late Victorian period's treatment of the Ripper murders as a source of macabre entertainment (which continues to this day), but can be understood to echo further De Quincey's own depiction of such horrifying violence as a subject of fine art in his "On Murder" essays, and the genre of popular crime literature that they were to inspire.[15]

Such textual hauntings from the East End's history of the "crimes that delight us" (191) can be further found in the narrative's self-aware citation of their influence on the neo-Gothic. The Limehouse Golem's crimes seem purposefully to invoke the horror tropes of the popular Gothic literary genres of the Victorian period, the "penny dreadful" and the "shilling shocker," that were often inspired by crimes or "popular melodramas" of the time (Lewis 2007, 84). In the novel, the Golem's crimes are serialised in this manner as "lurid episodes" written in "the purplest of prose" within those chapter's gruesome recounts of their horror in the "spirit of these garish tales" (84). It is an approach which the film's gory depictions of Kildare's imagined recreations of each murder by a potential Golem certainly evoke in their use of cinematic horror tropes of the slasher movie in these scenes. Ackroyd's contemporary narrator even suggests that the Golem's murders gave rise to performances of the "horror repertoire" shown at the "various 'blood tubs' or 'blood and thunder' playhouses where 'shockers' were the customary entertainment" (164), and both the novel and the film also feature the performance a "blood tub" play inspired by the original Ratcliffe Highway murders and the Limehouse Golem's crimes.

The contemporary narrator of the novel further proposes that the Limehouse murders inspired a "famous sequence of paintings by James McNeill Whistler, 'Limehouse Nocturnes,' in which the brooding presence of the riverine streets is conveyed by viridian green, ultramarine, ivory and black," and that the crimes influenced how "Somerset Maugham and David Carreras [...] first became aware of their fascination for drama," and further that Carreras "wrote a play based upon the Limehouse killings entitled *No Man Knows My Name*" (164). However, these are all fictional, imagined metatextual hauntings fabricated by Ackroyd for the purpose of the narrative's historical artifices.[16] Yet the contemporary narrator goes on to suggest that the Golem's crimes actually influenced the creation of one of the most famous Gothic fictions of the *fin de siècle*; "The murders in Limehouse led indirectly to *The Picture of Dorian Gray*, written by Oscar Wilde some eight years later, in which the opium dens and cheap theatres of that area play a large part in a somewhat melodramatic narrative" (164). The inclusion of these knowing allusions prompts an experience of the uncanny because they are absorbed into *Dan Leno and the Limehouse Golem*'s metatextual séance as literary phantoms that force the reader to acknowledge the Victorian *fin-de-siècle* Gothic works (and their contemporary adaptations) that have made the East End's past so famous for precisely the kind of violent crimes which are self-reflexively depicted under the cover of the "notorious pea-soupers of the period, so ably memorialised by Robert Louis Stevenson and Arthur Conan Doyle, [which] were quite as dark, as their literary reputation would suggest" (43). Indeed, we find these authors' most well-known characters are further parodied in Ackroyd's narrative.

Elizabeth Cree's secret night-time transformations from a respectable middle-class woman to a deviant gentleman murderer, who prowls the East End in search of forbidden releases, mimics the equally duplicitous titular character of Stevenson's *Strange Case of Dr. Jekyll and Mr. Hyde* (1886). Like Dr. Jekyll, Elizabeth appears to become increasingly monopolised by her alternate identities—her masculine characters—eventually carrying them off the stage and onto the theatre of the city's streets for night-time strolls to "see the *other* world" as "a regular masher" (153; emphasis added); just as Jekyll's identity is weakened by the strength of Hyde's, through such actions Elizabeth, too, becomes similarly consumed until her own fragile sense of self is surrendered to the aggressive power offered by her own Hyde-like "brute that slept within" (64), her Gothic doppelgänger: the Limehouse Golem. Such similarities can be further found between Wilde's doppelgänger protagonist Dorian Gray, who sees decadent living as an art form, and Ackroyd's own who instead views a sensational death in this way. Dorian and Elizabeth thus reflect one another in their attitudes to art in that they both see art or artful living to be more real and offer more reality than life itself. This attitude is precisely what is projected through the creation of their monstrous doubles, for each seemingly supernatural manifestation of the monster only ever exists in the form of a piece of art. The monstrosity of Dorian's double is literally embodied within an artwork of himself, while Elizabeth's double is embodied in a monstrous character that she crafted both as a piece of theatrical performance art and as a work of fine art through the fabricated diary of the Limehouse Golem. One can conclude, then, that Ackroyd self-reflexively evokes the established depiction of the city's East End from Wilde's novel as well as Stevenson's, and indeed the kind of doppelgänger monsters that they created within them, in order to fashion his own within an equally Gothic neo-Victorian London.

Therefore, the ways in which Ackroyd's narrative conveys the uncanny influence that the city's spirit of place seems to have over Elizabeth in the creation of her Limehouse Golem similarly recalls how London itself appears to shape the formation of the similarly divided doppelgänger characters of these famous late-Victorian Gothic works. "Identity and the city," Linda Dryden reminds us, "are crucial to the imaginative representation of the divided self" in the modern Gothic (2003, 17). Ackroyd invokes the "sinister, crepuscular London" of the neo-Victorian Urban Gothic made famous by such depictions in Stevenson's and Wilde's texts that he self-reflexively references in the construction of his imagined city, and which likewise appears to function as "a haven for strange powers, a city of footsteps and flaring lights, of houses packed close together, of lachrymose alleys and false doors" (38). The film's cinematography similarly evokes the legacies of this imagery of the city, recreating 1880 London as it is described in Ackroyd's narrative alongside specific visual references of its neo-Victorian screen legacies. This parallel is evoked by drawing a stark contrast between the cool fog-wreathed figures of the dimly lit cobblestoned streets of a London bathed in ominous shadow regardless of whether it is night or day, and the bright warmth that radiates from the bawdy world of the Victorian music hall inside the bustling theatre's intricately detailed gas-lit interiors, lively overcrowded audience and colourful stage performers.

Throughout the novel, the city's influence on characters and events is made explicitly clear to the reader in both the first-person accounts found in the Golem's diary and the commentary of the contemporary third-person narrator who repeatedly draws our attention to such observations. For example, the contemporary narrator describes how "ordinary Londoners" responded to the Limehouse Golem murders with such a "frenzied interested" that it appeared as if "they had been waiting impatiently for these murders to happen—as if the new conditions of the metropolis required some vivid identification, some flagrant confirmation of its status as the largest and darkest city in the world" (88). This idea that the city itself has some kind of malevolent spectral influence over its inhabitants is shared by Elizabeth, who admits to an awareness of its power over her and actively indulges in it. Writing as the Limehouse Golem, she describes an uncanny prescience of such a feeling on her way to commit the murder of Solomon Weil: "it seemed to me as if the whole city were trembling in anticipation of some great change; at that moment, I felt proud to be entrusted with its powers of expression. I had become its messenger as I walked towards Limehouse" (85). As the story unfolds, in both the novel and the film, it becomes clear that the decrepit area of Limehouse is more than just a suitably Gothic setting for the narrative's crimes, but that the historic spirit of place for this "accursed and desolate spot" (238) in the city appears to be governed by its macabre legacy of murder.

In Ackroyd's narrative, then, it is indeed the "labyrinthine city of the modern Gothic imagination [that] is, in part, responsible for the creation of the monsters that roam its streets" (188). Hence, the Limehouse Golem can be read to be a monstrous incarnation of the Gothic *genius loci* of London's East End, textually embodied in the very act of naming the monster after the infamous district itself. This idea is further articulated by Ackroyd's contemporary narrator who finds that in the wake of the Golem's murders: "It was as if some primeval force had erupted in Limehouse, and there was an irrational but general fear that it would not stop there but would spread over the city and perhaps even the entire country. Some dark spirit had been released, or so it seemed, and certain religious leaders began to suggest that London itself—this vast urban creation which was the first of its kind upon the globe—was somehow responsible for the evil" (2007 [1994], 162). By establishing his own monstrous Gothic doppelgänger character as a product of London's East End, an area of the city with a gruesome history that has been further enhanced by the legacy of the late-Victorian Gothic imprinted upon it, Ackroyd effectively evokes the "Gothic *of* a city rather than just in a city," for as Robert Mighall suggests, "that city needs a concentration of memories and historical associations" (2007, 57) to create the atmosphere of the Urban Gothic. These historical associations may be found to exist within the real city of London; however, the memories of these associations are most intensely concentrated within Ackroyd's *imagined* London as a literary palimpsest of textual hauntings such as those previously established in the late-Victorian Gothic London inhabited by Doctor Jekyll and Dorian Gray alongside their neo-Gothic Victorian afterlives.

In *Dan Leno and the Limehouse Golem*, Ackroyd manipulates each of these visions to create his own textually haunted city, which is in Wolfreys' words "at once immediately apprehensible to the modern, popular imagination—one fed not only on neo-Victorian fiction but also […] on dramatised versions of Victorian novels" (2004, 129). It is a process that the recent cinematic adaption of Ackroyd's novel as a neo-Victorian horror film thus makes literal. Furthermore, it is a process that plays on the uncertainty that is inherent to the uncanny by affirming the neo-Victorian's "power of re-enactment," to quote Marie-Luise Kohlke and Christian Gutleben, "by re-imagining metropolises and urban experiences that may or may not ever have existed as represented" (2015, 35). Since, as Hutcheon has proposed, the past can only be known through the traces of its textual remains, both factual and fictional, this power of re-enactment must be considered as an essentially metafictive endeavour, for it is always "a question of representing, that is, of constructing and interpreting, not of objective recording" (2002 [1989], 70). While the historical reality of the city portrayed in the novel and its adaptation is certainly dictated by the neo-Victorian Gothic's "stock literary devices for staging the *Grand Guignol* urban experience" (Wolfreys 2004, 157), it is in the acknowledgement that they are *self-reflexive re-enactments* that this chapter's understanding of neo-Gothic narrative as a form of textual haunting can be found, revealed in the metatextual (*mise-en-)séances* of these doppelgänger texts. One could argue, then, that the famous nineteenth-century pantomime turn for which the real Dan Leno was so well known that haunts both texts encapsulates not just Ackroyd's neo-Gothic vision of Victorian London's East End, but Goldman's adaptation of it too, for once more "here we are, *again!*"

Notes

1 See Prosser (2014, 2015 and 2019).

2 Ackroyd parodies these spiritualist practices in *English Music*, in the theatrical "*séances*" Clement and Timothy Harcombe perform for their followers, the "Harcombe Circle," at the Chemical Theatre in Hackney during the 1920s, which Ackroyd explains in the novel's "Acknowledgements" were inspired by the real Victorian medium Daniel Home and his book, *Incidents in My Life* (1863).

3 For a few examples of such scholarship, see Boehm-Schnitker and Gruss (2014), Mitchell (2010), Arias and Pulham (2009), Kohlke (2008, 1–18) and Kohlke and Gutleben (2010, 2011, 2012, 2015 and 2017) who, as coeditors of Rodopi's *Neo-Victorian Series*, have further pursued the neo-Victorian in this manner throughout their edited collections.

4 Note here that Ackroyd changes the actual historical date of the Ratcliffe Highway massacre of the Marr family by John Williams from December 1811 to 1812, and that altering historical facts is one of his most common ways to deliberately falsify official history when reconstructing it as a part of his own counterfactual narratives.

5 In the court transcript that forms chapter 23 of the novel, Elizabeth's lawyer Mr. Lister refers to "your account of your early life" (130), which suggests that the first-person narrative we have been previously reading is in fact part of the trial's documents.

6 See "*The Limehouse Golem.*"

7 For some representative examples of such scholarship, see Onega (1999, 134–47; 2011, 267–96), Mergenthal (2002, 123–39), Lewis (2007, 80–87), Pulham (2009, 157–79), Robinson (2011, 150–69), Taube (2015, 93–110), Ganteau (2015, 151–74), Komsta (2015, 60–79) and Chalupský (2016, ch. 3 and 5).

8 In his introduction to the collected essays, Morrison lists the influence De Quincey's writing had on the works of his contemporaries, as well as their continued impact on these genres and their authors in the twentieth- and twenty-first centuries, which includes Peter Ackroyd's *Hawksmoor* and *Dan Leno and the Limehouse Golem*.

9 Interestingly De Quincey's essay has also been previously read by Ackroyd's character Detective Hawksmoor in his earlier novel *Hawksmoor*: "It had been in this district [St George's-in-the-East], as Hawksmoor knew, that the Marr murders of 1812 had occurred—the perpetrator being a certain John Williams, who, according to De Quincey whose account Hawksmoor avidly read, 'asserted his supremacy over all the children of Cain.'" He was transformed, again according to De Quincey, into a "mighty murderer" and until his execution he remained an object of awe and mystery to those who lived in the shadow of the Wapping church" (2010 [1985], 142).

10 De Quincey refers to John Williams' murders as "immortal" throughout his essays but it was of course De Quincey himself who immortalised the Ratcliffe Highway murders and their perpetrator in his own works, which certainly seem to form their own neo-Gothic narrative.

11 The title of Coventry Patmore's poem, *The Angel in the House* (1854), in which he ascribes his wife with all the attributes of the "perfect woman," has since been popularly used to describe the Victorian ideology of the separate spheres, in which the Victorian feminine ideal was, in simple terms, a selfless mother and a devoted wife who dedicated their life to the moral protection of the private, domestic sphere.

12 See Lewis (2007, 83–84).

13 Patricia Pulham even suggests that the Golem's murder of Solomon Weil points towards the mysterious disappearance of Jewish scholar David Rodinsky from his Spitalfields flat in the 1960s (2009, 165).
14 For further discussion of the sociocultural impact of the Ripper murders on Victorian public reforms, and indeed the growth of Gothic literature of doubles during the period, see Dryden (2003, 45–73).
15 For further discussion of the Ripper murders and the New Journalism movement and their impact on Victorian society and literature, see Ridenhour (2013, 15–42).
16 Although Onega has interestingly suggested that an ironic connection can be found with the real Somerset Maugham for the similarities between the eponymous protagonist of Maugham's first novel *Liza of Lambeth* (1897) and the early life of Ackroyd's Lambeth Marsh Lizzie (2011, 277–78).

Bibliography

Ackroyd, Peter. *Chatterton*. New York: Grove Press, 1987.

———. *English Music*. London: Hamish Hamilton, 1992.

———. *The Great Fire of London*. 1982. London: Penguin Books, 1993a.

———. *The Last Testament of Oscar Wilde*. 1983. London: Penguin Books, 1993b.

———. *The Trial of Elizabeth Cree: A Novel of the Limehouse Murders*. New York: Doubleday, 1995.

———. *London: The Biography*. 2000. London: Vintage, 2001.

———. "London Luminaries and Cockney Visionaries." In *Peter Ackroyd. The Collection: Journalism, Reviews, Essays, Short Stories, Lectures*, edited by Thomas Wright, 341–51. 2001. London: Vintage, 2002.

———. *Dan Leno and the Limehouse Golem*. 1994. London: Vintage, 2007.

———. *The Casebook of Victor Frankenstein*. London: Chatto and Windus, 2008.

———. *Hawksmoor*. 1985. London: Penguin Books, 2010.

Arias, Rosario, and Patricia Pulham. Introduction to *Haunting and Spectrality in Neo-Victorian Fiction: Possessing the Past*, edited by Rosario Arias and Patricia Pulham, xi–xxvi. New York: Palgrave Macmillan, 2009.

Boehm-Schnitker, Nadine, and Susanne Gruss, eds. *Neo-Victorian Literature and Culture: Immersions and Revisitations*. New York: Routledge, 2014.

Chalupský, Petr. *A Horror and a Beauty: The World of Peter Ackroyd's London Novels*. Prague: Karolinum Press, 2016.

De Quincey, Thomas. "On Murder Considered as One of the Fine Arts." 1827. In *Thomas De Quincey On Murder*, edited by Robert Morrison, 8–34. Oxford: Oxford University Press, 2006.

———. "Postscript [To On Murder Considered as One of the Fine Arts]." 1854. In *Thomas De Quincey On Murder*, edited by Robert Morrison, 95–141. Oxford: Oxford University Press, 2006.

———. "Second Paper on Murder Considered as One of the Fine Arts." 1839. In *Thomas De Quincey On Murder*, edited by Robert Morrison, 81–94. Oxford: Oxford University Press, 2006.

Dryden, Linda. *The Modern Gothic and Literary Doubles: Stevenson, Wilde and Wells*. Basingstoke: Palgrave Macmillan, 2003.

Ganteau, Jean-Michel. "Vulnerable Visibilities: Peter Ackroyd's Monstrous Victorian Metropolis." In *Neo-Victorian Cities: Reassessing Urban Politics and Poetics*, edited by Marie-Luise Kohlke and Christian Gutleben, 151–74. Amsterdam: Rodopi, 2015.

Gibson, Jeremy, and Julian Wolfreys. *Peter Ackroyd: The Ludic and Labyrinthine Text*. Basingstoke: Palgrave Macmillan, 2000.

Heilmann, Ann, and Mark Llewellyn. *Neo-Victorianism: The Victorians in the Twenty-First Century, 1999–2009*. Basingstoke: Palgrave Macmillan, 2010.

Hogle, Jerrold E. "The Gothic Ghost of the Counterfeit and the Progress of Abjection." In *A New Companion to the Gothic*, edited by David Punter, 496–509. Hoboken: Wiley-Blackwell, 2012.

Home, Daniel. *Incidents in My Life*. London: Longman, 1863.

Hutcheon, Linda. "'The Pastime of Past Time': Fiction, History, Historiographic Metafiction." *Genre: Forms of Discourse and Culture* 20, no. 3–4 (1987): 285–305.

———. *The Politics of Postmodernism*, rev. 2nd ed. 1989. London: Routledge, 2002.

Kohlke, Marie-Luise. "Introduction: Speculations in and on the Neo-Victorian Encounter." *Neo-Victorian Studies* 1, no. 1 (Autumn 2008): 1–18.

Kohlke, Marie-Luise, and Christian Gutleben, eds. *Neo-Victorian Tropes of Trauma: The Politics of Bearing After-Witness to Nineteenth-Century Suffering*. Amsterdam: Rodopi, 2010.

———. *Neo-Victorian Families: Gender, Sexual and Cultural Politics*. Amsterdam: Rodopi, 2011.

———. *Neo-Victorian Gothic: Horror, Violence and Degeneration in the Re-imagined Nineteenth Century*. Amsterdam: Rodopi, 2012.

———. *Neo-Victorian Cities: Reassessing Urban Politics and Poetics*. Leiden, the Netherlands: Brill Rodopi, 2015.

———. *Neo-Victorian Humour: Comic Subversions and Unlaughter in Contemporary Historical Re-visions*. Leiden, the Netherlands: Brill, 2017.

Komsta, Marta. *Welcome to the Chemical Theatre: The Urban Chronotope in Peter Ackroyd's Fiction*. Frankfurt: Peter Lang GmbH Internationaler Verlag der Wissenschaften, 2015.

Lewis, Barry. *My Words Echo Thus: Possessing the Past in Peter Ackroyd*. Columbia: University of South Carolina Press, 2007.

The Limehouse Golem. Dir. Juan Carlos Medina. Number 9 Films, 2016.

"*The Limehouse Golem*." HanWay Films. https://www.hanwayfilms.com/the-limehouse-golem.

Mergenthal, Silvia. "'Whose City?' Contested Spaces and Contesting Spatialities in Contemporary London Fiction." In *London in Literature: Visionary Mappings of the Metropolis*, edited by Susana Onega and John A. Stotesbury, 123–39. Heidelberg, Germany: Carl Winter Universitätsverlag, 2002.

Mighall, Robert. "Gothic Cities." In *The Routledge Companion to Gothic*, edited by Catherine Spooner and Emma McEvoy, 54–62. London: Routledge, 2007.

Mitchell, Kate. *History and Cultural Memory in Neo-Victorian Fiction: Victorian Afterimages*. Basingstoke: Palgrave Macmillan, 2010.

Morrison, Robert. Introduction to *Thomas De Quincey On Murder*, edited by Robert Morrison, vii–xxvii. Oxford: Oxford University Press, 2006.

Onega, Susana. "An Interview with Peter Ackroyd." *Twentieth Century Literature* 42, no. 2 (1996): 208–20.

———. *Metafiction and Myth in the Novels of Peter Ackroyd*. Columbia, SC: Camden House, 1999.

———. "Family Traumas and Serial Killing in Peter Ackroyd's *Dan Leno and the Limehouse Golem*." In *Neo-Victorian Families: Gender, Sexual and Cultural Politics*, edited by Marie-Luise Kohlke and Christian Gutleben, 267–96. Amsterdam: Rodopi, 2011.

Prosser, Ashleigh. "The Abhuman City: Peter Ackroyd's Gothic Historiography of London." In *The Gothic and the Everyday: Living Gothic*, edited by Lorna Piatti-Farnell and Maria Beville, 69–82. Basingstoke: Palgrave Macmillan, 2014.

———. "'No Place Like Home: The Chronotope of the Haunted House in Peter Ackroyd's *The House of Doctor Dee*." *Aeternum: The Journal of Contemporary Gothic Studies* 2, no. 1 (June 2015): 1–19. www.aeternumjournal.com/issues.

———. "Resurrecting *Frankenstein*: Peter Ackroyd's *The Casebook of Victor Frankenstein* and the Metafictional Monster Within." *Australasian Journal of Popular Culture* 8, no. 2 (September 2019): 179–96.

Pulham, Patricia. "Mapping Histories: The Golem and the Serial Killer in *White Chappell, Scarlet Tracings* and *Dan Leno and the Limehouse Golem*." In *Haunting and Spectrality in Neo-Victorian Fiction: Possessing the Past*, edited by Rosario Arias and Patricia Pulham, 157–79. New York: Palgrave Macmillan, 2009.

Ridenhour, Jamieson. *In Darkest London: The Gothic Cityscape in Victorian Literature*. Plymouth: Scarecrow Press, 2013.

Robinson, Alan. *Narrating the Past: Historiography, Memory and the Contemporary Novel*. Basingstoke: Palgrave Macmillan, 2011.

Shiller, Dana. "The Redemptive Past in the Neo-Victorian Novel." *Studies in the Novel* 29, no. 4 (1997): 538–61.

Stetz, Margaret D. "Neo-Victorian Studies." *Victorian Literature and Culture* 40, no. 1 (2012): 339–46.

Stevenson, Robert Louis. *Strange Case of Dr Jekyll and Mr Hyde*. 1886. Oxford: Oxford University Press, 2006.

Taube, Aleksejs. "London's East End in Peter Ackroyd's *Dan Leno and the Limehouse Golem*." In *Literature and the Peripheral City*, edited by Ameel Lieven, Jason Finch and Markku Salmela, 93–110. Basingstoke: Palgrave Macmillan, 2015.

Wilde, Oscar. *The Picture of Dorian Gray*. 1891. Oxford: Oxford University Press, 2006.

Wolfreys, Julian. *Victorian Hauntings: Spectrality, Gothic, the Uncanny and Literature*. New York: Palgrave, 2002.

———. *Writing London: Materiality, Memory, Spectrality*. Basingstoke: Palgrave Macmillan, 2004.

———. "Notes towards a Poetics of Spectrality: The Examples of Neo-Victorian Textuality." In *Reading Historical Fiction: The Revenant and Remembered Past*, edited by Kate Mitchell and Nicola Parsons, 153–71. Basingstoke: Palgrave Macmillan, 2013.

Chapter Seven

SPECTRAL FEMALES, SPECTRAL MALES: COLONIALITY AND GENDER IN NEO-GOTHIC AUSTRALIAN NOVELS

Kate Livett

The Gothic is an Ur-mode in Australian literature for several reasons: It was popular historically in the eighteenth and nineteenth centuries during which colonisation took place and white-Australian culture took root in the colonies (Turcotte 1998; Gelder 2012, 381); "Australian National Identity," consolidated at the moment of federation of the colonies in 1901, took its literary form in what is known as 1890s Realism, a realism heavily saturated with the Gothic; and finally but perhaps most significantly, the cultural psyche of the nation is built upon the repression—and its return—of the horrors of violence on the colonial frontiers—eeriness and brutality of all kinds, including rape, murder and massacres of Aboriginal people. This psyche is insistently expressed in the literature of the nation; in both high and popular forms (Weaver 2009), Australian literature is and always has been awash with Gothic terror, grotesquerie, secrets and hauntings.

It is in this context that the present chapter makes a claim for a neo-Gothic zeitgeist in Australian literature, in which fundamental tropes of the Female Gothic are recast in a twenty-first century light (or, perhaps better, darkness). Three novels, two of them multiple award-winners—*The Night Guest* by Fiona McFarlane (2013) and *The Swan Book* by Alexis Wright (2013)[1]—and one an overlooked novel by an author whose other works are also acclaimed, *The Engagement*, by Chloe Hooper (2016 [2012]), are three works that deploy in updated form some classic Female Gothic conventions. In their revisions, or repressions, to the classic Gothic tropes of the haunted house, the menacing male, criminal plotting and intrigue in relation to money and property, and doubles/doppelgängers and ghostly figures, these novels reflect contemporary social and cultural concerns of race and gender in both Australia and global modernity more broadly.

The spectrality central to the Gothic form aligns in these novels with the spectralising operations of contemporary globalised modernity. Perpetuating the capitalist-colonial structures that have always worked to the benefit of the white male subject, these ghosting forces of globalisation overcome the individual men in these novels but continue to secure their hierarchical power at the top of the structure of privilege. Through this rendering spectral of the (always-already absent) Father, these Gothic villains increase their power through the course of these three narratives, ultimately triumphing over not just the female and the racialised, colonised subject, but over time itself. In escaping chronology, the spectral male overcomes the challenges to his structural domination posed by feminism and postcolonialism. In this hegemonic triumph, these novels present powerful critiques of the vexed assumption of a postfeminist, post-postcolonial world.

The return of the repressed (ideology)

The return of the repressed inheres in the Gothic form. As Diana Wallace has recently asserted, "to say something is 'Gothic' is […] to imply that it is obsessed with the return of the past" (2013, 4). For the Female Gothic of the eighteenth and nineteenth centuries, the repressed historical culture that threatened to return was the Catholic Medieval world (Killeen 2013, 145–61; Sage 1988). In the Australian context there are several key understandings of the nature of this returning repressed. In his analysis of nineteenth-century literature, Gerry Turcotte contends that "from its inception the Gothic has dealt with fears and themes which are endemic in the colonial experience: isolation, entrapment, fear of pursuit and fear of the unknown" (1998, 10).

From the outset, the Gothic was connected to British colonisers' culture and literary traditions but transported to a new environment in which Aboriginal people and the landscape were cast as the Gothic threat. First Nations novelist Melissa Lucashenko argues that this view is ongoing in the contemporary treatment of Aboriginal people by Migaloo, or non-Aboriginal, people because the "very presence of Aboriginal people is disturbing. To them we are not people, but rather a metaphor for the past" (2001, 132). Ken Gelder and Jane M. Jacobs critique this white anxiety and argue that Gothic hauntings are symptomatic of the unsettledness of colonial culture (1994, 23–24).

Most recently, critics have discussed the possibility of an Aboriginal Gothic genre; indeed, Katrin Althans posits that Aboriginal writers and filmmakers such as Sam Watson, Tracey Moffatt, Kim Scott and Alexis Wright have used the Gothic mode to subvert the British/European Gothic tradition so that white colonisers are cast as the repressed monstrous threatening Indigenous reality (2012, 29). Althans defines these works as demonstrating an Aboriginal Gothic subgenre that "usurp[s], appropriate[s] and eventual[ly] transform[s] the master discourse" (10).

All three schemas of threatening colonialism as the return of the repressed are evident in *The Engagement, The Night Guest* and *The Swan Book*. Hooper's *The Engagement* explicitly rehearses what Gelder and Jacobs have called the (politically) "productive potential" of the "unsettling" Australian landscape (1994, 24). The heroine, Liese, rehearses a contemporary postcolonial perspective that views the Gothic male villain's ancestral sheep station property as stolen land (100). The villain, Alexander, insists unapologetically on his right to own the land. In the respective attitudes of the heroine and villain, then, the novel displays the contemporary anxiety about the return of repressed colonial attitudes.

McFarlane's *The Night Guest* presents an elderly white middle-class female, Ruth Field, whose past is intimately tied to original colonial activities; she was the child of a white religious missionary family in Fiji. Ruth is recently widowed and living in an isolated beach house in a seaside town in New South Wales. Declaring herself to have been sent by the government (2013, 9), the middle-aged unspecified-racialised woman, Frida, who comes to work as a domestic old-age carer, is experienced by Ruth through her white perspective in terms of the original colonial Gothic: the uncanny strangeness of the non-white Other. Ruth's colonial perspective is complicated and critiqued by the operations of the novel.

The Swan Book's ever-multiplying complexities in regard to the return of the repressed are generated by its Aboriginal-Gothic critique of white colonisers and the fundamental threat they pose to Aboriginal people and the environment. The future setting of *The Swan Book*, as well as the non-realist poetic density of its language, invoke multiple layers of historical repression and return. Within the temporality of *The Swan Book*'s future setting, the current present of real-world contemporary Australia is the past, and there-fore a doubly uncannily returning present. *The Swan Book* imagines a globalized future in which white hegemonic culture still prevails, with the tokenistic complicity of a few assimilated Aboriginal people, to mean that "*even an Aboriginal man in Australia can get elected by the common Aboriginal-hating people to be the Head of State in Australia*" (2013, 283; emphasis in original). If, as Fred Botting states, the Gothic "resonates as much with anxieties and fears concerning the crises and changes in the present as with any terrors of the past" (2012, 14), *The Swan Book*'s future setting mobilizes anxieties about the present to the maximum degree by showing how they might continue to play out in the immediate future.

Haunted houses

Haunted houses are the Gothic trope and site of this return of the repressed that, in spe-cific ways, demonstrate their imbrication in the capitalist-colonialist structures that seem to have returned with force in globalisation. Each heroine is imprisoned in a house, as frequently occurs in classic Gothic narratives, fulfilling Marie Mulvey-Roberts' observa-tion that "heroines confined within castles represent the containment of women within patriarchal social and legal structures" (2016, 109). White middle-class Ruth and Liese have the rights to legal ownership and control including over (haunted) houses that drives the novels' narratives. For *The Swan Book*'s Oblivia, an impoverished Aboriginal girl, questions of material ownership are so far from her purview as to be irrelevant. Her home is the swamp to which she wishes to return after being abducted and imprisoned in a city apartment building.

In *The Engagement*, the legal and economic independence of middle-class women in global capitalism is the basis of identity for the heroine but becomes a condition threatened by the explicit and implicit transactions represented in the novel. Postfeminist, female legal, economic and psychic independence are negotiated through the tensions between property ownership and the uncanny nature of houses, and the relationships of both to metaphors of psychic control. The heroine, Liese, a late-twenties/early-thirties Englishwoman temporarily living in Melbourne and working as a real-estate agent, meets the Gothic villain, Alexander Colquhuon, in the context of the city and within the comingled postfeminist, global-capitalist economies of sex and real estate. Liese is showing Alexander apartments for sale, and they meet regularly for casual sex at vacant properties, sex for which Alexander pays Liese in cash. Liese tells the reader she had not set out to sell sexual services for money but is grateful for the extra income, saying, "I liked being paid. I liked it very much" (2012, 68), "I owed money you see" (27).

An explicit and open economy of real estate for sale is the reason for Liese's meeting of Alexander, and it is the site that enables the fantasy of and the subsequent actual contracting of monetary exchange for sex. The fact that Alexander does not own these houses, is not the master of the mansion, reflects the characters' ostensible gender equality in a structure in which Liese has significant bargaining power and sexual agency.

In traveling to the Outback, and Alexander's ancestral home, however, Liese enters the truly haunted space that is entirely his domain. The novel opens at a time after their city arrangement has become routine, with a new development—a letter from Alexander to Liese invites her to stay the weekend at his rural property and be paid for the whole time period as an extension of their current practice. Liese accepts and it is in this homestead, his Gothic mansion, that he begins his thorough, Gothic, persecution of her: "With a rush of vertigo, I sensed my imprisonment. In the entrance hall I tried the door-handle again even though I knew it was locked. The reality of this situation struck me with a mixture of dread—fierce, immediate, intuitive—and something close to hilarity; a kind of sick humour, a humour that made me feel sick. Of course this would be happening, I thought, of course it would. Here was the punishment for my own transgressions. I was now utterly in a stranger's house, and this time I did not have a key" (55).

Liese is horrified to realise the relationship between her attempted control over her sexuality within the vacant spaces and the punishment it provokes in Alexander. The interior of his house is represented as Gothic with glass cases of dead birds providing "uncanny décor" (49–50). Unlike with the vacant houses of their city trysts, Alexander is the owner of this room and this house. Having entrapped Liese in the house, he asserts upon her the control to which he has structural access, which includes a forced marriage after which Liese describes her entrapment in the house in explicitly Gothic terms: "Lying in the narrow bed I felt like I'd been buried. The house was wheezing, making strangely human noises. The glass panes of the window rattled, then there was silence. *No one knows where I am*" (109; emphasis in original). Isolation and entombment within a haunted house controlled by a malevolent historical ideology embodied in a specific man are the Gothic punishments of psychic persecution that Liese undergoes for taking the risk of challenging the masculine prerogative of desire and economics.

The situation in *The Night Guest* is the mirror image of Liese's relationship to economic capital and property ownership; it is precisely Ruth's possession of the house and the money from her marriage that is the reason she is targeted by her old-age caregiver Frida and her boyfriend George. This is a classic scenario of the Gothic in which the heroine's money and property are the cause of her value to the villain, in the tradition of the Female Gothic, made exemplary by Ann Radcliffe's *The Mysteries of Udolpho* (1794), in which both the young heroine Emily St. Auburn and her aunt Madame Cheron are kept hostage for their financial values: Count Montoni marries Madame Cheron to obtain what he believes to be her considerable fortune (1836 [1794], 93) and imprisons his wife and her niece in the castle, later trying to sell Emily, literally, to Count Morano (138). In *The Night Guest*, Although Ruth now owns the house, the master of the house was her husband Harry, and his death has not equated with her taking over this mastery. There is an emptiness, a vacuum where his power was, that neither the visiting Richard (romantic hero of her youth) nor her absent sons can fill.

Ironically, in moving from a married state to one of post-marriage independence, Ruth is beset by menace. Diana Wallace engages with Mary Beard's argument that in pre-eighteenth-century law women were subject to the authority of their male relatives and once married were effectively "civilly dead" (Beard 1946, 78).[2] Wallace analyses Beard's argument, identifying that "the language of spectrality used by Beard [...] suggests the particular power of the Gothic to express the erasure of women in history" (2013, 2). In the character of Ruth, McFarlane presents a female subject of the present who initially seems to be in a post-marriage condition, legally alive rather than civilly dead. But as her haunted house attests, it is precisely because she now owns that house that her status as an independent, property-owning subject makes her a target for exploitation. Ruth's personal gender identity and the specifics of her age mean that she is tied to an anachronistic female passivity and helplessness and becomes besieged in her own home like the heroines of eighteenth-century Gothic (Ferguson-Ellis 1989, 48–52). Rather than bringing the recalcitrant modern female subject to his own house, as the neo-Gothic villain of *The Engagement* does to Liese, the absence of a (protective) male authority in Ruth's house leaves space open for the villains to move in and haunt her. She is a neo-Gothic heroine threatened by the return of the pre-feminist Medieval of the civilly dead female, and the non-white Other feared by the colonial female.

The literal houses and metaphorical minds haunted by menacing Others and villainous males in *The Engagement* and *The Night Guest* are evident in Wright's *The Swan Book*, too, but are doubled by the inclusion of the nation of Australia itself as an isolated, "empty yet spectrally occupied" house of control, imprisonment and the return of the repressed. Acclaimed Aboriginal novelist Kim Scott says: "Some people are starting to think about: can we graft a contemporary Australian community onto its indigenous roots? [...] Can you anchor a shimmering nation state via those regional indigenous roots?" (2015, 19). Wright's novel can be read as an imagined future in which the nation has not tried to do this; rather, it has continued to assimilate and/or marginalise Aboriginal people within white hegemony and law. The nation as a haunted house is a trope within what Althans calls Aboriginal Gothic literature. Althans argues that the "neocolonial uncanny" sometimes "makes the haunted house stand for the Australian nation" (2012, 17). Within the haunted mansion of Australia are multiple local places, occupied by different groups of revenants, spectres, ghosts and ghouls—the Australian population—who may or may not already be dead. Like the Gothic mansion of Edgar Allan Poe's *The House of Usher* (1839), this neo-Gothic future Australia is a building being reclaimed by nature. In *The Swan Book* this eerie reclamation is a forceful and rapid flood/jungling caused by climate change. As her name suggests, Oblivia herself is a spectre who haunts the house that is Australia. First, she is the spirit of the tree from which she is reborn after violent trauma; then she lives in the swamp, haunting the wrecked ship on which her "rescuer," the white woman Bella Donna, lives. Finally, abducted by

Warren Finch, she experiences a brief stay in a white family's suburban home and is then imprisoned in an apartment block in the city where the "building was a cage" (2013, 234). Later, the reader follows her leaving and her joining the mass refugee walk out of the city, back towards the country, where her homelessness means that she has become a wandering spectre, continuing to haunt the nation. In each of her houses—home and continent—Oblivia *is* the ghost who haunts it. The haunted houses of *The Swan Book*, then, are about capitalist ownership to the extent that it is the "ownership" of the nation by the polluting, violent, structurally impoverishing forces of capital that has *already* been the site of the heroine's spectralisation.

Spectral femininity

It is through their entrapment in these haunted houses and nations that the heroines of these novels become, to use Rebecca Munford's helpful term, the "spectral feminine" (2016, 120), by which she means characters "condemn[ed] […] to perennial incompleteness, unable to present fully as embodied subjects" (133). Hence, spectral femininity is commensurate with disempowerment and loss of the legal and economic rights. In *The Engagement* and *The Night Guest* the heroines Ruth and Liese presumed these rights were theirs and the narratives trace their progressive spectralisation, culminating in their metaphorical and actual deaths, respectively. Oblivia in *The Swan Book*, however, has been rendered ghostly already, before the events of the novel begin; she is a spectre from the outset. Munford stresses that "ghostly representations and narrative effects make present experiences of social invisibility and historical dispossession" (121), which is certainly the case with Oblivia. Key, also, is the connection Munford makes from the level of the signifier, between the spectre and the spectacle/specular (120). The hauntings of these three novels range across different inflections of vision, spectralisation and knowledge. Ultimately, however, the very ghostliness of these female figures means that their lack of material force prohibits change in the domain of the real.

The Engagement explicitly traces the spectralisation of the modern woman, Liese, by the villain, Alexander Colquhuon, as she charts in the first person the progressive disintegration of her independence and confidence ending, finally, in her spectralisation to herself. From the beginning of the interlude at Alexander's house he sets out to break down the understood and transparent economy of their relations and to destroy Liese's previously secure sense of desire, self and agency. He calls her a "slut" and a "nymphomaniac" (139), says he is in love with her (90), tells her she needs rescuing through marriage (109) and imposes a violent rejection of understood terms of their sexual interactions (77). He forces her to "accept" his proposal of marriage (100), discusses their engagement in front of several other people (204–6), invades her past through stalking and presents her with the history of her own sexual activities as a narrative of pathological perversion (170–76). Finally, he rejects her at the altar because of her sexual past (243), and by the end of the weekend has effectively spectralised Liese to herself, so that by the time he drives her back to the city she is rendered speechless, physically passive (246) and mentally disintegrated: "I would leave his house and spend months, years wondering what had happened between us while he continued unscathed, a seemingly eligible pillar of the community" (245). She is now ghosted by the violent neo-Gothic hatred of the male perspective on her agency and is spectralised to the reader, to whom she seems a shadow of her former self.

The spectralising of Ruth in McFarlane's *The Night Guest* is enacted partly by Frida and her boyfriend George, who are, from Ruth's perspective, Gothic villains. Taking advantage of Ruth's advanced age, Frida manipulates her into signing over her money, thus effectively spectralising her—in the age of capital she is "civilly dead" (Beard 1946, 78). Moreover, this civil death is followed by her actual death at Frida's hand. At a textual level, Ruth is consistently spectralised through the collapse of time inherent in the "apparitional language" of the Gothic genre itself (Munford 2016, 121). Through absence of physical description of her ageing body, alongside detailed backstories of her young adult years in Fiji, Ruth appears as a kind of original Gothic heroine of the eighteenth century such as Emily St. Auburn of *The Mysteries of Udolpho*, Ellena Rosalba in *The Italian* (1797, 68) and even the titled women in Walpole's *The Castle of Otranto* (1764): Hippolita, Matilda and Isabella—logical yet feminine, intelligent yet passive and subject to the physical and symbolic force of powerful male figures. Attributable to the past of her British missionary childhood in Fiji with its already antiquated gender ideas including female deportment, these qualities also function, ironically, as features indicative of age.

The literal return of Ruth's past in the present, in the figure of her first love-interest Richard Porter, now 80 years old, significantly adds to the temporal ambiguity that effects her spectralisation. In this ambiguity, Ruth acts upon her past in the present, finally consummating her relationship with Richard (124–26). This uncanny belated action recalls Liese's crossing of the uncanny boundaries in her sex with Alexander in vacant houses. Ruth and Richard's sex, occurring decades too late, is an anachronism; however, it is without effect—Richard simply leaves as they both knew he would, and he does not save Ruth from Frida and George. A victim of the uncanny temporality, Ruth suffers the fate identified by Chris Baldick, who suggests that "for the Gothic effect to be attained, a tale should combine a fearful sense of inheritance in time with a claustrophobic sense of enclosure in space, these two dimensions reinforcing one another to produce an impression of sickening descent into disintegration" (1992, xix). Caught within the merging binaries of past and present, age and youth, Ruth is ghosted in all of these, trapped in her own house until she is ejected even from there by Frida, left to die in the garden from exposure overnight. Her fate demonstrates that the tragic lives and deaths of older women in Gothic novels act as "dreadful reminders that transgressing the laws of patriarchy is often fatal to oneself and others" (Davison 2009, 102). Due to her age, Ruth's son Jeffrey ironically infantilises her, dismissing her fears about the phantom tiger prowling the house by night with which the novel opens. He is wrong to do so—this haunting does actually presage the very real threat of Frida and George, but Jeffrey understands it only as a substantiveless symptom of old-age dementia.[3]

The collapsed binaries caused by the figure of the spectre extend from Ruth to Frida as well; they are doubles of one another in a colonial inversion in which Frida is inevitably spectral. Frida occupies both collapsed binary opposites of being simultaneously a racialised Other preying on an elderly white woman, and a victimised middle-aged woman working in manual labour for the service of the more privileged, and who does actually care for Ruth and provides her with the companionship she is missing. Part of Ruth's anachronistic colonial identity is that she is a colonising subject who fears the non-white as Other and, through Ruth's perspective, the novel represents Frida in these terms as a Gothic Other not unlike the madwomen of the British Gothic tradition (Stein 1983, 123; Talairach-Vielmas 2016, 31–45). Ironically, Ruth is correct about the spectral otherness of Frida, but from the wrong perspective; Frida is eventually spectralised by her boyfriend, George, through the same mechanism of financial disempowerment and abandonment that that couple has effected upon Ruth. Frida's dead body is found in the sea, washed up on the rocks (275). The reader is given a dual perspective on the two women throughout, with Frida consistently presented by the text as a different-yet-similar mirror of Ruth. According to Frida she, like Ruth, is living in a family home marked by the absence of a formerly protective family member—in Frida's case her dead mother (79)—a home that is now, also like Ruth's, occupied by a threatening presence, Frida's "brother" George, who in the denouement turns out to be her boyfriend (273). Frida tells Ruth that George has in fact re-mortgaged her house and spent all the money (214). Thus, Frida appears as a spectre in Ruth's house because she has been already spectralised before the narrative present, by the villainous male George.[4] As with the threat to Ruth's property and economic independence that Frida and George pose, Frida herself is threatened by George's abuse of her finances, telling Ruth that she needs "to protect my inheritance," "or he'd let it go to the piss" (79). Like Ruth, Frida fails to maintain her economic independence, and her attempted theft of Ruth's property is a direct consequence of male exploitation of her own rights to capital.

Liese and Ruth are rendered spectral at the end of their respective texts, while Frida as a racialised female character is doubly spectralised—an operation seen also in Wright's *The Swan Book*, which begins with the spectrality of its heroine, Oblivia, in all intersecting categories of identity: gender, race and age. Her name is "Oblivion Ethyl(ene) officially" she tells us herself (2), "significantly so named," as Susan Sheridan notes (2017, 199), because Oblivia is literally a ghost. For Aboriginal writers and Aboriginal culture, Australian temporality is always-already both pre- and post-European colonisation, both of which exist in tandem with and eclipsed by Indigenous cosmology of Deep Time. In the context of Gothic literature, the sidelining of Indigenous time and space creates a "hauntology," in Derrida's terms (1994 [1993], 6),[5] seen in *The Swan Book* in that all the characters in the novel are in a sense both alive and already dead, revenants and spectres who haunt the hegemonic culture. With literary spectres of Pynchon's *Gravity's Rainbow* (1973) (whose historical depiction of a World War II world is a kind of post-apocalyptic world itself), the language of *The Swan Book* is a haunted language; an ironic, satirical tone that saturates the novel with the doubleness of culture, the unavoidable lostness that haunts all language in a Lacanian sense, overdetermined by the literal and symbolic losses that attend Aboriginal identity. However, even within this world of revenants and ghosts, Oblivia's spectralisation is nonetheless specific.

Oblivia's spectral femininity is defined by her post-life condition; she is a neo-Gothic heroine who begins the novel having already suffered the worst of violent abuse by males, having been gang-raped. She is the figure of the limit of abject identity: "A little girl was lost. She had fallen into the deep underground bowel of a giant eucalyptus tree

[…] Everyone had forgotten that she even existed—although, apparently, that did not take long" (2013, 7). Born a second time from out of the roots of the tree where she lay, Oblivia does not speak. The reader hears her thoughts, through omniscient focalised perspective, but at no time during the novel does she have the power to speak from her own position back to those who speak at/to her. Abducted by Warren Finch and the genies, Doom, Mail and Hart, his bodyguards, and driven off to the city towards a new life as Warren's wife, the group stops in a particular part of country overnight, and Oblivia "knew it was a ghost place" (200) and thinks they are wandering "*just like ghosts! Perhaps they had already crossed over into that world. Would she escape? Do ghosts escape?*" (192; emphasis in original). Oblivia is haunted by the ghosts of her kin, the Harbour Master and the old woman, both occupants of the swamp, and still living in the first chapters of the book. After their deaths they transition seamlessly into ghostly inhabitants of Oblivia's mind. As she arrives in Sydney, worried about tales she has heard from the spirit of Bella Donna about "*women and girls who have disappeared*" (192; emphasis in original), the Harbour Master says, "*Don't worry, you are dead already*" (192; emphasis in original).

Once imprisoned in the apartment block in the city, Oblivia is further spectralised through the doubling of herself on television. The Harbour Master ghost draws Oblivia's attention to another Oblivia on the television who is confident, glamorous and accompanies Warren Finch in his governmental duties. Oblivia does not recognise this other self: "She quickly noticed the really small things that were totally opposed to how she thought about herself. Where were the downcast eyes for instance? Why the lack of self-consciousness? Where was the shame? How could she have agreed to let people stare at her like that?" (255).[6] Oblivia becomes aware that parts of her life have been stolen and ghosted by Finch: "It had taken numerous glimpses of seeing herself masquerading around the place as Marlene Dietrich, for the girl to realise that Warren Finch was stealing parts of her life for his own purposes. *Yes, that was how he was covering up his mésalliance of a marriage with her.* She did not know how it happened, but somehow, a part of her life was being lived elsewhere with her husband. She came and went into a different life which Warren Finch returned through the television" (255–56; emphasis in original). The images of herself and Finch returned through the television is the return of both heroine and villain as the repressed ghosts haunting the nation. Oblivia grows increasingly angry about Warren's spectralising of her, an anger that replaces the "terror of the Gothic heroine [which is] simply that of being confined and then abandoned, and beyond that, of being, in an unspecified yet absolute way, completely surrounded by superior male power" (Ferguson-Ellis 1989, 46).

Spectral males

Liese, Ruth, Frida and Oblivia are spectralised by villainous males who themselves become spectralised, as this section will show, in a system in which individual male authority is trumped by the vicissitudes of the ideological forces of globalisation. These spectral females are oppressed by men who are realist characters; they are villains, but material ones. However, in all three texts male spectrality is fundamental. The males, too, become circumscribed by Castle's observations of the mechanisms in Radcliffe's Gothic

(1995, 137). Specifically, Radcliffe's "apparitional language," which "makes ambiguous the boundaries between life and death, present and absent" (Munford 2016, 121). In all three novels these binaries are overdetermined, polysemous and contextual, for their operations are determined by the particularities of textual circumstance. In each there is a different kind of victory by the men. Their material situations differ, but each has left the female characters defeated, as their masculinity affords them the capacity of realignment with the dominant ideologies of culture. The alignment of personal and abstract is most seamless in *The Engagement*'s Alexander, whose private perversions do not challenge public law. George, in *The Night Guest*, is ostensibly the most victorious, yet the novel concludes with him pursued by legal authorities. In his criminality he is mirrored by the law-abiding ghostly male Jeffrey, Ruth's son. The status of Warren Finch in *The Swan Book*, described by the novel as an "archangel" (2013, 119) and by himself as "post-racial" (122), occupies the most evidently allegorical function as the symbol of the Law of the Father. Each to some degree escapes into abstract hegemony, returning to the circuits of structural power that have always supported them.

Alexander of *The Engagement* is the least literally spectralised of the males, but he does achieve a spectral power through the use of incoming written and photographic texts. He sends anonymous letters to himself detailing Liese's sexual activities from her teenage years with disturbingly accurate details. For Liese his uncanny familiarity with her private past creates a sense of his omniscient power. Noting that it could have been Liese who wrote the letters herself, Peter Kirkpatrick says that readers "need to ask ourselves whether Liese is the victim that she presents herself to be, the reluctant Gothic heroine, or whether she is in control all along and playing a role in a game which she herself initiated all those months before" (2017, 98–99). Whether responsible for the letters and initially originating this game or not, the ultimate effects are the same: it is her psychic breakdown that is effected, not his; in fact, he becomes a haunting presence in own private memories.

The letters also raise the spectre of madness. When he accuses her of writing the letters to him, and she retorts that it was he who sent them to himself, he says, "But who'd actually do that? Only someone who was mad" (243). So, if she has sent the letters then he pronounces her mad, and she is therefore the female subject whose sexual fantasies are a symptom of her general madness, in the Gothic tradition (Stein 1983; Talairach-Vielmas 2016), or, alternatively, if he is the sender, he is cheerfully pronouncing himself mad, inscribing himself as a Gothic villain who has exceeded the boundaries of logical reason and normal power. As the reader knows, such a male will not be punished by the system, but more likely rewarded, and will "continue[] unscathed, a seemingly eligible pillar of the community" (Hooper 2016, 245). Either way, she cannot win this game.

In *The Night Guest* two absent male figures negotiate spectrality for the consolidation of their respective power. George is an eerie and spectral presence from the moment Frida appears, delivering Frida to Ruth's house in his taxi each day, but never emerging from the car and unseen by either Ruth or the reader; Frida thinks, "Anything could be lurking in that drive: a tiger, or a taxi" (2013, 52), yet George is more literally present on the scene than Jeffrey and Phillip. Phillip is the most absent, not entering into the narrative at all, and Jeffrey is only present via his haunting of the telephone line whenever he senses disruption to the plan of waiting-out his mother's death to obtain the house and money (133–37). He is forced to appear when she dies, but this form of presence only serves to display his essential lack of authority and control within the structures that have led to Ruth's demise (271). Nonetheless, he does inherit the house, if not the money. George, who has stolen Ruth's money, now becomes entirely spectral, having sped off in his taxi beyond the limits of the text (229). In doing so, he abandons Frida, leaving her as trapped, isolated and disempowered as Ruth, only more so, as she is now wanted for criminal fraud. By the end of the novel, George and Jeffrey are left to fight it out in an abstract space beyond the narrative where the "authorities" are going to find or not find George and recover or not recover Ruth's money. Both Frida and Ruth are dead.

Warren Finch, the villainous male of *The Swan Book*, is, like the heroine Oblivia, spectral throughout the novel, but unlike Oblivia, his spectral masculinity allows him to manifest his desire for power even after death. He appears at the Swamp as a visiting dignitary—the deputy president of the Government of Australia—early in the novel, in a moment in which both his materiality and his ghostliness are instantiated. In this scene he is referred to satirically as an archangel by the swamp people (2013, 119) though, iron-ically, they do not believe in his power any more than they believe in the "other so-called miracles for assimilation" (119). His angelic business is also parodied, as a miraculous spectacle that creates "more stars in the sky," and heralds a new era in which "all would be well," but which is simultaneously, as they say, yet another "God-given failure[]," in the face of which they are "incredulous" (119). Warren undermines his own superhuman aura by "look[ing] no different in appearance to anybody else living in the swamp" (118–19). The compound and comical irony of the Aboriginal perspective here is that Warren's ghostliness pertains to an inextricable conflation of the spiritual, the spectral and Castle's "ghostliness of other people" in industrial modernity (1995, 125).

This ghostly complexity characterises Warren throughout the text; Warren is more spectral than the spectral inhabitants of Australia, just as he is more powerful than an ordinary citizen due to his public roles as deputy president of the Australian Government (and archangel of the Swamp). Like Oblivia, Warren was originally from the swamp area, known for dancing with the Brolgas (2013, 122). Abducted in childhood and raised by a white family, his story is that of the Stolen Generation Indigenous people of Australia's recent past.[7] Having been raised in a white family, Warren becomes the first Indigenous deputy president of the Government of Australia (123). As a colonized subject assimilated into the hegemony, he is preoccupied with power and his visibility throughout the nation:

> These days he was far more excited about how the world danced for him from way up high, or in the couch-grass backyards of every Australian city, its towns, and right down to any far-flung, buffel-grass infested corner of the country [...]. All people liked to dance for a gift from God. The Warren Finch dance. He was the lost key. He was post-racial. Possibly even post-Indigenous. His sophistication had been far-flung and heaven-sent. Internationally Warren. Post-tyranny politics kind of man. True thing! He was long gone from cardboard box and packing crate humpies in the remote forgotten worlds like this swamp. (122–23)

From this point of Warren's most solid embodiment, he becomes increasingly spectral, disappearing once Oblivia is ensconced in the apartment block, The People's Palace

(234). After seeing herself rendered as a phantom on television, she realises that *he* has become spectral to *her*. "She could not remember him—had no idea, even what he looked like unless she saw him on the television" (265). The Harbour Master obsessively watches Warren and Oblivia on television, living a spectral life: "You could not avoid the fact that Warren's life was being lived at a higher percentage elsewhere with the glamorous 'promise' wife, the First Lady of whatnot, than being wasted in hanging around, and minding reality in a swan-filthy apartment" (267).

Ultimately, because of his doubled subjectivity as colonised-become-coloniser, there is profound pathos in Warren's neo-Gothic villainy. In returning to the swamp to collect his promise-wife, Oblivia, he is told by others about the rape and identifies that the law of the nation failed to protect her from violence: "*They had not protected you. Nobody did.* [...] *Their job was to protect you. That was the law*" (231; emphasis in original). But, of course, as the deputy president he *is* the law. He wields his power to obliterate the law's abject Other, the swamp people whose failure to protect Oblivia (or Warren himself, who was abducted from the swamp as a child) is itself a direct result of disempowerment by the law in their imprisonment in the detention camp that is the swamp. Warren strikes out at the material corollary of colonialism, not its invisible operations, ordering the Army to blow up the swamp (230). In doing so he destroys Oblivia's home.[8] Believing he is changing the system that spectralised Oblivia, he repeats the colonisers' practices.

Warren's assassination is itself a spectral spectacle—it is unclear who has shot him, and his status as alive or dead is ambiguous. Even if she has done it—she is unclear about this herself—this act does not work to solidify Oblivia's sense of self. She finds herself somehow outside in a storm standing next to the (now presumably ghost of) Warren and moves off "into the ghost fog" (279). Like the false culmination of relations between Ruth and Richard in *The Night Guest*, the killing of Warren is evacuated of transformational force: it brings about no change to colonial or gender structures.

The authorities refuse to allow Warren's Aboriginal kin to bury his body (288), and eventually people begin to believe that "*Warren Finch was not dead*" (292; emphasis in original). This is Oblivia's view, too, as she hops out of the semi-trailer carrying his corpse around the country in the "*Spirit of the Nation*" tour: "She watched the semitrailer roaring up the highway from the ghost town's park [...] *There he goes*, she thought of Warren Finch, *he's still holding on to power, still searching for the ultimate paradise. Yep!* The same stories you hear about power. A dead man was still making people run after him" (301–2; emphasis in original). After his death he dissolves into a sign, his transcending materiality. Warren has become a constantly visible spectre of the figure of power itself, moving but always somewhere on the highways of Australia: a spectral entity who escapes specific location, always just out of reach—the spectralised Father of the Law in post-postcolonial global capitalism.

After his death Oblivia "deterritorializes" herself again, in Deleuzo-Guattarian terms (1987 [1980], 3, 56, 87 and 307), in a line of flight that is ironically a walk through floodwater, carrying a young swan that can neither fly nor swim.[9] As she walks she converses with the flocks of (ghost?) swans,[10] and eventually, "Her mind [is] only a lonely mansion for the stories of extinction" (333), she becomes a ghost again, as she has always-already been. She "walks around the old dry swamp pretty regularly they say, and having seen her where there is a light moving over the marshes in the middle of the night, like a will-o'-the-wisp, they thought that they had heard her screaming, *kayi, kayi kala-wurru nganyi, your country is calling out for you*, which they described was just like listening to a sigh of a moth extending out over the landscape" (334; emphasis in original).

These twenty-first century Female neo-Gothic tales demonstrate an absence of the original Gothic logic in which, for authors like Radcliffe, "order is restored" (Smith 2007, 33). Metatextually performing their own uncanniness, these Australian neo-Gothic texts show that the destructive elements of the historical past since the fundamental shift from the Medieval into Enlightenment modernity onwards have never actually *been* repressed. Accordingly, they cannot be re-repressed. As a result, the destructive operations of these returning historical structures are not curtailed at the end of any of these novels but allowed to play out to their fullest.

Notes

1 In 2014 *The Night Guest* was: longlisted for the Guardian First Book Award (United Kingdom); and shortlisted for multiple major Australian literary awards. It won the New South Wales Premier's Literary Awards (Glenda Adams Award) and the Sydney Morning Herald Young Novelist Award. Also in 2014, *The Swan Book* was shortlisted for the Miles Franklin Literary Award, the Stella Prize, the NSW Premier's Literary Awards and the Victorian Premier's Literary Awards, and was the winner of the ALS Gold Medal Award. Chloe Hooper's first novel, *A Child's Book of True Crime*, was shortlisted for the Orange Prize (2002), and Hooper's nonfiction narrative of the death-in-custody of Cameron Doomadgee on Palm Island, *The Tall Man: Death and Life on Palm* Island (2008), won multiple prizes. Hooper's *The Engagement* received no attention in the literary prizes and awards of its publication year.

2 Diana Wallace, in her Introduction to *Female Gothic Histories*, discusses historian Mary Beard's argument, in *Woman as Force in History*, about the legal status of women in marriage during the Medieval period (2013, 2). Writing in 1946 and analysing William Blackstone's Commentaries on the Laws of England 7th Edition (1775), Beard argues that a woman was essentially "civilly dead" once she was legally married, as her rights were subsumed into, and assumed as subject to, those of her husband (78–79). Wallace analyses and builds upon Beard's use of Gothic imagery in her discussion of the legal status of women.

3 Malte Völk notes the intersection between dementia and the menacing atmosphere in the novel, referring to the "build-up of tension through dementia symptoms" (2017, 62).

4 Frida's narrative of herself is revealed as, of course, fictional: her mother is still alive and well and living in Perth (2013, 274). Ironically, Frida turns out to have been, not Fijian, but "English, apparently. The father was from New Zealand—half Maori" (274).

5 Rebecca Munford uses Derrida's concept of "hauntology" to develop her argument about "spectral femininity" in her essay in *Women and the Gothic* (2016, 119–34).

6 In his essay on "The Uncanny," Sigmund Freud summarises Otto Rank's study on the double, or döppelganger: "The double was originally an insurance against the extinction of the self" but in later historical periods "becomes the uncanny harbinger of death" (2003 [1919], 142).

7 In 1997 the Australian Human Rights Commission released its report into the Stolen Generations of Aboriginal and Torres Strait Islander children who were forcibly taken from their families by the Australian government during the twentieth century. This report contained the testimonies of over five hundred of the many tens of thousands of Indigenous people who were the subject of state-directed removal, as children, from their families. Many of them never saw their families again, and many parents of these children were never told where the government had placed them (1997, Part 2), effectively destroying families and resulting in major intergenerational trauma (Part 3).

8 The horrifying abuse–revenge cycle that Warren partakes in is discussed by law and litera-ture scholar Honni Van Rijswijk, who argues that Oblivia cannot speak of having been raped because it would allow the law to justify revenge punishment and " reinforce law's habit of instrumentalizing violence—the history of the law's violent interventions on the basis of the story of one Aboriginal subject harming another, a practice evident from the Aborigines Protection Acts of the twentieth century to the Northern Territory Intervention still in force" (2015).

9 Named after a bird, Warren Finch is also a symbol of potential deterritorialisation.

10 For an analysis of weather, climate and the figure of the swans in Wright's novel, see Jane Gleeson-White (2016, 29–39).

Bibliography

Althans, Katrin. *Darkness Subverted: Aboriginal Gothic in Black Australian Literature and Film*. Göttingen: Bonn University Press, 2012.

Atkinson, Meera. *The Poetics of Transgenerational Trauma*. New York: Bloomsbury Academic, 2017.

Baldick, Chris. Introduction to *The Oxford Book of Gothic Tales*, edited and introduction by Chris Baldick, xi–xxiii. Oxford: Oxford University Press, 1992.

Beard, Mary R. *Woman as Force in History*. New York: Macmillan, 1946.

Botting, Fred. "In Gothic Darkly: Heterotopia, History, Culture." In *A New Companion to the Gothic*, edited by David Punter, 12–24. Oxford: Wiley-Blackwell, 2012.

Bringing Them Home: Report of the National Inquiry into the Separation of Aboriginal and Torres Strait Islander Children from Their Families. Australian Human Rights Commission. April 1997. https://www.humanrights.gov.au/our-work/bringing-them-home-report-1997.

Castle, Terry. *The Female Thermometer: Eighteenth-Century Culture and the Invention of the Uncanny*. New York: Oxford University Press, 1995.

Davidson, Jim. "Tasmanian Gothic." *Meanjin* 48, no. 2 (1989): 307–24.

Davison, Carol Margaret. *Gothic Literature 1764–1824*. Cardiff: University of Wales Press, 2009.

Deleuze, Giles, and Felix Guattari. *A Thousand Plateaus: Capitalism and Schizophrenia*. 1980. Translated by Brian Massumi. Minneapolis: University of Minnesota Press, 1987.

Derrida, Jacques. *Spectres of Marx*. 1993. Translated by Peggy Kamuf. New York: Routledge, 1994.

Ferguson-Ellis, Kate. *The Contested Castle: Gothic Novels and the Subversion of Domestic Ideology*. Chicago: University of Illinois Press, 1989.

Freud, Sigmund. "The Uncanny." 1919. In *The Uncanny*, translated by David McLintock, 135–51. London: Penguin, 2003.

Gelder, Ken. "Australian Gothic." In *A New Companion to the Gothic*, edited by David Punter, 379–92. Oxford: Wiley-Blackwell, 2012.

Gelder, Ken, and Jane M. Jacobs. *Uncanny Australia: Sacredness and Identity in a Postcolonial Nation*. Melbourne: Melbourne University Press, 1994.

Gleeson-White, Jane. "Country and Climate Change in Alexis Wright's *The Swan Book*." *Swamphen: The Australasian Journal of Ecocriticism and Cultural Ecology* 6 (2016): 29–39.

Hooper, Chloe. 2012. *The Engagement*. Maryborough, VIC: Penguin, 2016.

Horner, Avril, and Sue Zlosnik. "No Country for Old Women: Gender, Age and the Gothic." In *Women and the Gothic: Edinburgh Companion*, edited by Avril Horner and Sue Zlosnik, 184–98. Edinburgh: Edinburgh University Press, 2016.

Killeen, Jarlath. *The Emergence of Irish Gothic Fiction: Histories, Origins, Theories*. Edinburgh: Edinburgh University Press, 2013.

Kirkpatrick, Peter. "'*Dear nightmare*': Chloe Hooper's *The Engagement* as Gothic Romance." *Southerly* 77, no. 3 (2017): 85–105.

Lucashenko, Melissa. "'But You Don't Look Like a Metaphor': Migaloo Thinking about Aboriginal People." In *Changing Geographies: Essays on Australia*, edited by Susan Ballyn, Geoff

Belligoi, Kathy Firth, Elisa Morera de la Vall and Bill Phillips, 127–34. Barcelona: Australian Studies Centre, University of Barcelona, 2001.

McFarlane, Fiona. *The Night Guest*. Maryborough, VIC: Penguin, 2013.

Mulvey-Roberts, Marie. "The Female Gothic Body." In *Women and the Gothic: Edinburgh Companion*, edited by Avril Horner and Sue Zlosnik, 106–19. Edinburgh: Edinburgh University Press, 2016.

Munford, Rebecca. "Spectral Femininity." In *Women and the Gothic: Edinburgh Companion*, edited by Avril Horner and Sue Zlosnik, 120–34. Edinburgh: Edinburgh University Press, 2016.

Radcliffe, Ann Ward. *The Mysteries of Udolpho*. 1794. London: J. Limbird, 1836. https://archive.org/details/mysteriesofudolp00radc.

———. *The Italian, or The Confessional of the Black Penitents*. 1797. Edited and introduction by Frederick Garber. Oxford: Oxford University Press, 1981.

Sage, Victor. *Horror Fiction in the Protestant Tradition*. Basingstoke: Macmillan, 1988.

Scott, Kim. "Interview: Can You Anchor a Shimmering Nation State via Regional Indigenous Roots?" In *Giving This Country a Memory: Contemporary Aboriginal Voices of Australia*, edited by Anne Brewster, 2–21. Amherst, NY: Cambria Press, 2015.

Sheridan, Susan. "Feminist Fables and Alexis Wright's Art of the Fabulous in *The Swan Book*." *Hecate* 43, no.1/2 (2017): 197–214.

Smith, Andrew. *Gothic Literature*. Edinburgh: Edinburgh University Press, 2007.

Stein, Karen F. "Monsters and Madwomen: Changing Female Gothic." In *The Female Gothic*, edited by Juliann E. Fleenor, 123–37. Montreal: Eden Press, 1983.

Talairach-Vielmas, Laurence. "Madwomen and Attics." In *Women and the Gothic: Edinburgh Companion*, edited by Avril Horner and Sue Zlosnik, 31–45. Edinburgh: Edinburgh University Press, 2016.

Turcotte, Gerry. "Australian Gothic." In *The Handbook to Gothic Literature*, edited by Marie Mulvey-Roberts, 10–19. Basingstoke: Macmillan, 1998.

Van Rijswijk, Honni. "Encountering Law's Harm through Literary Critique: An Anti-elegy of Land and Sovereignty." *University of Technology Sydney Law and Research Series*, 2015. classic.austlii.edu.au/au/journals/UTSLRS/2015/35.html.

Völk, Malte. "Driving, Not Losing, the Plot: Narrative Patterns in Implicit and Explicit Fictional Representations of Dementia." *Open Cultural Studies* 1 (2017): 55–65.

Wallace, Diana. *Female Gothic Histories: Gender, History and the Gothic*. Cardiff: University of Wales Press, 2013.

Walpole, Horace. *The Castle of Otranto*. 1764. In *Three Gothic Novels*, edited by E. F. Bleiler, 3–106. New York: Dover, 1966.

Weaver, Rachael. "Colonial Violence and Forgotten Fiction." *Australian Literary Studies* 24, no. 2 (2009): 33–53.

Wright, Alexis. *The Swan Book*. Sydney: Giramondo, 2013.

Chapter Eight

"WE ARE ALL HUMANS": SELF-AWARE ZOMBIES AND NEO-GOTHIC POSTHUMANISM

Karen E. Macfarlane

We are all humans, but some of us are just more mortal than others.

Braidotti (2013, 15)

It has become a sort of primal scene in zombie narratives: the moment of misrecognition, of uncertainty, the moment when a survivor sees the zombie of a lover or child or friend and, refusing to believe that it is dead, approaches and is often consumed. These scenes, whether the survivor falls prey to the undead or is saved by a companion, enact some of the central elements encoded in the figure of the zombie. In fact, in a significant number of zombie narratives, the living protagonists question not only what the zombies are, but who they had been. In almost all zombie stories there is a moment when protagonists look at an approaching horde of the undead and wonder at their loss of individuality. Zombies are, then, fundamentally concerned with interdependent issues of identity, subjectivity and the limits of the human. Or, perhaps more accurately, they make visible a preoccupation with the fundamental uncertainty that shapes and underlies these issues. Zombies unsettle binary structures—alive/dead, human/non-human, even self/other—and straddle the lines in between, disturbing and disrupting categories and systems. In traditional/Romero[1] zombie narratives, the kind in which clearly monstrous, unthinking walking corpses are pitted against a band of living human survivors, the conflict is often articulated as a battle between the human and its other: the dead, the zombie, the undead, the monster. But zombies are not easily or irretrievably other. As Barbara, the protagonist of *Night of the Living Dead* (1990), says, "They are us. We are them and they are us." In this sense, many contemporary zombie narratives can be thought of as fundamentally posthuman, embracing the ways in which posthumanism challenges assumptions about the category "human" as definitive and stable. But even in these narratives, as the "primal scene" suggests, this distinction is borne of desperation; the awareness that "humanity" is not, ultimately, a category that cannot be clearly defined. This indeterminacy opens the space for the neo-Gothic, self-aware[2] zombie, a figure from which the category "human" is not definitively removed or elided at death and which exchanges the Romero zombie's metaphorical connections with voracious consumerism and mindless labour under industrial capital with metonymic associations to the spectrality of neoliberal capital, the isolation of neoliberal subjectivity and the vertiginous flow of information and identity in networked culture. In these zombies, categories slip, destabilising them and reworking their definitions. The neo-Gothic zombie opens up a space for thinking of "a world where humanity is threatened not by extinction but by definition" (Alberto 2017, 113).

The uncanny familiarity of the zombie, in both its traditional (i.e. the contemporary or "Romero zombie") and posthuman forms, invites dangerously destablilising misrecognition. Texts that reimagine the zombie as a subject make visible and critique posthuman fantasies of disembodiment in a neoliberal, digitally networked age. The zombies in these texts are not only sentient, but self-aware: introspective and individual. As such, they reimagine the sort of disembodiment that we see in the twenty-first century cybersubject's fusion with digital technologies as a nightmare of undifferentiation that reflects on the horror of Western culture's increasingly disembodied, networked existence. The all-too-embodied figure of the self-aware zombie is a nightmarish manifestation of the posthuman dream of disembodiment. This dream began to be articulated as early as the 1950s when Alan Turing posited that "under specific circumstances it would be impossible to distinguish between computer and human intelligence" (quoted in Herbrechter 2013, 92), a concept that became "a widespread delusion" in Western culture and which N. Katherine Hayles famously rejected, insisting that consciousness and embodiment were necessarily interdependent (1999, 1). The act of unmooring consciousness from the body, the articulation of Cartesian/liberal humanist dualism, informs some of the central debates in critical posthumanism and in philosophical discussions of zombies and consciousness. For my purposes, these arguments will open a space for thinking specifically about how the self-aware zombie's refusal of that dualism, through its insistent and horrific embodiment, can be seen to be thinking through some of the complex interconnections between resistances to the limits neoliberalism places on subjectivity, posthuman discussions of death and consciousness and life in digitally networked culture. Zombies—traditional zombies—are "an inherent part of life in network culture" (Macfarlane 2018, 244) and are at their core digital monsters, reflecting both the terror of disembodiment in cyberspace and the horror of the networked age. Their corporeality reminds us of the materiality of technology and of the body that interacts with it.

Twenty-first century subjectivity is increasingly constructed in terms of interactions with the products of technological corporations which define and limit the ways in which we communicate. Our experiences are fragmented through the use of targeted algorithms that generate individualised consumer and entertainment "experiences." These algorithms filter information, news, consumer products and politics down to an almost impossibly narrow focus calculated and dispersed by the spectral corporations behind the networks, making subjects in networked culture paradoxically isolated even as they participate in the profusion of information flows online. The contemporary subject becomes not a citizen, or even a consumer in the neoliberal sense, but what Daniel Zamora describes in a recent interview with Niklas Olson as a "sovereign consumer" (2019). Zamora makes it clear that he doesn't "understand the sovereign consumer as a real individual or as a fixed concept but as an analytical umbrella term for a range of ideas asserting that free consumer choice is the defining feature of the market economy." The contemporary subject can be thought of, then, as one of a multiplicity of isolated, invisible bodies behind screens linked to corporate entities that control what they see, what they consume, how they interpret the world that they are increasingly physically removed from. The subject is one of an infinitude of minds experientially circulating in cyberspace but trapped in bodies in a Gothic travesty of posthuman fantasies of disembodiment.

This fantasy was made popular by proponents of transhumanism who, according to Hayles, thought "of information as a kind of bodiless fluid that could flow between different substrates without loss of meaning or form" (1999, xii) and so human identity could be thought of as "essentially an informational pattern rather than an embodied enaction" (xii). If human identity is informational, then the blending of human and machine was, according to Hans Moravec in 1988, conceptually possible and so "machines can, for all practical purposes, become human beings. You are the cyborg, and the cyborg is you" (quoted in xii). But in the digitally networked twenty-first century, questions of the relation between the user and the network are perhaps not as much about "enacted" embodiment as about the "projected" image (Herbrechter 2013, 93) generated at their intersection. In this sense, contemporary posthumanism "remind[s] information of its forgotten or repressed materiality" (94). So, if the cyborg, as human disembodied and downloaded into the machine, might have been the ideal figure for thinking through the relation between nascent computer technologies and subjectivity in the latter part of the twentieth century, it is the self-aware zombie, as fundamentally embodied but subject to the imperatives of neoliberal cybersubjectivity, that best explores the imperilled definitions of the human in twenty-first century digital culture. In networked digital culture, the body is reimagined as incidental to the focus of online exchanges, as simply the material device that is necessary for initiating the connection with the network so that life can be lived, disembodied, online. The body is "in our contemporary societies [...] no longer the allocation of a tangible identity, the irrevocable incarnation of a subject, or its being-in-the-world, but a construct, an interface, a terminal, a volatile object."[3]

In this sense, while the traditional zombie, which is most often read as limitlessly metaphorical, can be seen to draw attention to the horror of the material in our relation to networked culture, its embodiment reminding us of our visceral responses to life online, the self-aware zombie picks up where its predecessor left off, metonymically gesturing both backward to the tropes of zombie narratives and outward to questions of the possibility of consciousness and humanity in network culture. Self-aware zombies are a relatively recent addition to the zombie canon. While there are examples of intelligent zombies in earlier films and fiction, most famously those in *Return of the Living Dead* (1985) and in Robin Becker's novel *Brains: A Zombie Memoir* (1994), the possibility of zombies retaining individuality only really started to appear in the early part of the twenty-first century. Films like Romero's *Land of the Dead* (2005) and *Fido* (2007) hinted that zombies could potentially retain vestiges of their former selves, and novels like David Wellington's *Monster Island* (2006) explored the possibility of fully functioning, self-aware members of the walking dead. It is probably a coincidence that the self-aware zombie begins to appear just as digital and networked technologies became more and more integrated into the lives of individuals in the early parts of the twenty-first century but that both technologies and the consciousness of the zombies have become more sophisticated as the century has progressed can, I would argue, be fruitfully connected. Zombies are, after all, monsters, figures that act as a "'fantasy screen' upon which viewers and readers inscribe […] meaning. The monster [is] a remarkably mobile, permeable, and infinitely interpretable body. The monster's body, indeed, is a machine that, in its Gothic mode, produces meaning and can represent any horrible trait that the reader feeds into the narrative. The monster functions as monster, in other words, when it is able to condense as many fear-producing traits as possible into one body" (Halberstam 1995, 10, 21). Traditional zombies are, then, truly monstrous. They are meaning-making figures that take on and generate multiple and simultaneous narratives of anxiety and horror. They have come to stand for mindless, repetitive work, rampant consumerism, the potential for the spread of viral pandemics, conservative fears of migrant populations and on and on. The potential meanings encoded in the figure of the zombie are as unstable as its physical characteristics, slipping (un)easily between and within categories of race, gender, class, ability. As Marc Leverette has argued, the zombie's "undecidable status falls as the slash between human/nonhumans, us/Other, living/dead, at once telling us explicitly about ourselves while often serving as a critical commentary on what we might become tomorrow" (2008, 202). Zombies have, in short, "become the most enduring, expressive and consummate metaphor for our [contemporary] crisis in meaning" (Vervaeke et al. 2017, 4).

The zombie legend is deeply rooted in West-African and Haitian spiritual practices and in the history of trans-Atlantic slavery. The contemporary zombie is "a direct result of the neocolonial occupation of Haiti (1915–1934) where after the figure was reshaped and rebranded with the mark of a new society's concerns" (Lauro 2017, x). The embodiment of these new concerns was introduced in George A. Romero's *Night of the Living Dead* (1968) and consolidated in its sequel, *Dawn of the Dead* (1978). The mindless, shambling, voracious, flesh-eating hordes of zombies in the latter film, in particular, invited associations with the reduction of the individual to mindless labourer and consumer within systems of industrial capital, a connection that, as Sarah Juliet Lauro notes, "follows the lineage of the zombie's folkloric origins in imagery [that exposes] the greed of the colonial oppressor" (ix). In contemporary culture, zombies continue to reflect, and reflect on, their historical associations with oppression and disenfranchisement. As Sheryl Vint has suggested, the fact that zombies do not appear as individuals makes them an appropriate "symbol for disenfranchised labor" (2013, 135). They are, she argues, "a way for working through the alienation of capitalist extraction of surplus value: They mirror how human living labor is turned into a dead thing, a commodity" (135). As "creatures physically indiscernible from ordinary human beings, but altogether bereft of conscious experiences" (Heil 2003, 3), zombies are truly monstrous, embodying incoherence and rupturing stable systems of signification. In the twenty-first century the shift from industrial capital to financial/informational capital has given the zombie a new (un)life as a way of thinking through "the ideological manipulation" (Blake 2015, 27) to which the subject is exposed when it becomes a cybersubject. In contemporary manifestations, the zombie "gives a gruesome, rotting face to those most dreadful anxieties that haunt our world" (Leverette 2008, 202) and functions as "a means of exposing and exploring the impact of neoliberal economies as the social and cultural organization of the world, and, in turn, the models of subjectivity available to its inhabitants" (Blake 2017, 105).

It is around these limited, precarious "models of subjectivity" under neoliberal social and economic practices that the self-aware zombie's potential meanings begin to res-onate. Neoliberalism is, as Herb Wyile has argued the "drink of choice since the 1980s" (2013, 29), a cocktail of "free market policies, privatization, financial deregulation and speculation, and corporate enterprise over government-led decision making [...] appar-ently without alternative" (Murnane 2016, 230). Neoliberalism is not only an economic system, but it is also a series of cultural and social practices that regulate and shape the construction of the individual subject. Neoliberal social practices police the meanings and movements of the individual body even as they control the narratives through which the stories of the individual can be told. In the neoliberal world "social space disappears as a communal form, replaced by a global system in which individuals circulate in the flows of money, information, and desire as consumers of property and commodities" (Botting 2001, 139). So, as Wendy Brown has argued, "the model neoliberal citizen is one who strategizes for her or himself among various social, political, and economic options, not one who strives with others to alter or organize these options" (2005, 43). The context of unregulated consumption, commodification, technological ascendance, depersonalisation and borderlessness positions the subject under neoliberalism as isolated from social and political communities through the imperative of neoliberal competition. George Monbiot has pointed out that "when neoliberalism fell apart in 2008 there was [...] nothing. This is why the zombie walks" (2016). Yet, neoliberal policies and social practices persist, even after its ostensible demise during the global financial crisis, and this persistence is why, I would argue, the zombie talks.

With the neoliberal subject's focus on self-interest, the zombie's meanings resonate less in images of a mindless horde and instead become manifest in the figure of the singular self-aware zombie. Most self-aware zombies are, in fact, unique figures in their narratives. R in Isaac Marion's *Warm Bodies* is, initially at least, one of the few zombies in the airport capable of "focused thought" (2011, 5); Jack Barnes in Becker's *Brains: A Zombie Memoir* speculates that "I couldn't be the only corpse with consciousness, the only brain-eater with a brain. I wasn't entirely alone. Was I?" (2010, 20); and, like Scott Kenemore's Peter Mellor in *Zombie, Ohio*, Jack eventually finds that his abilities allow him to lead a "zombie band" (2011, 96) hunting humans in the empty landscape of post-apocalyptic America. Each of these figures is isolated from the zombies around them partially because of their inability to speak (Jack is only able to write, and R is monosyllabic for most of the novel) or because of their unique condition as a rational agent. These zombies, with all of their isolated introspection, work to think through the implications of the complex, layered, reality, "apparently without alternative" (Murnane 2016, 230), that is contem-porary culture.

In spite of being identified as dead, these talking, thinking zombies continue on with their un-lives, fully aware of their identities, their relationships and their place in the world. While other intelligent undead figures, such as mummies in nineteenth-century fiction, have appeared in folklore and popular narratives, the zombie itself has always, even in its original form as part of West African religious practice, been characterised by the radical removal of the self from the body. In the stories of the self-aware zombie the opposite is true: the mind and the body are intimately and, indeed, inextricably connected. The nature of this physicality, and what it means to be a subject that is so fundamentally embodied, appears in what can be categorised as two narratively and theoretically distinct types of self-aware zombies in popular culture. The first type, which is my primary focus here, appear in works such as David Wellington's *Monster Island*, Daryl Gregory's *Raising Stony Mayhall* (2011) and, perhaps most famously, Isaac Marion's *Warm Bodies*. These novels focus on zombies who, except for their ability to think rationally, would otherwise be indistinguishable from their horror film cousins and retain most of the characteristics of the monster; they are "denizens of the borderland, [that] have always represented the extremities of transgression and the limits of the order of things" (Herbrechter 2013, 86). The second category is what I have called the "de-monstered" (Macfarlane 2012, 114) monster, which appears in television series such as *Santa Clarita Diet* (2017–19) and *iZombie* (2015–19), and in novels such as Diana Rowland's *White Trash Zombie* (2009–present) series. In the latter narratives, the zombie protagonists are not truly monsters. Monstrosity (or more specifically, being zombies or undead) here is set out as simply another way to think about difference. Sheila, Liv and Angel, the zombies in these works, lead all but normal lives: going to work, shopping, being with family and friends. Their difference lies, especially after *Santa Clarita*'s Sheila is given a serum to stabilise her unpredictable body, in their appetites. Their need for human flesh (on Sheila's part) and brains (on Liv's and Angel's) drives the generally light-hearted plots of these series and solidifies their fundamentally conventional, fundamentally moral core. Liv and Angel work in coroners' offices and, in scenes reminiscent of a cooking show *iZombie*'s, Liv cooks and eats the brains of the dead as a way of helping to solve their murders, while Sheila only eats what she calls "bad people" (Nazis and blackmailers), often in the form of a smoothie. In this sense these are fully domesticated zombies, "heimlich monsters" (Greenberg 2013, 124) whose presence elicits pleasure rather than fear in their audiences by playing on and with the "category collisions implicit in [their] disengenuousness" (124). Like the "mainstreamed" vampires of *True Blood* and the *Twilight* series of novels and films, these protagonists' identities are fundamentally stable. The change in their bodies and their appetites and indeed their afterlives is incidental to the larger plot in which (minor) differences are accommodated and middle-class[4] identities are partially destabilised in a safe and fundamentally conservative way. These are decidedly human, rather than posthuman, zombies.

The posthuman zombie negotiates many of the same fault lines as the "heimlich monster," all the while never losing the radical potential for disruption encoded in the figure of the monster. The role of monsters in popular culture is to be irretrievably Other. In this position it "creates a sense of vertigo, [it is] that which calls into question our (their, anyone's) epistemological world view, highlights its fragmentary and inadequate nature" (Mittman 2013, 8). As a figure that challenges and questions, monsters "are overdetermined signifiers" (Edwards 2015, 14) that are integral to hegemonic cultural systems even as they pose fundamental challenges to the underpinnings of those systems. While the heimlich and de-monstered monsters focus on the potential for change inherent in the figure, then, that their representation is emptied of the horror of (mis)recognition undermines their potential for radical critique.

The heimlich zombie potentially participates in a twenty-first century trajectory of the Gothic that Catherine Spooner has called "happy Gothic." For Spooner, "happy Gothic" uses traditional Gothic imagery emptied of the "gloomy and miserable or scary and horrid" (2017, 3), and as a result its narratives are generally "positively inclined" (3). Although there is a positive element to some of the works that focus on self-aware zombies—as, for example, in the redemptive focus of *Warm Bodies*—self-aware zombies maintain the fundamental characteristics of their predecessors in the Gothic, even as they work through very twenty-first century preoccupations with a fear of technologically inflected undifferentiation, formlessness and "undeath" (Shaw 2009, 253). In these neo-Gothic texts, the self-aware zombie's position self-reflexively plays out the fact that "past images and forms [are] worn too thin to veil the gaping black hole of objectless anxiety" (Botting 2014, 298) in the twenty-first century. If traditional zombie narratives are structured around the struggle to maintain human subjectivity in the face of the "contagious antisubjectivity" of the zombie horde that is "a collectivity of anti-characters that actively works to negate/subsume all characters" (Swanson 2014, 387), then the appearance of the self-aware zombie threatens not only the world of the narrative in which they appear but also the metanarrative of the zombie itself. As the focalising consciousness of the text, the zombie point of view reconfigures the questions that zombie narratives have always asked: questions about the unstable divisions between self and other, human and nonhuman and, significantly, the increasingly imperceptible distinction between life and death in Western culture and science.

The traditional zombie embodies the limits of death, decay and non-identity, but in the context of posthuman necropolitics, self-aware zombies push these limits to their absolute logical extreme. They embody what Megan Stern calls "death without limits" (2008, 351), an ontological space created by technological interventions within medical practices that "postpone the moment of death, in some cases indefinitely" (Shaw 2009, 253). The spectre of endlessly embodied death in life that contemporary medical technology makes possible is the Gothic inversion of fantasies of transcendent subjectivity in both spiritual and technological discourses.

In discussions of posthuman disembodiment, cybernetic existence is theorised as a fantasy of transcendence, a "freedom from history and materiality" (Chun 2006, 13) that can continue even beyond death. Indeed, death seems to be all but defeated in cyberspace. Posthumous messaging and posting, not a fantasy but very much a reality of contemporary digital communication, allows the dead to continue to post on social media and elsewhere. Services like Dead Switch, Ghostmemo, DeadSocial and others are "computational processes [and...] algorithms that directly animate the dead by automating [their] social media posts" (Arnold et al. 2018, 4) enacting an online, disembodied version of an individual and allowing them to continue their lives as "posthuman, posthumous" (Marion 2011, 57) consciousnesses. Identity can thus not only be dispersed online in life, it can continue, zombie-like, after death. Contemporary culture is haunted by the "spectre of 'undeath'" (Shaw 2009, 253), of the ways in which "techno-utopianism" (252) makes death indeterminate. It is troubled by the ways in which neoliberal economies spectralise labour, capital and subjectivity and by the concept that the subject can be disembodied, dispersed and, as Colson Whitehead's Lieutenant says, his life is on "the cloud. It was all of me up there. The necessary docs and e-mails and key photographs. The proof" (2011, 92). This clash between the material and the immaterial makes the focus of contemporary cultural anxieties "objectless," as Botting has suggested. Paradoxically, while the zombie itself is all too embodied, its presence, and in particular the presence of its neo-Gothic incarnation, makes visible the horror of the "black hole" (Braidotti 2013, 131) that both Botting and Braidotti describe as a central metaphor for contemporary culture.

In her discussion of death and posthumanism, Braidotti suggests that it is "the inhuman conceptual excess: the unrepresentable, the unthinkable and the unproductive black hole that we all fear" (131). Death's unrepresentability is best thought about in terms of the zombie: excessively corporeal, excessively dead but somehow never adequately inhabiting these definitions. The zombie's body is unstable, disintegrating, and its movement contradicts the stillness that is traditionally associated with death. The zombie raises questions of what, exactly, defines death, what constitutes its limits, how it can be thought and how it can be represented in the discourses of the living. In this sense, it is death, not the zombie, that is the focal point of all zombie narratives. The questions that the zombie poses by its very existence, by its inadequate and unstable representations, explore the fact that death is "not a limit, but […] a porous threshold" (131). For Braidotti, questions about death and neoliberal economic, cultural and technological practice are intimately connected to each other. In the necropolitics that are an integral part of advanced capitalism, she argues that "the human becomes subsumed into global networks of control and commodification that have taken 'Life' as the main target" (64). Similarly, the increasing emphasis on technological intervention in extending life or modifying its terms has led to what Roger Luckhurst has called "the New Death" (2015, 84).

Extended by medical technologies and redefined by committees of scientists, the New Death is not a moment, not a "decisive rupture" (85), but instead a series of gradations and shifting definitions, a "temporal process" (88). Tracing technological interventions into death, Luckhurst notes that the shift in the late 1960s from understanding death to be the moment when the heart ceases to beat to being instead determined by the technological monitoring of the level of a patient's brain activity redefined dying as a space of undefinability, "an uncertainly extensive biotechnical domain after life but before death" (88). Similarly, Barry Murnane has argued that "medicine and new technologies have turned death into an ambiguous state of polysemic potential and uncertainty" (2015, 119).

This uncertainty about death is, of course, nothing new. In the nineteenth century, European cultures were similarly uneasy about the lack of empirical evidence that could determine the moment of death. Stories of premature burials revealed the "disquieting liminality of near death states" (Behlmer 2003, 208) and a pervasive distrust of the Men of Science who attempted to define them. While there are few verifiable stories of premature burial, the power of the image reveals a general anxiety about the limits of medical/scientific knowledge and fuelled debates about the disconcerting porousness between states of being that should have been clearly separate (221; Mangham 2010, 15). As Edgar Allan Poe states in "The Premature Burial," "The boundaries that divide Life from Death are at best shadowy and vague. Who shall say where one ends, and the other begins?" (1965 [1844], 58–59). Similarly Charles Lever's narrator in "Postmortem Recollections of a Medical Lecturer," declared dead by this medical colleagues but conscious and all too aware of what is happening around his body, queries, "What then is death? Could it be, that though coldness wrapt the suffering clay, passion and sense should still survive—that while every external trace of life had fled, consciousness should still cling to the cold corpse destined for the earth. Oh! How horrible, how more than horrible! The terror of the thought" (2014 [1836], 198). Articulating the horror of the liminal space between life and death, these stories explore the Gothic implications of the Cartesian/liberal humanist division between body and consciousness. What Poe and Lever are describing here is similar to what ultimately became known as "locked in syndrome," a state "in which cortical activity is unequivocally preserved amidst catastrophic collapse of the voluntary muscular and nervous system" (Luckhurst 2015, 89). Being "locked in" an inert body again reinforces the persistence of Cartesian/liberal humanist conceptions that insist on a mind/body split and which conceptualise identity as an essence that is somehow separate and separable from the body.

While the nineteenth-century texts posited this living death as a state of immobility, isolation and tortured consciousness, the appearance of the Romero zombie in 1968— coincidentally (or not) as Luckhurst points out, the same year as the Ad Hoc Committee of the Harvard Medical School "relocate[d] death from the heart to the brain" (88)— reimagined this image as its inverse: as physical mobility with a nightmarish lack of consciousness. What drives traditional stories of zombies is that, particularly as a part of a mindless horde, zombies have been emptied of individuality, identity and any sort of subjectivity. In the space between these subject-less zombies and fully self-aware zombies is perhaps the most horrific imagining of this figure. Truly hybrid, blending the horror of nineteenth-century stories of live burial with tropes of the ambulatory corpse, zombies in Jonathan Maberry's novel *Dead of Night* (2011) and its sequel, *Fall of Night* (2014), open a space for thinking about the zombie in terms of ontology, abject corporeality and posthuman alienation.

Dead of Night begins with all of the standard conventions of a zombie thriller: the unexplained reanimation of the dead, frightening encounters with zombies, an embattled enclave of survivors and questions about the nature of the undead and their difference from the living upon whom they feed. As the scientist who introduced the zombie parasites to this world explains it, "In order to discuss this [...] we have to step outside of our normal scientific lexicon. We are not discussing life or death as we have always known it. Those have always been the only two states of existence [...] This is a third state of existence" (Maberry 2011, 183). The "third state" is not, it turns out, the mindless one that characterises Romero zombies, or the ideal transcendence of transhumanism, but is rather a nightmarish state of being fully aware inside of a zombie body, able to "feel everything. Every. Single. Thing" (54). Maberry's "locked in" zombie feels the "jolts in his legs with each clumsy step. The protest of muscles as they fought the onset of rigour even as they lifted his arms and flexed his hands. The stretch of jaw muscles. The shuddering snap as his teeth clamped shut around the young police officer's throat" (54). Helpless, trapped in a body that "no longer belonged to him [but which] existed around him. He existed within. Disconnected from control but still connected to every single nerve and sensory organ" (55), Maberry's zombies are startlingly reminiscent of Poe's and Lever's protagonists: helpless witnesses to the fate of their bodies. The Cartesian/liberal humanist split between the mind and body is maintained in these stories, and the horror that is played out is that of the breakdown of the order that it posits: the failure of the "self, the consciousness, the personality, the everything" to break away from the "lifeless clay" (Maberry 2014, 18). Tethered to the body, the self is "hovering, floating, aware but no longer in control of the meat and bone that had once been its home [...] a ghost haunting that stolen home of flesh and blood" (18). Like the consciousness/body split that characterised the nineteenth-century stories, Maberry's zombies are still very much liberal humanist figures in which the mind, the essence, of the individual is understood to be separate and separable from the body. These divided figures play out Gothic fears of a liminal state: both/neither alive and/nor dead. Both Maberry and Lever use the image of the "self" as a ghost, as an immaterial entity held hostage by their all-too-material bodies. Looking into the eyes of a zombie, Maberry's protagonist, Dez, "thought that she caught the flicker of something else; it was as if she looked through the grimy glass of a haunted house and saw the pale, pleading face of a ghost. In the second before the thing lunged at her, Dez saw the shadow of the little girl screaming at her from the endless darkness" (2011, 250). The shadow of the self that Maberry describes here reinforces the nightmare of the mind/body split that has plagued humanist culture and finds its Gothic image in these stories of live burial and haunted zombies.

The posthuman, neo-Gothic zombie, though, shifts the emphasis in these stories away from the mind/body, material/immaterial binary and even, impossibly, away from the spectre of death. If traditional zombies are "Thanatos in drag" (Leverette 2008, 195) whose persistence represents a "mourning of life" (Abbott 2016, 160), then the trajectory that contemporary zombie narratives have followed, from Romero's monsters to Maberry's unwilling passengers in their highjacked bodies to Kenemore's Peter Mellor who describes himself as "an unusually intelligent, self-aware zombie" (2011, 160) who is able to wonder "was I 'human'? Did I dare make that claim?" (160) shifts the paradigm of the living dead as unambiguous other to an almost infinitely variable series of characters whose narrative presence works through the implications of the New Death, of posthuman fantasies of disembodiment and of the limits of online subjectivity. Peter's embodied existence beyond death, his persistence as a speaking, thinking subject challenges the continued viability of binary definitions in a digitally networked world. The self-aware zombie represents a move from the referentiality and stability of the horror/Gothic zombie narrative to a neo-Gothic reimagining of the nature of the subgenre itself.

Zombie narratives are, like most Gothic texts, formulaic and referential. Traditional zombie stories are characterised by self-reflexive gestures to the zombie canon as well as the repetition of standard tropes, plots and characters. When the zombie becomes the self-defining centre of the narrative, though, it disrupts that referential chain. This disruption is more than simple reversal in which the monster becomes the self and the human becomes the other; it is a Deleuzian rupture in which the stable meanings of the traditional Gothic narrative explode outward, spiralling away from the original text but always and significantly connected to it. Traditional zombie narratives are built on the establishment and maintenance of binary oppositions, but the introduction of the self-aware zombie as the focaliser of the text refuses the stability of that binary, refuses the simplicity of that structure and, instead, reveals "human" as a performative narrative and discursive position. In Kenemore's *Zombie, Ohio*, Peter was a philosophy professor at a small liberal arts college who wakes up from a car accident to find himself in the middle of a zombie uprising, and himself as one of the undead: "No pulse. No sensation. No breathing. I was dead. Except, of course, I *wasn't*. I was walking and talking and thinking (to some extent, anyway) [...] But I *was*. I *existed*. Didn't I? A line from my training in philosophy came to me: 'I think, therefore I am.' [...] I was definitely thinking. So I definitely *was*. But *what* was I?" (2011, 30). If the human is a "subject (one who is conscious of his/her self) marked by rational thinking/intelligence, who is able to plot his/her own cause of action depending on his/her needs, desires, wishes, and, as a result of his/her actions, produces history" (Nayar 2014, 5), then Peter, in spite of being clearly dead (the top of his skull was shaved off during the accident and his body decomposes as the narrative progresses) and reanimated, should still be "human." He is also a zombie, also dead, also animate, also thinking, also craving brains; "what" he is is a series of supplements. That the zombie can define *himself* and, perhaps more significantly, define himself as possibly human initiates a series of posthuman speculations about the category "human" as an assemblage, as a construct that is defined by exclusions, "expelling the animal, the plant and the machine" (30). Peter's contemplations about what he is, though, are not structured around exclusions, but are assembled through inclusions. He is alive *and* he is dead *and* he is moral *and* he is thinking and the list goes on. What Peter *is* refuses categorisation. He is not only the singular thinking zombie in the novel, he is a narrative: stories are told about him, he tells stories about himself, to himself, creating his "I" as a series of supplementary narrative gestures. Like *Warm Bodies'* R, Peter and other self-aware zombie narrators are discursive monsters,[5] playing with the instabilities of definition and the fault lines of generic conventions.

While questions of what it is to be human appear in almost every encounter with the zombie, when the zombie takes on the role of organising consciousness in the text, the terms of those questions shift and shatter under the weight of multiple, even infinite, possibilities. Its subjectivity pushes backward and outward into the meta-narrative of the subgenre. Without the stabilising gravity of the binary, the zombie loses its metaphorical status as monster/symbol/excess/"fantasy screen." The resulting metonymic zombie opens up questions and associations, not simply erasing or straddling, but refusing the narrative, ontological and generic lines that have shaped the traditional zombie narrative. So these works become unpredictable, extrageneric and not so much referential as associative. Narratives that are controlled by self-aware zombies spiral off into any number of different directions. Daryl Gregory's *Raising Stony Mayhall* resists the very corporeality of the zombie. Stony continues to exist as a disembodied consciousness at the end of the novel, persisting in an "accidental afterlife" (2011, 412) in which he can communicate with his family and participate in the lives of his community. In other works, like Corey Redekop's *Husk* (2012) and Marion's *Warm Bodies*, subjectivity is thoroughly embodied. Marion's zombies experience the memories of the people they kill when they eat their brains and Redekop's zombies continue to live in their own brains, even when those brains are fragmented, consumed and discarded. In these works, the zombie's ordering consciousness disorders the expectations of the subgenre at once drawing on the tropes and rupturing their meanings.

The metonymic nature of the self-aware zombie infects its narrative then, rendering it metonymic in form as well. There are no clear generic conventions for this figure: they participate in and reinforce traditional elements of the subgenre even as they reorient and disrupt it. The metonymic form reflects on the ways in which information and identities can be multiplied and dispersed, fragmented and assembled online. It is through the figure of the self-aware zombie that, through its destabilised reflection of issues of identity in twenty-first century networked culture, humanity, posthumanity, articulates and neo-Gothically reimagines these complex relations in a form that, itself, refuses to conform to a stable generic formula. They are themselves agents of misrecognition.

It would seem paradoxical that the zombie, of all potential monsters, could serve as the monstrous manifestation of twenty-first century anxieties and preoccupations about the layered implications of life in a digitised world which "promotes a culture of consumerist individualism that has refashioned global subjectivity itself—the neoliberal subject being presented as a fluid, mobile, and hybridised entity whose traditional markers of identity (class, ethnicity, region, gender, or sexuality) have been deemed irrelevant" (Blake and Aldana Reyes 2016, 5). Posthuman fantasies of dispersed, incorporeal existence "remind us that embodiment becomes more complex and more diffuse" (Jones 2010, 192) as the varied technological and scientific interventions of the twenty-first century bring into being what had previously only been the stuff of science fiction. Technologies that enable online subjectivity, technologies that turn death into an ambiguous, undefinable state, destabilise definitions of what it means to be human, even what it means to be alive, shifting the ground from clearly (if problematically) insisting on ontological categories of consciousness, responsiveness, memory, identity to dispersing these definitions onto machines, or medically or pharmacologically assisted bodies. But, for now at least, disembodiment can only be a "powerful illusion" (Hayles 1999, 47) because, as Hayles argues, these technologies are, themselves embedded in complex materialities—materialities of both the networks and the users—that are interdependent and inextricably connected. The self-aware zombie explores the Gothic implications of human subjectivity in neoliberal networked culture, unsettling the cybersubject's posthuman fantasies of disembodiment with its all-too embodied disruption of the binary constructions that underpin those fantasies.

Notes

1 By this term I mean the sort of zombie that George Romero introduced into Western popular culture in *Night of the Living Dead* (1968).

2 I am using "self-aware" here rather than "sentient" or "conscious" because this term reflects on the specificity of definitions of human ontology that I think characterises these figures. As I will

argue here, the zombie reflects and reflects on specific anxieties about the status of humanity, human life and definitions of humanity.

3 Translated by Herbrechter (2013, 96) from David Le Breton's *l'Adieu au Corps* (1999).

4 Rowland's Angel Crawford is the exception here: She first appears in the narrative as a down-and-out drug addict who, after her death and reanimation, becomes gainfully employed and begins to take college classes. For Angel, zombification means upward mobility.

5 See Anya Heise-Von Der Lippe (2018) for a nuanced discussion of the ways in which language and self-construction work in *Warm Bodies*.

Bibliography

Abbott, Stacey. *Undead Apocalypse: Vampires and Zombies in the 21st Century*. Edinburgh: Edinburgh University Press, 2016.

Alberto, Maria. "Forging Posthuman Identities in Comic Mitchell's *In the Flesh*." In *Posthuman Gothic*, edited by Anya Heise-von der Lippe, 109–24. Cardiff: University of Wales Press, 2017.

Arnold, Michael, et al. *Death and Digital Media*. New York: Routledge, 2018.

Becker, Robin. *Brains: A Zombie Memoir*. 1994. New York: HarperCollins, 2010.

Behlmer, George K. "Grave Doubts: Victorian Medicine, Moral Panic, and the Signs of Death." *Journal of British Studies* 42 (2003): 206–35.

Blake, Linnie. "'Are We Worth Saving? You Tell Me': Neoliberalism, Zombies, and the failure of Free Trade." *Gothic Studies* 17, no. 2 (2015): 26–41.

———. "Catastrophic Events and Queer Northern Villages: Zombie Pharmacology *In the Flesh*." In *Neoliberal Gothic: International Gothic in the Neoliberal Age*, edited by Linnie Blake and Agnieszka Soltysik Monnet, 104–21. Manchester, UK: Manchester University Press, 2017.

Blake, Linnie, and Xavier Aldana Reyes. Introduction to *Digital Horror: Haunted Technologies, Network Panic and the Found Footage Phenomenon*, edited by Linnie Blake and Xavier Aldana Reyes, 1–16. London: L. B. Tauris, 2016.

Botting, Fred. "Candygothic." In *The Gothic*, edited by Fred Botting, 133–51. Cambridge, UK: D.S. Brewer, 2001.

———. *The Gothic*, 2nd ed. London: Routledge, 2014.

Braidotti, Rosi. *The Posthuman*. Cambridge, UK: Polity Press, 2013.

Brown, Wendy. "Neoliberalism and the End of Liberal Democracy." In *Edgework: Critical Essays on Knowledge and Politics*, 37–59. Princeton, NJ: Princeton University Press, 2005.

Chun, Wendy Hui Kong. *Control and Freedom: Power and Paranoia in the Age of Fiber Optics*. Cambridge: MIT Press, 2006.

Currie, Andrew, dir. *Fido*. Roadside Attractions/Samuel Goldwyn, 2007.

Edwards, Justin D. Introduction to *Technologies of the Gothic in Literature and Culture: Technogothics*, edited by Justin D. Edwards, 1–16. New York: Routledge, 2015.

Fresco, Victor. *Santa Clarita Diet*. Netflix, 2017–19.

Greenberg, Harvey Roy. "Heimlich Maneuvers: On a Certain Tendency of Horror and Speculative Cinema." *PSYART: A Hyperlink Journal for the Psychological Study of the Arts* 7 (September 2001). December 6, 2013. http://psyartjournal.com/article/show/greenberg-heimlich_maneuvers_on_a_certain_tendency.

Gregory, Daryl. *Raising Stony Mayhall*. New York: Del Rey Books, 2011.

Halberstam, Judith. *Skin Shows: Gothic Horror and the Technology of Monsters*. Durham, NC: Duke University Press, 1995.

Hayles, N. Katherine. *How We Became Posthuman: Virtual Bodies in Cybernetics, Literature, and Informatics*. Chicago: University of Chicago Press, 1999.

Heil, John. *From an Ontological Point of View*. Oxford: Clarendon Press, 2003.

Heise-Von Der Lippe, Anya. "'I Keep Saying Brains': Posthuman Zombie Narratives." *Horror Studies* 9, no. 1 (2018): 69–85.

Herbrechter, Stefan. *Posthumanism: A Critical Analysis*. London: Bloomsbury, 2013.

Jones, Steve. "Technologies of Isolation: Apocalypse and Self in Kurosawa Kiyoshi's *Kairo*." *Japanese Studies* 30, no. 2 (2010): 185–98.

Kenemore, Scott. *Zombie, Ohio: A Tale of the Undead*. New York: Skyhorse Publishing, 2011.

Lauro, Sarah. Juliet. "Introduction: Wander and Wonder in Zombieland." In *Zombie Theory: A Reader*, edited by Sarah Juliet Lauro, vii–xxiii. Minneapolis: University of Minnesota Press, 2017.

Lever, Charles. "Post-Mortem Recollections of a Medical Lecturer." 1836. In *Gothic Evolutions: Poetry, Tales, Context, Theory*, edited by Corina Wagner, 195–200. Peterborough, ON: Broadview Press, 2014.

Leverette, Marc. "The Funk of Forty Thousand Years; or, How the (Un)Dead Get Their Groove On." In *Zombie Culture: Autopsies of the Living Dead*, edited by Shawn McIntosh and Marc Leverette, 185–212. Lenham: Scarecrow, 2008.

Luckhurst, Roger. "Biomedical Horror: New Death and the New Undead." In *Technologies of the Gothic in Literature and Culture: Technogothics*, edited by Justin D. Edwards, 84–98. New York: Routledge, 2015.

Maberry, Jonathan. *Dead of Night: A Zombie Novel*. New York: St. Martin's Griffin, 2011.

———. *Fall of Night*. New York: St. Martin's Press, 2014.

Macfarlane, Karen E. "The Monstrous House of Gaga." In *The Gothic in Contemporary Literature and Popular Culture: PopGoth*, edited by Justin D. Edwards, 114–34. New York: Routledge, 2012.

———. "Zombies and the Viral Web." *Horror Studies* 9, no. 2 (2018): 231–47.

Mangham, Andrew. "Buried Alive: The Gothic Awakening of Taphephobia." *Journal of Literature and Science* 3, no. 1 (2010): 10–22.

Marion, Isaac. *Warm Bodies*. New York: Emily Bestler Books, 2011.

Mittman, Asa Simon. "Introduction: The Impact of Monsters and Monster Studies." In *The Ashgate Research Companion to Monsters and the Monstrous*, edited by Asa Simon Mittman with Peter J. Dendle, 1–14. Farnham: Ashgate, 2013.

Monbiot, George. "Neoliberalism: The Ideology at the Root of All Our Problems." *The Guardian*, April 15, 2016. https://www.theguardian.com/books/2016/apr/15/neoliberalism-ideology-problem-george-monbiot.

Murnane, Barry. "George Best's Dead Livers: Transplanting the Gothic into Biotechnology and Medicine." In *Technologies of the Gothic in Literature and Culture: Technogothics*, edited by Justin D. Edwards, 113–26. New York: Routledge, 2015.

———. "*In the Flesh* and the Gothic Pharmacology of Everyday Life; or Into and Out of the Gothic." *Text Matters* 6, no. 6 (2016): 227–44.

Nayar, Pramod K. *Posthumanism*. Cambridge, UK: Polity Press, 2014.

O'Bannon, Dan, dir. *Return of the Living Dead*. Hemdale Film Corporation, Orion Pictures, 1985.

Poe, Edgar Allan. "The Premature Burial." 1844. In *18 Best Stories by Edgar Allan* Poe, edited by Vincent Price and Chandler Brossard, 58–72. New York: Doubleday, 1965.

Redekop, Corey. *Husk*. Toronto: ECW Press, 2012.

Romero, George A. *Night of the Living Dead*. Image Ten, Continental Distributing, 1968.

———, dir. *Night of the Living Dead*. 21st Century Film Corporation, Columbia Pictures, 1990.

———. *Land of the Dead*. Atmosphere Entertainment, Universal Pictures, 2005.

Romero, George A., and Susanna Sparrow. *Dawn of the Dead*. New York: St. Martin's Press, 1978.

Rowland, Diana. *My Life as a White Trash Zombie*. New York: DAW Books, 2011.

Shaw, Debra Benita. "Technology, Death and the Cultural Imagination." *Science as Culture* 18, no. 3 (2009): 251–60.

Spooner, Catherine. *Post-Millennial Gothic: Comedy, Romance and the Rise of Happy Gothic*. London: Bloomsbury, 2017.

Stern, Megan. "'Yes:—No:—I Have Been Sleeping—and Now—Now—I Am Dead': Undeath, the Body and Medicine." *Studies in History and Philosophy of Biological and Biomedical Sciences* 39, no. 3 (2008): 347–54.

Swanson, Carl. "'The Only Metaphor Left': Colson Whitehead's *Zone One* and Zombie Narrative Form." *Genre* 47, no. 3 (2014): 379–405.

Thomas, Rob, et al., producers. *iZombie*. Spondoolie Productions, Warner Bros, Television, 2015–19.

Vervaeke, John, Christopher Mastropietro and Filip Miscevic. "A New Zeitgeist." In *Zombies in Western Culture: A Twenty-First Century Crisis*, edited by John Vervaeke, Christopher Mastropietro and Filip Miscevic, 1–8. Cambridge, UK: Open Book Publishers, 2017.

Vint, Sheryl. "Abject Posthumanism: Neoliberalism, Biopolitics, and Zombies." In *Monster Culture in the 21st Century: A Reader*, edited by Marina Levina and Diem My T. Bui, 133–46. London: Bloomsbury Academic. 2013.

Wellington, David. *Monster Island: A Zombie Novel*. Philadelphia: Running Press, 2006.

Whitehead, Colson. *Zone One*. Toronto: Doubleday, 2011.

Wyile, Herb. "Neoliberalism, Austerity, and the Academy." *English Studies in Canada* 39, no. 4 (2013): 29–31.

Zamora, Daniel. "How Neoliberalism Reinvented Democracy: An Interview with Niklas Olsen." *Jacobin*, April 2019. https://www.jacobinmag.com/2019/04/neoliberalism-democracy-consumer-sovereignty.

Chapter Nine

NEO-GOTHIC DINOSAURS AND THE HAUNTING OF HISTORY

Jessica Gildersleeve and Nike Sulway

Marie-Luise Kohlke and Christian Gutleben have identified the neo-Victorian Gothic as a mode particularly suited to political and ethical cultural engagement, precisely for the way in which it disrupts any "uniform" contemporary iteration of the Gothic; by returning to the past, the neo-Gothic "rekindle[s] an intensely disturbing desire that unsettles norms and redefines boundaries once more" (2012, 2). Indeed, the Gothic[1] more generally attends to the social and cultural problems faced in the contemporary moment, precisely through its interest in the strange, the abject and the Other. This chapter examines the dinosaur narrative as a particular kind of neo-Gothic uniquely positioned to address the collapse of moral, spatial and historical boundaries. Addressing a selection of early dinosaur narratives, as well as the range of films in the *Jurassic Park* series (1993–2018), this chapter will explore the dinosaur as a figure of the limit of our Gothic imagination, that is, the point at which the known world reaches the boundaries of the unknown or other. In particular, however, the chapter will focus on the specific engagement with Gothic tropes in the most recent *Jurassic Park* film, *Jurassic World: Fallen Kingdom* (2018): the isolated mansion, the rich benefactor, the orphan child, the presence of family secrets and the haunting or stalking figure. In the embedding of the conventional Gothic within a contemporary context concerned with environmental collapse, the dinosaur and its impossible presence is reinvigorated as a problem exceeding our capacity for conservative solution.

The *Jurassic Park* films, and in particular *Jurassic Park: Fallen Kingdom*, are perhaps most commonly and readily recognised (and marketed) as works of science fiction, rather than Gothic or neo-Gothic works; however, in their focus on the moral and ethical questions raised by scientific research, and particularly with the moral problems associated with creating (and destroying) artificial, unnatural or hybridised life, these works harken back to a long-standing narrative tradition in which the Gothic and science fiction intermingle.

Perhaps the most obvious precursor of this intermingling of the Gothic and science fiction is Mary Shelley's *Frankenstein, or The Modern Prometheus* (1818), in which the scientific research of the eponymous character results in the creation of an unnamed (and perhaps unnameable) monster who threatens the integrity of Frankenstein's mind, body and family. As in the *Jurassic Park* films, *Frankenstein*'s central scientific novum is the combination and reanimation (or de-extinction) of previously extinct bodies.[2] Both texts focus on and remain concerned with the incapacity of the scientist-creator to control or contain the resulting monstrous creations. *Frankenstein*, as with the *Jurassic Park* films, reveals a concern with uncanny, unnatural and uncontrolled reproduction and with the collapse and reformation of family structures.

This mingling of the Gothic and science fiction, linked to a strong focus on both the morality of scientific research generally and reproductive or life-creating technology in particular, as well as questions of maternity, family and reproduction, is echoed across a range of texts. These include works such as the *Alien* franchise (1979–2017), with its ruined space stations, impregnating aliens, uncanny mothers and orphaned children, and Octavia Butler's *Lilith's Brood* novel trilogy (1987–89), which also focuses on the ethical and moral problems that are a result of interracial and interspecies hybrid reproduction in a Gothic cultural landscape of familial secrets, the haunting figures of the Ooloi, unnatural pregnancies and "half-breed" children, and a concern with the abject nature of reproductive bodies and processes. The tradition thus exhibits a persistent concern with uncanny or unnatural reproduction, and in particular with the ethical and moral challenges faced within familial and social structures when the de-extinct, reanimated and/or hybrid offspring of the future refuse to live within the moral architecture of their creators when they reject their biological, social and moral heritage.

Despite our perpetual fascination with prehistoric creatures, dinosaurs feature surprisingly infrequently in contemporary narratives, perhaps because of the imagined consequences such a confrontation might produce. Indeed, for Allen A. Debus, "in fiction, dinosaurs and other prehistoric animals reflect our aspirations, human tendencies, contemporary understanding of nature, earth history and, perhaps especially, our fears" (2006, 18). Jules Verne's *Journey to the Centre of the Earth* (1864) is perhaps the earliest work to feature dinosaurs. The intrepid explorers of Verne's narrative first encounter the bones of dinosaurs and other prehistoric creatures, such as mastodons, before witnessing a violent ocean struggle between an *Icthyosaurus* and a *Plesiosaurus*, creatures that at first confuse the young narrator because of their apparent combination of various characteristics of other animals, such that they become a kind of hybrid of the known world of the surface. This hybridity is the source of the travellers' fear of a prehistoric human—part-humanoid, part-ape. Indeed, it is this creature that appears to provoke a greater threat to their safety than the thrashing dinosaurs who had ignored their presence; its uncanny familiarity is such that they recognise the creature's potential for human violence and aggression.

Arthur Conan Doyle's novel *The Lost World* (1912) may be seen in some ways—not least in its title—as the clearest predecessor of the *Jurassic Park* novels by Michael Crichton (*Jurassic Park* (1990) and *The Lost World* (1995)) and their later adaptation as a highly successful film franchise. In Doyle's narrative, a group of scientists travel to a South American jungle where it is rumoured dinosaurs still exist. As in *Journey to the Centre of the Earth*, it is not only the dinosaurs that are to be feared, but the human characters as the group becomes entangled in a war between two tribes, the most violent of which appears to have similar features to the human-ape of Verne's novel. The explorers are ultimately able to escape and return to England with a stolen *Pterodactyl* egg, determined to prove the existence of the dinosaurs; however, the baby *Pterodactyl* escapes in the tussle of the crowd, flying free over the city. Doyle's final image of the uncontrollability of the dinosaurs and of such explorers or scientists recurs a number of times in the *Jurassic Park* films, as a birdlike shadow crosses an ocean sunset, disturbing our sense of the familiar and representing the disruption to the known world to come.

Finally, in Ray Bradbury's short story "A Sound of Thunder" (1952), dinosaurs become the favoured target of time-travelling, exotic animal hunters. Although they are careful to kill only those creatures for which death is momentarily imminent, one panicked hunter steps off the designated path, causing an unnecessary dinosaur death. The party returns to their own time to discover irrevocable change, including the suggested presence of dinosaurs in the modern age. The anxiety produced at the end of this story is thus a neo-Gothic one as the thought-dead past returns to disrupt and reconfigure the "hypermodern" (Kohlke and Gutleben 2012, 2) present.

These three examples describe the first two "'ages' of popular interest in dinosaurs" described by Debus: that is, "the traditional life-through-time phase of emphasis, roughly 1800 to World War II's aftermath—a plausible beginning of the Anthropocene epoch"; this is followed by the "inner turmoil" of the Cold War "and the dawning realisation that mankind might create its own extinction—gone like the dinosaurs […] in a puff of smoke" (2016, 199). In each of these early dinosaur narratives, then, it is not simply the dinosaurs themselves that figure the threat; rather, it is unregulated and unethical human behaviour that causes concern at best, or horrific disruption at worst. The third phase, however, "emphasises when dinosaurs assumed a more humanoid guise and configuration, thus enhancing their ability to directly *forewarn* (not simply through metaphor) but also by relying on their majesty, innate language and intelligence to remind us of what happened to them" (199; emphasis in original). It is perhaps for this reason that two particular figures in the *Jurassic Park* films take such a hold. The first of these are the *Velociraptors* first featured in *Jurassic Park* (1993), and later metamorphosing into the *Indominus Rex* and *Indoraptor* of *Jurassic World* (2015) and *Fallen Kingdom*—they are "veritable monsters not only due to their inherent savagery, but also for their crafty, menacing intellect […] qualities far too human-like for our comfort" (Debus 2006, 126). That the *Raptors* open doors with their claws, function as a family or community and stand almost eye-to-eye with a human adult are all ways in which they mimic the human. The *Raptors* are most closely echoed, however, by young Maisie Lockwood (Isabella Sermon), the human clone equivalent to the dinosaurs in *Fallen Kingdom*—herself an "unholy" figure, to borrow the term of John Hammond, the original creator of Jurassic Park. By tracing these uncanny transgressions of time, space and the human/animal, in the first part of this chapter, we will consider the ways in which the *Jurassic Park* films seek to manage such breaches. We then turn to a more specific consideration of the construction of familial values, particularly motherhood, as central to the films' conservatism. Ultimately, the neo-Gothicism of these films is at work to return us to questions of human power and responsibility but places these within a conservative discourse of love and compassion.

The central conceit of each of the *Jurassic Park* films concerns the collapse of spatial and temporal boundaries, such as the failure or determined rupture of the fences and walls designed to contain the dinosaurs, which then permits them to invade the space of the humans. However, it also describes the dinosaurs' originary return. Created through

DNA splicing in which the dinosaur DNA is combined with various other animals in order to bring it to life, and from the first shot of the first film in which a small reptilian eye is exposed by a claw probing at the crack in its egg, the dinosaurs break down the boundaries of past and present through their uncanny return. It is therefore this ability to permeate such boundaries—that is, their Gothic abjection—that constitutes the dinosaurs' threat, not only to human life, but to social, moral, temporal and spatial order. Indeed, the *Jurassic Park* films do not only call up the abject in their plots; rather, they are abject in their very generic hybridity, their splicing of the Gothic and its progeny, science fiction. To be sure, even as each narrative is ostensibly presented according to the generic conventions of science fiction, they are always and everywhere interrupted by its Gothic foundations. In the most recent film in the series, *Fallen Kingdom*, these foundations resist containment, dominating the screen in the depiction of the isolated castle and its dungeons, museums and craggy cliffs, as well as its uncanny families. It is this explicit return of the tropes and conventions of the Gothic within the science fiction narrative that makes *Fallen Kingdom*'s abjection neo-Gothic. By returning to the genre's most readily identifiable roots, the film constructs a desire to return to traditional narrative and by extension traditional values. Its conservatism, therefore, implores for the restoration of narrative and moral order, made explicit by chaos theorist Dr. Ian Malcolm (Jeff Goldblum) asserting this very same desire in the court hearing that frames the narrative.

To be sure, the dinosaurs of the *Jurassic Park* series constitute a literal irruption of the thought-dead past into the ongoing present. In this sense, they are spectral or liminal figures, a point underscored by the giant hologram of a dinosaur that fills the atrium of the reception building in *Jurassic World*. That Claire Dearing (Bryce Dallas Howard), the Park's operations manager, simply walks through this ghostly image, rather than regarding it with the awe of the others in the room, suggests a disrespect for this uncanny return associated with her authorisation of the creation of the *Indominus Rex*, a dinosaur itself made spectral by its ability to camouflage and thus, like a ghost, to appear as if from nowhere, as when it fools Claire into thinking that it has escaped from its cage. The dinosaurs can also be read as a refiguration of the uncanny undead of classic Gothic horror films, such as zombies and vampires: they are the resurrected dead.

It is in this sense that Maisie is the human equivalent of the dinosaurs. She is the cloned granddaughter of Benjamin Lockwood (James Cromwell), a nostalgic reproduction of his beloved daughter, and therefore a ghostly repetition of the past. She is the image from Lockwood's old photographs made real. That "Maisie" means "pearl" suggests the way in which she is cultured or created, merely a simulacra of the real or natural. However, Maisie is also, of course, a child, and thus symbolically representative of the future in general as well as Lockwood's legacy in particular. That she survives the film with her newly created family—"parents" Claire and Owen Green (Chris Pratt), Claire's lover and the animal behaviourist responsible for training the *Velociraptors*—suggests a disrupted future, because it is one in which she should not exist. Indeed, when they return to Lockwood Manor with the captured dinosaurs, Eli Mills (Rafe Spall) identifies the pair as "the parents of the new world," meaning a world inhabited by de-extinct weaponised dinosaurs trained to obey human commands. Yet, that the film depicts them as Maisie's pseudo-parents further underscores the similarity between Maisie and the dinosaurs. Ultimately, it is Maisie who is responsible for freeing the dinosaurs trapped in her grandfather's basement dungeon moments after Claire and Owen have silently agreed that it is safest to let them die, asserting "I had to [save them]. They're alive. Like me." In part such a view expresses a conservative pro-life sentiment akin to that expressed by the judge in the framing courtroom scenes, when he asks Malcolm if they should leave the fate of the dinosaurs in God's hands. However, the point also aligns with the dinosaur narrative's overarching warning about the humanoid threat of these creatures. That is, it is not simply that the freed dinosaurs now represent a threat to the human population as a new predator at the top of the food chain, but that their abject human–animal characteristics give them the power to choose their behaviour, most clearly exhibited when Blue, the most human of Owen's *Raptors*, chooses freedom over joining her pseudo-father in effective captivity.

As a function of its neo-Gothicism, then, the *Jurassic Park* series not only suggests a fear of the return of the past, but also of the way in which the entirely curated or created, rather than resurrected, dinosaurs—the *Indominus Rex* and the *Indoraptor*—represent a literal and embodied collision of the clearly defined past and the blurred and abject future within a single body. This is the "neo-Jurassic" period to which Malcolm refers in *Fallen Kingdom*; the new era of Jurassic World is one in which our conceptualisations of time, history and the future no longer apply—indeed, one in which they might be entirely eradicated with the death of the human race and the victorious "de-extinction" of the dinosaurs. It is in the face of this threat that many of the paleo-scientists in each film take on the role of moral guardians—not of the dinosaurs, but of human history and civilisation. They are scientists of the long-dead, of bones and archaeological sites, now confronted with living, breathing, breeding, fighting, live animals. As such, the palaeontologists, in particular, are often resistant to the ethics of the Jurassic Park project: to them, dinosaurs belong to and have their proper place in the past, meaning that they are also improper, abject bodies in the present.

For this reason, the parks are set up with a strong emphasis on what are thought to be impenetrable boundaries between the landscapes that belong to the dinosaurs and the human spaces. However, since, in their abjection, "Gothic texts […] create porous worlds where social, political, spiritual, physical, geographical, and personal boundaries are […] permeable" (Yang and Healey 2016, 3), it is always true in the films that problems arise when either species transgress these boundaries. For example, the scenes that take place in the outdoors of the islands emphasise their primitiveness, their archaic and uncivilised wildness, including volcanoes, wild storms and impenetrable jungles. Within these spaces, which are the proper spaces of the dinosaurs, the humans are most at risk. "Gothic landscapes," Sharon Rose Yang and Kathleen Healey have it, "are a lens by which cultures reflect back their darkness hidden from the light of consciousness" (5). As such, moving into these wild spaces results in increased threats to human life and thus often constitutes the site of human death: this is the case for each occasion when the human characters engage in pseudo-safari expeditions in small vehicles. When such expeditions take place at night or during a storm, events that involve "power and sensory obfuscation […] leav[ing] characters unable to orient themselves, unable to assert human power to perceive a shifting, even hostile, nature, let alone to control or define it"

(5–6), these threats are increased. This is described, for example, in the first encounters with the dinosaurs in *Jurassic Park*, such as when the *Velociraptor*s are delivered to their pen during a stormy night, devouring a park worker who ventures too close, and when the *Tyrannosaurus Rex* escapes its large, fenced field, terrorising Dr. Alan Grant (Sam Neill) and his young charges. The scenes inside the "human" spaces, however, emphasise technological, corporate, capitalist and militaristic aspects of human civilisation. Within these spaces, dinosaurs are the interlopers who are out of place and most under threat. Though they still embody a threat to humans here, it is also where they are mostly likely to be caged, beaten, shot and killed. The dinosaurs are mostly defeated or contained within such human or civilised spaces.

Yet, the space occupied and ruled by the dinosaurs grows and expands as the series progresses, a Gothic reversal of human colonisation, until finally at the end of *Fallen Kingdom* they encroach on the human space to the extent that they threaten the human species. In *Jurassic Park*, it takes only one (Gothic) storm to destroy power to the fences that contain the dinosaurs and thus to enable their freedom. Very quickly, the distinction between inside and outside, the human space and the dinosaur space, the civilised and the wild, is collapsed, made abject, as rain floods the park's buildings and the *Velociraptor*s enter the cafeteria and kitchen. This distinction is never restored, so that in *The Lost World* (1997), the *Tyrannosaurus Rex* escapes the ship that has transported it to San Diego, wreaking havoc on the city and even invading the suburban, domestic space as it searches for its offspring, while in *Jurassic World* Zach and Gray discover the original reception building of Jurassic Park, now taken over by jungle. Moreover, the dinosaur space appears to expand in a kind of uncanny mutation. Although Isla Nublar had in *Jurassic Park* seemed to be an isolated, singular place, the later films in the franchise reveal that Isla Nublar is part of a small archipelago of five similar islands, *Las Cinco Muertes* (the five deaths), across which the dinosaurs now roam and reproduce, uncontrolled by human intervention. More particularly, each of these islands can also be seen to operate as a kind of Gothic estate: each is home to a large manse, surrounded by parks, fields and enclosures for its exotic pets; moreover, the failure of this estate means that it becomes a ruin out of which is born the monstrous progeny of a new park.

Lockwood's estate in *Fallen Kingdom* can thus be seen not as an anomaly but rather as the latest in this line of neo-Gothic reproduction. Although it is located in California, the extreme long shots of the mansion's position on a cliff make it appear as if it, too, is on an isolated island. That this large, old and imposing building with the highly ornate façade of Gothic architecture is usually shown from the outside at night, in the rain, with blurred and flickering lights in the windows, reinforces its mimicry of the storms that lash the jungles of Isla Nublar and Isla Sorna in the earlier films. It is this Gothic estate that houses (or contains) Maisie, the humanoid-dinosaur equivalent, who is never apparently permitted beyond its walls. Like the estates of Isla Nublar and Isla Sorna, moreover, this uncanny estate is not simply a home, but also includes a number of non-domestic spaces, such as a museum with exhibits of various dinosaur species either as articulated skeletons or in dioramas with suitable painted and plaster scenery. It also features an underground genetics lab in the sub-basement, similar to that on the earlier islands, and in which Dr. Henry Wu (B. D. Wong) creates the dinosaurs; a series of cells for keeping imprisoned dinosaurs; and a massive auction room, or theatre, in the round. The Lockwood estate therefore masks its secret function, suppressing its most obvious sites of imprisonment and scientific experiment in its multiple and expansive basements, just as Isla Nublar had masked the experimental island of Isla Sorna. It is in these out-of-sight spaces that the most serious moral transgressions are committed and where we thus reach the limits of ethical behaviours.

Reaching the depths of the Lockwood estate thus constitutes our arrival at the most significant ethical questions raised by the neo-Gothicism of the *Jurassic Park* films and where the direct conflict between creating, causing or permitting life or death takes place, both literally in this space as Claire, Owen and Maisie debate freeing the trapped dinosaurs, and within the narrative frame, as this decision is shown alongside Malcolm's determination that "we altered the course of natural history. This is a correction." That Maisie is directly implicated in this discussion is telling, for it points up the ways in which it is the humanoid aspect of the dinosaurs that makes them both most sympathetic and most threatening. The decision in Lockwood's basement is an echo of the earlier scene in which the erupting volcano on Isla Nublar destroys the remaining dinosaurs on the island, itself an echo of their original extinction 65 million years ago. The clouds of smoke frame a lone *Brachiosaurus* standing on the dock, apparently forlornly watching the boat, its last chance to escape, disappear. It is a tragic moment, underscored by the fact that the *Brachiosaurus* was the first full dinosaur seen in *Jurassic Park*, and thus bringing the reignited life of the dinosaurs full circle. But it is made most tragic by the *Brachiosaurus'* familiarity, by the way in which it is, if not entirely personified, at least made domesticated, safe or friendly, akin to a cow or an elephant. The tragic death of the *Brachiosaurus* as synecdoche for the dinosaurs as a whole suggests the way in which, over the past few decades, dinosaurs have "become an iconic, socially-culturally relevant breed of animals. The fact that dinosaurs were victimised by environmental devastation caused by an asteroid (or comet) impact at the peak of their evolutionary development cast them as the most tragic characters of all time" (Debus 2006, 146).[3]

Fallen Kingdom, as with many of the preceding films in the *Jurassic Park* franchise, reveals an uneasy fascination with uncontrolled reproduction, and in particular the uncontrolled and uncontrollable reproduction of the feminine. In one sense, as A. Robin Hoffman argues in relation to the films *Rosemary's Baby* (1968) and *Alien* (1979), *Fallen Kingdom* is fascinated by "humans potential to incubate, literally, their own destruction" (2011, 239). Perhaps more significantly, the film betrays both a fascination for, and an unease with, a future populated by female clones—a future in which male bodies are not necessary to ensure the futurity or survival of either human or dinosaur species, as well as one in which patriarchal and capitalist power and authority are not sufficient to control reproduction. This failure of reproductive control is a recurrent one in the *Jurassic Park* films: it is one of the key narrative triggers in the first film in which the ability of the all-female population of dinosaurs to reproduce (evidenced by the *Velociraptor* eggs Dr. Alan Grant finds in a nest), and their capacity to constantly escape the confines of the park's various enclosures, are what combine to make them an uncontrollable threat to the naïve dreams of John Hammond to produce a controlled, sterile, stable and profitable miracle. This problem recurs in each film, with the capacity of the female dinosaurs to both spontaneously reproduce "in the wild" and escape the control of their creator-owners perpetually both ignored or downplayed by the capitalists and patriarchs of the films. In *Fallen Kingdom*, the belief that the dinosaurs can and should be socially controlled is a persistent one, and one to which both the film's sympathetic characters and its antagonists ascribe. Here, control of the dinosaurs is strongly linked to the ethics of both social and biological parenting.

For the film's sympathetic characters, such as Owen, socialisation of the dinosaurs occurs within a protective, nurturing and curiosity-driven space. In flashbacks to Owen's work with Blue and her clone sisters as infants, Owen is shown being physically affectionate, feeding and playing with the dinosaurs. He describes the young Blue as "showing unprecedented signs of compliance" as well as signs of "concern, hyper-intelligence, cognitive bonding" and curiosity. Most significantly, Blue is described and shown as expressing empathy and familial care, comforting Owen when he displays signs of weakness rather than attacking him as her clone-sisters do. At the same time, it is clear that Owen's relationship with the dinosaurs is an ambivalent one. He is keenly aware of and alert to the threat of violence from his small charges, and is careful to teach the other humans responsible for the care of the dinosaurs not to let their guard down: not to put too much trust in the pseudo-familial, the pseudo-human bonds of caretaker and animal. While Owen displays affection for, admiration of and curiosity about his dinosaur daughters, he remains aware of their difference and of the magnitude of the threat they represent to human life. Twice during the film, he explicitly refuses to protect Blue: when Claire tries to convince him to come to the island and help to extract the dinosaurs, saving them from extinction, she tells him that Blue is alive. "You raised her, Owen," she says. "You spent years of your life working with her. You're just gonna let her die?" His reply is brief and nonchalant: "Well. Yeah." Later, as has already been discussed, both Owen and Claire make a decision not to save the dinosaurs trapped in the basement of Lockwood Estate.

While Owen recognises the limits of parental nurture in controlling the violence that is natural to the de-extinct dinosaurs, Henry Wu expresses a strong belief in the necessity for, and power of, nurture. Although Henry is a geneticist and biotechnologist, his faith in the capacity of science to create controllable weaponised dinosaurs is limited. As he tries to explain to Eli, genetic manipulation is a precise but also somewhat mysterious process. In a tense encounter with Eli in which he is pressured to provide genetic and scientific responses to Eli's military and economic desires, Henry asserts that "a wolf, genetically, is barely distinguishable from a bulldog, but within that grey area is art." For Henry, however, it is nurture (not nature) that is the essential missing ingredient in the creation of an ideally weaponised *Indoraptor*, and for that he requires Blue, a "behavioural specimen" hand-raised by Owen with the necessary qualities of "recognising authority" as well as "empathy, obedience, everything the prototype we have now is missing." As Henry tells Eli: "To get the next iteration under control it needs to form a familial bond with a closely related genetic link. It needs a mother!" Parenting here—specifically, mothering, with its implicit association of care, as opposed to fathering, more simply procreation—is a social means of instilling both a recognition of (male, military, capitalist) authority and obedience to that authority. But the mothering that Henry requires is not the natural or instinctive mothering that has occurred on Isla Nublar or any of the other islands, and which has resulted in a population of "wild" dinosaurs that are both too populous and too uncontrolled to be useful as much more than "seed money." He neither seeks nor values the mothering that has erupted outside of the control of military-industrial capitalist hetero-patriarchy of Jurassic Park. Instead, what he (and Eli) require is a result of unnatural, cross-species nurture: the mothering that a male human modelled for a female dinosaur.

The narrative problem of uncontrolled dinosaur reproduction is intriguingly echoed and refracted in considerations of the dismantling of family structures and legacies throughout the franchise, and in particular in *Fallen Kingdom*. Each of these considerations reflects persistent concerns, within both the Gothic and the neo-Gothic, and perhaps particularly in American iterations of both fields, with the dismantling of identity, and dissolution of the individual, the family and—by extension—the (patriarchal and capitalist) nation. As Martin argues, "The gothic coheres, if it can be said to cohere, around poetics (turns and tendencies in the dismantling of the national subject), around narrative structuration, and in its situation of the reader at the border of symbolic dissolution" (1998, vii). There are, in particular, three themes within the film that focus on these aspects of the neo-Gothic: the collapse or ruin of the patriarch's power; the recursive construction and destruction of pseudo-family units; and the dissolution of familial bloodlines and legacies as reflected in the figure of the motherless daughter.

The *Jurassic Park* films offer a series of paternalistic creators—father-Gods—whose power is substantial and even miraculous, but also a thing of the past.[4] From the first film's John Hammond to *Fallen Kingdom*'s Benjamin Lockwood, these doddering, benevolent, wealthy and loving, but naïve and ultimately powerless, grandfather figures are established as those who have, usually in the prehistory of the films, set in motion the creation of both the dinosaur populations and their own families and are attached to them, but have lost any of the control or authority they might once have possessed. Lockwood is Maisie's caretaker and protector, the coinventor of the genetic cloning technology that resulted in the de-extinction of dinosaurs, and a man of enormous wealth. Within the film he is shown as affectionate towards, but almost disinterested in, his "granddaughter," instead preferring to gaze nostalgically at photographs of his dead daughter and leave Maisie to the benevolent neglect of her nanny. In some ways, Maisie Lockwood is a literary echo of her namesake, Henry James' Maisie Farange (*What Maisie Knew* [1897]). Both Maisies are surrounded by and steeped in death: Maisie Lockwood in the death of her mother and grandfather, as well as the multiple victims of the dinosaurs who escape their enclosures on Lockwood Estate; Maisie Farange in a macabre association with Mrs. Wix's dead daughter. As Sam B. Girgus has argued, "The dead girl becomes a symbol for Maisie of her own deadness" (1979, 96). This echoes the ways in which various dead and de-extinct characters in *Fallen Kingdom*, from Maisie's sister/mother to the *Indoraptor*, reflect Maisie's status as a de-extinct or resurrected version of Lockwood's daughter, and her function as a symbol of the possibility of the death of the (naturally reproduced) human species. James' novel also focuses on the collapse of Maisie's family: a corruption and descent from wealth and privilege, and the relative safety of a nuclear family. At the novel's end—as at the end of *Fallen Kingdom*—Maisie is offered a choice between her dissolute mother and Mrs. Wix (her nanny). Both Maisies pass into the future of their narratives not with their natural or genetic family, but with a newly constructed pseudo-family with an uneasy or unresolved commitment to her/their care.

The Maisie of *Fallen Kingdom*, like the cloned dinosaurs of whom she is a human echo, is wholly unmothered, despite Henry's assertion that mothering is a necessity. Lockwood is similarly disconnected from the ways his other legacies—his wealth and the technology he pioneered—are being managed in the present by his dishonest, ambitious and financially motivated aide, Eli Mills. Confined to his bedroom, hooked up to intravenous drips, Lockwood is powerless to nurture, protect or control his genetic, financial or intellectual heritage.

The central role of various female characters in *Fallen Kingdom*—in particular the clone, Maisie—reflects Ellen Moer's assertion that "Ann Radcliffe firmly set the Gothic in one of the ways it would go ever after: a novel in which the central figure is a young woman who is simultaneously persecuted victim and courageous heroine" (1977, 91). Maisie becomes a central figure in the latter half of the film: a young woman who is both a victim (of familial collapse and of violent threats from both dinosaurs and men) and a heroine (as saviour of the dinosaurs). Further, as noted by Wolff (1979) in her discussion of filmic narratives, the Gothic provides a framework for explorations of the secret or secretive and obscure structure of female identity within spaces that are simultaneously threatening and exciting, and in relation to male figures who are ambiguously exciting or enticing, and threatening. Maisie's identity as secret and secretive, obscure and obscured, is strongly reflected in her status as the "motherless" daughter of the Lockwood household, and in her relations to the various threatening and protective male figures who offer her protection, including her "grandfather," Eli and Owen. Furthermore, both Maisie and the *Indoraptor* are lab-based genetic creations and, thus, motherless children, positioned as imperfect mirror images of each other. This is true both in terms of their genetic or biological make-up (Maisie is a clone of her mother, and the *Indoraptor* has been hybridised from the DNA of various extinct and de-extinct dinosaurs) and in terms of their social functions. For Eli, Maisie is as much intellectual property, and a potential source of income, as the *Indoraptor*. He makes this understanding of Maisie explicit when, at Lockwood's deathbed, he dismisses Iris from service as Maisie's nanny, refuting Iris' claim as the woman who raised her and understands her by asserting that he is "her guardian now [because] I understand her value." This conflict between the rights and responsibilities of various stakeholders in Maisie's guardianship is an interestingly warped echo of the conversation in which Claire tries to evoke Owen's protectiveness of Blue by reminding him that he raised her. While in the earlier scene Owen disavows any sense of ensuing responsibility for Blue, here Iris' attempt to claim her rights as Maisie's allo-mother are overridden by Eli's claim to both recognise and have authority over Maisie's financial and scientific value. Both Maisie and the *Indoraptor* are uneasily understood as motherless children—symbolic of the familial dissolution so central to Gothic and neo-Gothic narratives—and as scientific and financial assets. They are living inheritances that, in the absence of either a protective and nurturing mother or a powerful father (or grandfather), are vulnerable to the predations of capitalism and the military–industrial complex.

Thus, it is a central point of neo-Gothic concern throughout the *Jurassic Park* films that children have been shown as both literally and metaphorically abandoned by their mothers or relinquished into the care of insufficiently prepared allo-mothers. While Maisie has been raised by Iris, the film shows her role in Maisie's upbringing as, at best, ambivalent and inadequate. During the film, she interacts with her only rarely, telling her to go and see her grandfather or correcting her pronunciation. For the dinosaurs, the only appropriate or useful maternal influence shown or discussed in *Fallen Kingdom* (outside of the life-saving mothering of the pseudo-mothers during the various dinosaur attacks and stampedes) is Owen's mothering of Blue, which is strongly and repeatedly linked to the creation of dinosaurs who are obedient to (male) authority. The mothering that occurs spontaneously, and outside of male observation or control is, by comparison, both mysterious and suspect. By implication, the uncontrolled and unsupervised maternity of the dinosaurs, both in terms of their uncontrolled reproduction and their raising of their young, is the primary threat to humanity. It is, perhaps, significant that throughout the films, it is largely men and boys who are maimed, killed and eaten by the female dinosaurs. In some sense, the lack of appropriate, male-focused or male-educated mother figures for both Maisie and the *Indoraptor* lies at the heart of the film's anxiety about future generations of both children and dinosaurs: without a sufficient moral education, how will they form moral identities? Or, more particularly, how will they form moral identities that are centred on protecting and maintaining the patriarchal structures of human civilisation? As Malcolm's voiceover expresses during the closing scenes of the film, scenes in which dinosaurs and humans are seen cohabiting in urban and wild landscapes, "Genetic power has now been unleashed. Of course, that's going to be catastrophic [...]. We're gonna have to adjust to new threats that we can't imagine."

In these ways, the focus on family as a locus of care and control emerges through the repeated formation of a pseudo-family unit in each film: mother, father and child/children. Each of these families forms within the timeline of the film but falls apart in the years that pass off-screen. This recursive narrative is present from the first film, in which Dr. Alan Grant (palaeontologist) and Dr. Ellie Sattler (paleobotanist), the couple brought to Isla Nublar by John Hammond, initially question whether they each should or should not have children. Alan and Ellie form a pseudo-family unit with Hammond's two grandchildren, Tim and Lex, with the two allo-parents standing in for the children's absent parents as advisors, protectors and educators, such that by the end of the film Alan's reluctance to become a father has been overcome by his affection for Tim and Lex.[5]

Across the franchise, these pseudo-family units are oddly consistent, with a heterosexual couple functioning as parents, and the "children" (usually two in each film) slowly aging over the course of the series. While each of the prior film's central pseudo-families were mostly white and middle or upper class—the parents educated scientists and the children those of wealthy families (the Hammonds, the Kirbys)—in *Fallen Kingdom* the pseudo-children are not explicitly separated from a prior broken, absent or dysfunctional (albeit wealthy) family outside the archipelago. Instead, their own talents and education—Franklin is a computer technician while Zia is a paleo-veterinarian— uniquely position them as productive members of the imagined future. However, *Fallen Kingdom* also introduces Maisie, ultimately the child with whom Claire and Owen form a final familial bond. At the film's end, the three are shown together, driving along a coastal road in a family station wagon in the formation of a familial triad. However, unlike in the earlier films, the pseudo-family of Claire, Owen and Maisie is not a genetically linked or natural family (or potential family). Whereas *Jurassic Park* suggested that Alan and Ellie would marry and have children, the third film that the Kirby family would reunite after rescuing their son and *Jurassic World* that Claire and Owen would marry and reproduce, *Fallen Kingdom* offers a final image of a family made up of genetically unrelated individuals: a patched-together (Frankenstein) family headed out on the road into an uncertain and hybrid future.

Ultimately, the neo-Gothicism of the *Jurassic Park* films lies in the ways they construct an intense distrust of failed heteronormative families or those created within artificial (lab) conditions. Rather, the only family units that survive, even if only temporarily, are the pseudo-family units of the films, or those of the dinosaurs. The films also question the idea of heritage: of leaving a mark, of controlling the future. Malcolm is, in this sense, the series' fool-who-speaks-the-truth, its Cassandra, who perpetually identifies and predicts disaster, is ignored, belittled, questioned and injured, but persists.[6] Perhaps most powerfully, however, the films conservatively suggest the terrible consequences of the failures of appropriate (i.e. patriarchally oriented) motherhood, such that the logic of the films expresses an equation in which man creates offspring, offspring have no mothers, motherless offspring are immoral and immoral offspring destroy their fathers and their fathers' heritage. That these motherless offspring are resurrected or undead, moreover, suggests that any future in which they survive and thrive is itself a neo-Gothic one wherein the past is now the spectral future. As Dr. Malcolm asserts in response to Dr. Wu's claim that the all-female population of dinosaurs cannot breed in the wild, "Life, uh, finds a way," to be sure, but these dinosaur narratives suggest it is not a life of which we would want any part.

Notes

1 Martin and Savoy argue that "gothic cultural production [...] has yielded neither a 'genre' nor a cohesive 'mode' but rather a discursive field in which a metonymic national 'self' is undone by the return or its repressed Otherness" (1998, vii).
2 Darko Suvin (1979) first used the term *novum* (new thing) to refer to the scientifically plausible, but as yet undiscovered or unused, scientific technology or innovation used in science fiction narratives. For Suvin, the *novum*, which engenders cognitive estrangement (similar in structure and effect to Bertolt Brecht's *Verfremdung*) in the reader, is what distinguishes science fiction from fantasy.
3 Dinosaurs have been made friendly, unthreatening and sympathetic through their personification, especially in children's television, film, fiction and toys, such as *The Land Before Time* (1988–2016)—a series also coproduced by Steven Spielberg—*Dinosaur Train* (2009–present) and *Barney & Friends* (1992–2009). Yet, such depictions depend on an idea of dinosaurs as tamed and domesticated in their familiarity. It is of course true that "humans would never have evolved had the dinosaur reign continued unabated" (Debus 2006, 146). Indeed, it is precisely because the dinosaurs do not truly possess any of these characteristics that they threaten human life. For all their apparently human characteristics, the dinosaurs are ultimately wholly other, uncontrolled and uncontrollable.
4 Claire Dearing, for example, perceives the de-extinction of the dinosaurs as a miracle. She first describes the de-extinction this way early in the film, when Eli Mills takes her on a tour of Lockwood Estate. "What they did here was a miracle," she tells him. Later, while imprisoned

in the sub-basement, she says to Green: "Do you remember the first time you saw a dinosaur? The first time you see them it's like a miracle. You read about them in books, you see the bones in museums, but you don't really believe it. They're like myths, and then you see the first one alive."

5   The opening scene of *Jurassic Park III* (2001) suggests that Ellie and Alan have formed a nuclear family. However, this misrecognition is quickly undone when the failure of their romance is revealed and the children are shown to be the product of Ellie's marriage to another man. The same film focuses on another disrupted family: the divorced couple Paul and Amanda Kirby, whose son has become stranded on Isla Sorna. The Kirbys uneasily reconvene as a family, performing the familial tasks of mother, father and son: working together, demonstrating empathy for each other and protecting each other. In *Jurassic World*, we again see two children placed in the care of a non-parent: their aunt, Claire. As in *Jurassic Park*, Claire and Owen form a pseudo-nuclear family with Zach and Gray. Once again, the family unit at the heart of the film must work together to solve problems, and learn to communicate with and trust each other. A more diverse family unit is formed in *Fallen Kingdom*, although it nevertheless adheres to the established recursive pattern. Claire and Owen come together within the film's duration, but have not been together during the three years between the end of the previous film's narrative and the beginning of this one. Here, two of Claire's young employees at the Dinosaur Protection Group, Zia Rodriguez and Franklin Webb, function within the film as the couple's pseudo-children.

6   In Michael Crichton's book series Malcolm's injuries are by turns more explicit, extreme and long-lasting. At the end of the first book (*Jurassic Park*) Malcolm breaks his leg in a fall, is bed-bound and administered morphine that leads him to deliver often incoherent rants and is—at the novel's end—declared dead by the Costa Rican Air Force. In the sequel, *The Lost World*, Malcolm again suffers a leg injury, which this time results in a permanent physical disability.

Bibliography

Bradbury, Ray. "A Sound of Thunder." In *R Is for Rocket*, 11–29. New York: Doubleday, 1952.

Buchman, Peter, Alexander Payne and Jim Taylor. *Jurassic Park III*. Dir. Joe Johnston. Universal City, CA: Universal Pictures, 2001.

Butler, Octavia. *Adulthood Rites*. New York: Little, Brown and Company, 1997a.

———. *Dawn*. New York: Little, Brown and Company, 1997b.

———. *Imago*. New York: Little, Brown and Company, 1997c.

Connolly, Derek, and Colin Trevorrow. *Jurassic Park: Fallen Kingdom*. Dir. Juan Antonio Bayona. Universal City, CA: Universal Pictures, 2018.

Crichton, Michael. *Jurassic Park*. New York: Alfred A. Knopf, 1990.

———. *The Lost World*. New York: Alfred A. Knopf, 1995.

Crichton, Michael, and David Koepp. *Jurassic Park*. Dir. Steven Spielberg. Universal City, CA: Universal Pictures, 1993.

Debus, Allen A. *Dinosaurs in Fantastic Fiction: A Thematic Survey*. Jefferson, NC: McFarland, 2006.

———. *Dinosaurs Ever Evolving: The Changing Face of Prehistoric Animals in Popular Culture*. Jefferson, NC: McFarland, 2016.

Doyle, Arthur Conan. *The Lost World*. 1912. Mineola, NY: Dover, 1998.

Girgus, Sam B. *The Law of the Heart: Individualism and the Modern Self in American Literature*. Austin: University of Texas Press, 1979.

Hoffman, A. Robin. "How to See the Horror: The Hostile Fetus in *Rosemary's Baby* and *Alien*." *Literature Interpretation Theory* 22, no. 3 (2011): 239–61.

Jaffa, Rick, Amanda Silver, Derek Connolly and Colin Trevorrow. *Jurassic World*. Dir. Colin Trevorrow. Universal City, CA: Universal Pictures, 2015.

James, Henry. *What Maisie Knew*. 1897. New York: Library of America, 2003.

Koepp, David. *The Lost World: Jurassic Park*. Dir. Steven Spielberg. Universal City, CA: Universal Pictures, 1997.

Kohlke, Marie-Luise, and Christian Gutleben. "The (Mis)Shapes of Neo-Victorian Gothic: Continuations, Adaptations, Transformations." In *Neo-Victorian Gothic: Horror, Violence and Degeneration in the Re-imagined Nineteenth Century*, edited by Marie-Luise Gutleben and Christian Gutleben, 1–50. New York: Rodopi, 2012.

Martin, Robert K., and Eric Savoy, eds. *American Gothic: New Interventions in a National Narrative*. Iowa City: Iowa University Press, 1998.

Moers, Ellen. *Literary Women: The Great Writers*. New York: Oxford University Press, 1977.

Sanz, José Luis. *Starring T. Rex! Dinosaur Mythology and Popular Culture*. Translated by Philip Mason. Bloomington: Indiana University Press, 2002.

Shelley, Mary. *Frankenstein or The Modern Prometheus*. 1818. London: Penguin, 2018.

Suvin, Darko. *Metamorphosis of Science Fiction: On the Poetics and History of a Literary Genre*. New Haven, CT: Yale University Press, 1979.

Valerius, Karyn. "*Rosemary's Baby*, Gothic Pregnancy, and Fetal Subjects." *College Literature* 32, no. 3 (2005): 116–35.

Verne, Jules. *Journey to the Centre of the Earth*. 1864. Mineola, NY: Dover, 2005.

Wolff, Cynthia Griffin. "The Radcliffean Gothic Model: A Form for Feminine Sexuality." *Modern Language Studies* 9, no. 3 (1979): 98–113.

Yang, Sharon Rose, and Kathleen Healey. Introduction: "Haunted Landscapes and Fearful Spaces—Expanding Views on the Geography of the Gothic." In *Gothic Landscapes: Changing Eras, Changing Cultures, Changing Anxieties*, edited by Sharon Rose Yang and Kathleen Healey, 1–18. Houndmills: Palgrave Macmillan, 2016.

Chapter Ten

DOCTOR WHO'S SHAKEN FAITH IN SCIENCE: MISTRUSTING SCIENCE FROM THE GOTHIC TO THE NEO-GOTHIC

Geremy Carnes

Neo-Gothic stories have enjoyed immense popularity in contemporary popular culture. Science fiction in particular has developed a very productive relationship with the Gothic in the past several decades. It has often been claimed by scholars that such sci-fi Gothic demonstrates a fear of the future (or rather, a speculative future extrapolated from the rapidly changing present) in contrast to early Gothic literature, which feared the pre-modern past (or rather, a wilfully misrepresented version of the pre-modern past).[1] I would argue, however, that to make such a distinction is to yet again wilfully misrepresent the past, only this time it is not the pre-modern past, but early modernity, that is being misrepresented. The Gothic's original entry into mainstream culture in the 1790s came at a moment when many Britons found themselves as unsettled by the radical ideological and epistemological transformations of their present moment as they were critical of the ideologies and epistemologies of pre-modern Europe. In other words, fear of a revolutionary present or a terrifying future is nothing new to the Gothic. Indeed, it is one of its most essential elements.

In this chapter I aim to show that the contemporary neo-Gothic, especially neo-Gothic science fiction, has more in common with the earliest popular Gothic novels than is often acknowledged, and that their similarity is due in considerable part to the waning of public trust in science. For reasons I shall discuss, the status of science as a dependable foundation for knowledge about the world—a status it was just beginning to attain among European elites at the time of the Gothic's original rise to prominence—has been severely challenged in recent decades. Using episodes of the longest-running science fiction program on television, *Doctor Who*, as a case study, I will show how the loss of faith over the reliability of science has contributed to the effectiveness of the Gothic qualities of neo-Gothic science fiction. The neo-Gothic's contemporary popularity is largely due to the fact that the Gothic has always been the literature of modernity that most effectively reflects ideological and epistemological doubt, and our present moment is one of considerable doubt.

The notion that the early Gothic literary movement was initially pro-modernity is a common one. Fred Botting's comments on the early Gothic in his essay on the function of contemporary science fiction Gothic, "Aftergothic: Consumption, Machines, and Black Holes," aligns with this view:

> In the natural images, architectural ruins, and courtly customs frequently employed in a Gothic sublime, the past is appropriated and expelled in an attempt to separate a civilized, rational eighteenth century from its barbaric and feudal forbears. Remnants of the past— ruins, superstitions, passions—are attributes of an earlier epoch superseded by modern practices and qualities. Gothic figures thus mark turning points in cultural historical progress, points at which feudalism is apprehended and dismissed as a ruined past in a movement toward a more enlightened future. The momentum of change, however, carries with it anxieties: has the barbaric past really been surpassed? Have primitive energies and passions really been overcome? Gothic figures come to represent these anxieties and give them fearful form as monsters, ghosts, and demons whose return terrifies bourgeois normality and undermines ordered notions of civilized humanity and rational progress. (2002, 278–79)

In this understanding of the cultural work performed by the early Gothic, that work is to further the project of modernity and spread what we would now call a scientific worldview at the expense of traditional, and particularly religion-based worldviews. The early Gothic primarily fears the past; insofar as it holds fears about the modern present, it fears that the present is *insufficiently modern*. The early Gothic may sometimes doubt flawed humanity's ability to fully embrace modernity's ideologies of capitalism, liberty, and so on, and its scientific epistemology, but it does not call into question modernity's promethean promise that a better world would be possible if these ideals and ways of knowing *were* embraced. Only with the onset of science fiction Gothic in *Frankenstein* (1818) does Botting observe that science's capacity "to guarantee a comfortable future is brought into question"; subsequently, "scientific discovery is as much a threat as it is a promise" in Gothic fiction (2002, 279). Even then, the Gothic continues to function as "the dark underside of modernity" until, in the twentieth century, further ideological change creates a new role for the Gothic, which now "outlines the darkness of the postmodern condition" (281).

While I agree with much of Botting's analysis about the cultural work of the Gothic, I would argue that he (like many other scholars of the Gothic) overstates the early Gothic's faith in the project of modernity and the superiority of a scientific worldview. While *Frankenstein* may have been the first Gothic text to draw particular attention to (and critique) science, the question of whether the Gothic was generally pro-modern and pro-reason prior to *Frankenstein* is a perennial subject of debate among critics.[2] It is true that the Gothic could not have taken the form it did were it not for the spread of the ideologies and epistemologies we would recognise today as foundational to modernity and a scientific worldview. By the end of the eighteenth century, new social realities (with the help of Enlightenment intellectuals) had caused these modern ways of thinking and knowing to gain ground against those that had held sway in Europe for centuries.[3] Yet they were by no means firmly established—and indeed, their establishment received a powerful setback in the 1790s as the disasters of the French Revolution called into question the Enlightenment's promise that a society built upon reason would result in a peaceful and prosperous civilization. As it turned out, rationality could lead to barbarities just as terrible as those that had been the product of irrationality and super-stition. This decade, the 1790s, when both traditional and modern ideologies seemed, to many educated Britons, to be untenable was also the decade in which the Gothic transformed from a minor literary undercurrent into the most popular literary genre in Britain.[4] The Gothic, with its surreal, nightmarish worlds in which firm grounds for belief do not exist, was the literature needed by readers fearful of modernity yet forever cut off from pre-modernity.[5]

A brief consideration of major Gothic texts from this period bears out the genre's status as a product of ideological and epistemological doubt. True, these texts adopt a denigrating attitude towards pre-modern Europe, and some early Gothic writers (Mary Wollstonecraft and William Godwin, for instance) were fervent supporters of the ideal of reason. But the Gothic novels which played the greatest role in establishing the popularity of the genre were those that exposed a tension between anxieties about the barbarities of Europe's pre-modern past and anxieties about the crises of its revo-lutionary present. *Frankenstein*, simultaneously fascinated and terrified by the prome-thean prospects of modern science, is only the most overtly conflicted. The writer most associated with the Gothic's explosive popularity in the 1790s, Ann Radcliffe, is just as ideologically inconsistent, if not more so. Radcliffe's novels "promote aristocratic as well as bourgeois values, demonstrate both progressive and conservative political beliefs, and are at once feminist and anti-feminist," leading many modern critics to consider "this unresolvable conflictedness […] a definitive characteristic of Radcliffean Gothic" (Schmitt 1994, 855). Matthew Lewis' *The Monk* (1796), perhaps the decade's most widely read Gothic novel today, is at least as afraid of the modern revolutionary mob as of the Catholic Inquisition. In a highly influential reading of the novel, Peter Brooks positions it "at the dead end of the Age of Reason" and argues that it offers "one of the first and most lucid contextualizations of life in a world where reason has lost its prestige, yet the Godhead has lost its otherness" (1973, 249). It should come as no surprise that some critics have compared this period of terror and ideological crisis to our own postmodern moment.[6]

The early Gothic, then, is best understood not as a movement that worked to advance the project of modernity and spread of reason and science during the period of their rise, but as the literary expression of a moment of widespread uncertainty, and whose inconsistency rendered it, in the words of James Carson, "at once complicit with and critical of the Enlightenment" (1996, 265). Moreover, by understanding the early Gothic as a literature of doubt sparked by an often traumatic process of ideological and epistemological transformation, we find a stronger relationship between contemporary neo-Gothic literature and the early Gothic than Botting suggests. Indeed, contemporary neo-Gothic literature is more imitative of the earliest Gothic texts than much of the Gothic literature of the intervening centuries. In our postmodern (or post-postmodern, if you prefer) time, all ideologies, whether those of modernity or those which would seek to replace them, are considered suspect. Ideologically unmoored, contemporary Western culture finds itself in a position akin to that of 1790s Britain. The recent popu-larity of the Gothic may simply be due to our having recreated the conditions under which it first thrived.[7]

In demonstration of how the contemporary neo-Gothic has resurfaced the conflict between traditional and modern worldviews that sparked the early Gothic's popularity, in the remainder of this chapter I will examine some Gothic episodes in the long-running science fiction series *Doctor Who*. This program offers a unique opportunity for seeing ideological transformation play out in a single continuous narrative, as the show has aired from 1963 to 1989 (a period often referred to as Classic Who), and then from 2005 to the present day (a period known as New Who). Episodes of *Doctor Who* frequently portray conflicts between the scientific worldview (a term I will use to refer to the complex ideological and epistemological framework that supports the modern view of science as objective and as the ultimate arbiter of reality) and worldviews founded in religion or mysticism. While specific, real-world religions are not attacked on the show, the program generally has been, in both the Classic and New Who eras, implicitly and sometimes explicitly atheistic in outlook. As David Layton has argued, in *Doctor Who*, "religion and the supernatural are largely rejected as meaningful or valid ways of encountering the world," and the program "repeatedly demonstrate[s] flaws in the religious worldview" while "also demonstrat[ing] that a positive humanism, a secular worldview based upon science, reason, and the desire for truth, is a superior worldview to religion" (2012, 155).[8] That support for a secular, scientific worldview is another consistent feature of the program. Lindy A. Orthia, who has analysed attitudes and representations of science in the program in great detail, shows that these attitudes and representations have varied considerably over the years, ranging from "explorative ambivalence" in the programming of the 1960s, to the "atheist scientism" of the 1970s, to the "political post-modernism" of the 1980s and finally to the "myth-building hero worship" of the Doctor as a scientific genius in the New Who episodes of the 2000s. Yet throughout the series, the program treats science as the best means of understanding the universe, if at times one that is subject to misguided application (2010, 125).[9] In this chapter, I wish to focus on the two eras in which *Doctor Who* leans most strongly into the Gothic: the 1970s (a period in the program famous for its large number of Gothic episodes (111–12)), and the 2000s revival (which has consistently featured episodes with strong horror elements). Not entirely coincidentally, these two periods of the program are also those that raise the Doctor's scientific abilities to their most heroic pitch.

In the 1970s serials the Doctor (and, through him, the show as a whole) does not merely embrace a scientific worldview; he adopts an extreme scientistic ideology (103). In most serials of this era of the show, only scientific viewpoints are viewed as valuable, or even meaningful. The serials often portray mysticism as the source of the problems of a society (whether earthly or alien), from which that society must be rescued by the Doctor's science (110). Both Doctors from this era, Jon Pertwee's Third Doctor and Tom Baker's Fourth Doctor, repeatedly assert that all questions have scientific answers. Moreover, the Doctor embraces his identity as a scientist par excellence, as in this exchange from the "Colony in Space" serial:

Miner. Are you some kind of scientist?
Doctor. I'm *every* kind of scientist. (1971a)

Another serial from 1971 is one of the most fascinating examples of the program's scientistic ideology, as well as one of its most self-consciously Gothic productions: "The Dæmons." In this serial, the Doctor encounters a horned, goat-legged being called Azal, similar in appearance to popular depictions of the Devil. (All he lacks is the pitchfork.) He also resembles the Devil in possessing apparently supernatural power on an apocalyptic scale and in his ability to send gargoyle-like imps to do his bidding. His arrival is the result of a summoning ritual performed by a cult of robed men in the undercroft of a Gothic church. During the holiday of Beltane, he traps a small English town beneath a force field (the villagers of which—imperturbably English—carry right on with their Morris dancing and Maypole festival). The serial thus performs the classic Gothic move of linking Christianity with paganism, although in this case it is the Church of England that comes under critique, rather than the traditional Gothic villain, Catholicism. In short, the serial is filled to the brim with Gothic imagery deliberately evoking a premodern world of rural villagers practicing a mixture of Christian and pagan customs, who are threatened by apparently supernatural forces, the source of which is a being who appears to be the Devil himself.

The Doctor, of course, is having none of it. In his first scene, he criticises his young companion, Jo, for her New Age belief in the occult. When Jo presses him on how he can be so sure that there is no such thing as magic, he answers, "How? Well, I just know, that's all. Everything that happens in life must have a scientific explanation" (*Doctor Who* 1971b). The Doctor's position is strongly reinforced throughout the five episodes of the serial. At one point, after the characters have witnessed Azal's devil-like powers, the local witch Olive Hawthorne attempts to convince the Doctor, Jo and Captain Yates that they are dealing with the supernatural. Their exchange exemplifies the Doctor's certitude in the ability of science (and himself) to explain any problem:

Hawthorne. You're being deliberately obtuse. We're dealing with the supernatural, the occult, magic!
Doctor. Science.
Hawthorne. Magic!
Doctor. Science, Miss Hawthorne.
Yates. Look, whatever it is, how do we stop it?
Jo. And how can we stop it without knowing what it is?
Doctor. Well done, Jo. You're being logical at last. I'll turn you into a
Scientist. yet. Right, if there are no more interruptions, I'll tell you what it is.
(*Doctor Who* 1971b)

After this exchange, the Doctor proceeds to do just that. Azal, it turns out, is one of the Dæmons, an ancient and powerful race of alien scientists who have travelled throughout the universe running "experiments" in life. The Doctor explains that all of the devilish religious symbolism and black magic found throughout human history resulted from humanity's interactions with these beings and their technology. Earth is one of the Dæmons' experiments. Unfortunately, upon awakening, Azal decides that the Earth is a *failed* experiment, and determines to do what any scientist would do with a failed experiment: discard it and move on. Of course, the Doctor and Jo succeed in defeating Azal through the use of reason tempered with their humanistic values for life. As Orthia has noted, even when *Doctor Who* serials feature a scientist villain, science does not necessarily come under critique; often, the plot boils down to mad science being beaten by the Doctor's properly rational, life-affirming science (2010, 155). This serial follows that pattern.

Moreover, while the bad scientist is beaten, the supernatural is utterly vanquished. This is a common feature of the 1970s Gothic period of *Doctor Who*, in which the show proceeded to invent "a technoscientific explanation for paranormal phenomena," explaining away such Gothic mainstays as mummies, ghosts, zombies and pagan deities (112). But "The Dæmons" goes to an extreme, spending over two hours of airtime denying the existence of *any* knowledge outside of a scientific framework, and scoffing not only at Hawthorne's pagan witchcraft but also at Christian myths regarding the Devil and the Creation. Indeed, the program declares that insofar as Azal *is* the being that humans throughout history have perceived to be the Devil, it is the Devil, not God, who created life on earth and has served as humanity's guide. God is completely written out of the history of the universe. It is hard to imagine a children's television program airing today to have the boldness to make such a derisive dismissal of Christian belief.

In this serial, as in most of Classic Who, Gothic elements exist primarily to self-consciously repeat the victory of modernity over pre-modernity. The program raises Gothic, supernatural-seeming villains so that the Doctor's science and rationalism can explain them, contain them and strike them down. Especially in the scientistic 1970s period of the show, religious belief itself is implied to be a heresy against the unassailable Truth of science, with the Doctor serving as science's chief apostle and evangelist. (He'll make a scientist of Jo yet.) But precisely because the result of the conflict between religion and science is never in doubt in serials like "The Dæmons," these serials do not unsettle or disturb in the way that the most effective Gothic writing does. The serials of the 1970s, while they often deploy Gothic conventions in ways that recall the ideological and epistemological doubts that helped popularise the Gothic in the 1790s, do not truly share those doubts themselves. Whereas the early Gothic exhibits a loss of faith in both traditional *and* scientific worldviews, these serials have staunch faith in science and its capacity to triumph over any lingering threats from outdated worldviews. Even in serials where mad science endangers the world, *good* science steps in to save it.

In contrast, the program in its post-2005, New Who incarnation often *does* exhibit a truly Gothic loss of faith. *Doctor Who* has never hesitated to recycle its plots, and in one of the episodes of the program's revival, the Doctor encounters "the Devil" yet again. However, whereas in the 1970s episodes this encounter serves to reaffirm the Doctor's faith in the power of science to answer all questions, in the 2000s it has a much more disturbing effect on the Doctor, and his scientific worldview does not emerge entirely unscathed.

In the 2006 episodes "The Impossible Planet" and "The Satan Pit," the Doctor and his companion Rose travel to the future and visit a dingy space station called "Sanctuary Base," on a planet that is impossibly in orbit around a black hole.[10] The scientists of Sanctuary Base are attempting to drill into the centre of the planet to discover the force that allows it to avoid falling into the black hole. The Doctor celebrates the bravery and curiosity of these scientists, but their disregard for the feelings of the Ood, a hideous but friendly telepathic alien species they have enslaved, prevents the viewer from understanding these scientists as entirely positive figures. Even aside from the practice of slavery, something is amiss on this space station. There is a feeling of unease among the crew, and the numbers 666 keep appearing in seemingly unrelated situations.[11] It quickly becomes apparent that these scientists are, in traditionally Gothic fashion, meddling in forces they do not understand. Their drill reaches the subterranean ruins of an ancient alien civilization. Indeed, that civilization's writing cannot be translated by the Tardis (the Doctor's time machine), which has always been able to instantly translate any language in the history of the universe. Things turn ugly when a mysterious voice begins haunting the station, calling itself "the Beast" and projecting images of a horned, skinless monstrosity resembling the Devil. It also begins to possess members of the crew (turning their eyes red, of course), transforming the Ood into murderous monsters and turning one of the scientists into its avatar. Then an earthquake opens a chasm into which the Tardis falls, cutting off the Doctor and Rose's means of escape. This planet, we eventually learn, is nothing more than an elaborate dungeon cell for this ancient, powerful being, kept in orbit over a black hole so that the monster it contains may be destroyed should it ever prove necessary.

As the description above suggests, these episodes adapt many classic Gothic tropes to their futuristic, alien setting, creating a scenario in which it appears that demonic forces are at work. And, inevitably, the Doctor and Rose defeat this devilish threat, reasoning their way to solutions. Described thus, these episodes sound very much like a repeat of "The Dæmons." And some critics have attempted to read them as such. Sarah Balstrup argues that while the Doctor is forced to confront the limitations of his knowledge in these episodes, they do not challenge a scientific worldview. Rather, the episodes play with Richard Dawkins' theories about memes and their role in spreading religious beliefs. Balstrup sees these episodes as likening religion to "a cultural virus that the Doctor must fight in order to save humankind" and suggesting that God and the Devil are just ideas that have "no inherent power" beyond our belief in them (2014, 145, 150). Layton has also argued that these episodes exhibit the program's usual rational humanism. He observes that in dealing with the Beast, the Doctor repeatedly attempts to explain the Beast's activities rationally, stripping the supernatural down to the natural (2012, 151). Layton is correct that this is what the Doctor *attempts* to do, but unlike in "The Dæmons," where the unfolding of the plot ultimately proves the Doctor right, no such confirmation is granted to the viewer in these episodes. And if these episodes are critical of the power of religious beliefs, as Balstrup suggests, it needs to be added that they are *so* powerful that the Doctor's science is barely able to combat them. If not for an incredible stroke of luck in the show's closing moments, when the Doctor stumbles across his lost Tardis, the encounter would have ended in mutual destruction.

Indeed, the Doctor himself becomes increasingly unsure of the reliability of his scientific worldview. Consider, for instance, the following conversation between the Doctor and the Beast:

Doctor.   How did you end up on this rock?
Beast.   The Disciples of the Light rose up against me and chained me in the pit for all eternity.

Doctor.   When was this?
Beast.   Before time.
Doctor.   What does that mean?
Beast.   Before time.
Doctor.   What does "before time" mean?
Beast.   Before time and light and space and matter. Before the cataclysm. Before this universe was created.
Doctor.   That's impossible. No life could have existed back then.
Beast.   Is that your religion?
Doctor.   [...] It's a belief. (*Doctor Who* 2006)

The Doctor is clearly thrown off balance by the Beast's repeated claim to have existed since before time and space began (a claim corroborated by the fact that the Tardis does not recognise this civilization's writing), and by the Beast's suggestion that the Doctor's scientific understanding of the universe is itself a religion. Now, science is *not* a religion, but science *is* founded on unprovable beliefs, which the Doctor is acknowledging here, perhaps for the first time: the belief that the universe has unalterable laws such as the Laws of Causality and Induction; that those laws operate in the same manner across all time and space; that nothing outside of time and space exists, or if it does, that we can never interact with it. Unlike most scientists, the Doctor has never had to accept these beliefs as *mere* beliefs. As the owner of a teleporting time machine, he can verify through direct, empirical experience that the laws of the universe *do* operate consistently throughout time and space. In claiming to have existed since "before time," and thus, outside of the Tardis' navigational range, the Beast has made a claim that the Doctor is incapable of proving or disproving. All the Doctor can do is insist that the claim is impossible, even as he is forced to admit that his belief in its impossibility *is* only a belief. And by the end of the adventure, he has indicated several times that he realises this belief may be wrong. Pressed by one of the scientists at the station about whether he has "any sort of faith," the Doctor responds, "I [...] believe, I believe I haven't seen everything, I don't know. It's funny, isn't it? The things you make up, the rules. If that thing had said it came from *beyond* the universe, I'd believe it, but *before* the universe? Impossible. Doesn't fit my rule. Still, that's why I keep travelling. To be proved wrong" (*Doctor Who* 2006).

In his final confrontation with the Beast, the limits of the Doctor's concessions to its claims are telling. Face-to-face with a gargantuan, satanic monster chained in a fiery pit, the Doctor grants it the smallest acknowledgement he can: "I accept that you exist. I don't have to accept what you are, but your physical existence, I give you that" (*Doctor Who* 2006). We have come a long way from Pertwee's Doctor confidently asserting, "All right, I'll tell you what it is." Tennant's Doctor refuses to acknowledge anything beyond the bare, observable fact of the Beast's existence. Unlike in "The Dæmons," he cannot provide a rational explanation for this Devil-like being, but he also cannot accept that it *could* be the Devil, and so, he simply refuses to draw any further conclusions. This refusal comes not from a place of confidence in his understanding of what is possible and impossible but from a dogged determination to remain faithful to his *belief* of what is possible and impossible in spite of being brought face-to-face with a major challenge to that belief. This is not an expression of certainty that the scientific worldview is the only meaningful one, but a decision to entertain no other worldview, come what may. In the 1970s serial, Gothic tropes were deployed to raise the threat of the supernatural so that it could be soundly defeated by a confident scientistic hero. In these episodes from 2006, Gothic tropes are deployed in order to challenge the faith of that scientistic hero.

And challenged it is. The Doctor rants about other ideological frameworks within which the Beast might be understood, his voice derisive, yes, but his agitated demeanour indicating that his scorn is a tactic born from desperation, not confidence: "Have I got to, I don't know, beg an audience? Or is there a ritual? Some sort of incantation or summons or spell? All these things I don't believe in, are they real? Speak to me! Tell me!" (*Doctor Who* 2006). The Doctor demands answers, but he never receives them—nor do we. Conveniently, it is the Beast's silence at this moment that provides the Doctor with the clue he needs to understand not the Beast itself, but the Beast's plan to escape its prison: it has hidden its mind in one of the possessed crew members. With this discovery, the Doctor ceases to contemplate his epistemological quandary and immediately focuses on the concrete matter of devising a plan to destroy the Beast and save himself, Rose and the surviving crew members. He realises that there is a way that he can send the Beast into the black hole, but he also realises that in doing so, he will doom Rose to the same fate. In the midst of this new dilemma, the Doctor declares a new faith for himself: "So, that's the trap. Or the test, or the final judgment, I don't know. But if I kill you, I kill her. Except that implies in this big grand scheme of Gods and Devils that she's just a victim. But I've seen a lot of this universe. I've seen fake gods and bad gods and demi-gods and would-be gods, and out of all that, out of that whole pantheon, if I believe in one thing, just one thing, I believe in her!" (*Doctor Who* 2006). The Doctor carries out his plan, and, thanks to the lucky discovery of the Tardis, he and Rose find the means to save everyone in spite of the trap. He thus manages to regain his confidence by simply setting aside his doubts and focusing on the value of human relationships—not unlike the heroine of an Ann Radcliffe novel at the conclusion of her adventures.

Yet both we and the Doctor recognise this to be, at some level, a copout. The Doctor was not experiencing a crisis over his belief in other people; he was experiencing a crisis over his belief in the capacity of science to explain all phenomena. That crisis has been evaded, not solved. After their victory, Rose and the crew question him about his confrontation with the Beast, but the Doctor is determined not to revisit the questions that he had found so maddening:

Rose. What do you think it was, really?
Doctor. I think we beat it. That's good enough for me. (*Doctor Who* 2006)

Defeating the Beast is treated as an acceptable, if not entirely satisfactory, substitute for understanding it. And thus this Gothic tale ends in triumph over the villain, but not over the problem the villain represents. The monster that challenged the scientific worldview of the hero has been exorcised, but the exorcism cannot undo the fact that challenge was possible. Certainty can never exist once one recognises that one's worldview is a choice. The Doctor doubts.

What are we to make of this change to *Doctor Who*'s approach to the conflict between the supernatural and science, between traditional and modern ways of knowing, that is so central to the Gothic tradition? To close, I would like to offer some thoughts on the source of the doubts manifested in the New Who episodes, and what these doubts may mean for discussions of the broader Gothic resurgence in the early twenty-first century, particularly in science fiction.

First, this change represents a shift in the form of atheism underpinning the worldview espoused by the program. As we have observed, an atheistic tone has been a relatively consistent feature of the show since its inception, but that tone changed its pitch in New Who, when it was reimagined under showrunner Russell T. Davies' tenure (2005–10). A public atheist, Davies has often been identified with the New Atheist movement associated with high profile public intellectuals like Richard Dawkins and Christopher Hitchens. New Atheism is a confrontational atheism which sees religion as a dangerous force that must be actively combated. On multiple occasions, Davies has stated that his atheistic worldview and distrust of religion were integrated into *Doctor Who* and its spin-offs during his tenure, and several scholars have demonstrated how Davies' New Atheism influenced the portrayal of religious iconography and belief on these programs.[12] While it may seem paradoxical, I would suggest that this New Atheist influence is part of the reason New Who expresses more doubt in science than Classic Who. For the New Atheists, the eighteenth century's conflict between the Enlightenment and traditional religion, the conflict that fuelled the Gothic's popularity, has never ended. In their eyes, religious worldviews, rather than retreating in the face of triumphant science, are gaining strength. The scientific revolution could still ultimately end in science's defeat. From this perspective, the easy confidence in the triumph of science apparent in the classic series is nothing less than foolhardy complacency. In New Who, the subversion of the Doctor's scientific worldview by an ancient, destructive force expresses a real fear about the power of irrational, pre-modern forces at work in the modern world, a fear that Classic Who barely bothered to feign. Davies and his writers may retain confidence in their scientific worldview, but they do not have confidence that it will win the ideological struggle with resurgent religious worldviews.

But *are* they truly that confident in science? While the creators of New Who are certainly proponents of science and modernity, the whole tenor of New Who indicates that they are far less willing to fight openly under the standard of science than were the showrunners of the 1970s. As Orthia notes, those Classic Who episodes were made when there was "a very high level of public esteem for scientists in the West" (2010, 113). Today, the scientific community does not enjoy nearly that level of esteem. Some of the reasons for the loss of public trust in science have been manufactured by people acting in bad faith, particularly those behind the well-funded campaigns to sow doubt in climate science and prevent meaningful action being taken to prevent catastrophic climate change. But many reasons for this loss of trust are the result of real failures on the part of scientists and those who represent scientific work to the public. Scientists have been complicit in any number of harmful acts; the wilful blindness of scientists to the water crisis in Flint, Michigan, is only one recent example of scientists betraying the public trust. Moreover, since the 1980s, scholars of science and technology studies have actively worked to dismantle certain idealised conceptions of science as an objective, systematic pursuit of factual knowledge, free from ideological bias.[13] While *Doctor Who* retains a strong commitment to sceptical inquiry, it reflects the waning of the public's faith in the capacity of the scientific community, and perhaps of science itself, to save humanity from its most Gothic impulses. The scientists of Sanctuary Base, we should recall, are praised by the Doctor as exemplars of the human spirit of discovery. They are also slaveholders. Their futuristic science is not incompatible with supposedly pre-modern behaviour.

But the Doctor is still a heroic scientist in New Who, is he not? Doesn't this suggest that the program retains its faith in the promethean promise of science? I believe not, for two reasons. The first is that the Doctor is no longer a scientist. In Classic Who, the Doctor frequently associates himself with scientific pursuits (recall Pertwee's declaration: "I'm *every* kind of scientist"). However, Orthia has pointed out that, at least in the first four seasons of the program's New Who revival, the Doctor never once calls himself a scientist (2010, 85). While his scientific and technological genius is often responsible for saving the day, these are treated less as the attributes of a man committed to sceptical inquiry and scientific process than as heroic superpowers. This leads to my second reason for suggesting that the Doctor's heroism is not a sign of the program's continued confidence in science: The Doctor is *too* heroic. If the Doctor in Classic Who was science's apostle, the Doctor in New Who is its Messiah. Rather than treating science as a worldview available to all, New Who's hero worship of the Doctor instead treats science as a power beyond the grasp of ordinary mortals.[14] In transforming the Doctor from a scientist to a superhero who gestures vaguely towards science as the source of his powers, the program pays lip service to a scientific worldview while actually weakening its connection to it. Just as the Doctor deflected his own doubts about his scientific worldview in "The Satan Pit" by focusing instead on his personal faith in Rose, *Doctor Who* deflects viewers' doubts in the reliability of science by focusing instead on the personal heroism of the Doctor.

The neo-Gothic aesthetic that characterises the New Who era of *Doctor Who* has proven effective largely because it has developed in response to similar ideological and epistemological crises to those which gave rise to the Gothic in the first place. Most people in modernity—even very religious people—find religious frameworks by themselves to be inadequate for understanding the world, yet the primary alterative, science, has had its credibility attacked on multiple fronts. Once again, Western society finds itself without firm epistemological ground on which to stand. No wonder, then, that the neo-Gothic should flourish in twenty-first-century media, particularly in the genre that foregrounds conflicts within and surrounding science: science fiction. Until science overcomes this crisis of credibility—or until some new (or old) framework for understanding our world establishes itself as the dominant paradigm—the neo-Gothic is unlikely to diminish much in its appeal to modern audiences.

Notes

1 See, for instance, Fred Botting's claims about a modern form of science-fiction Gothic he terms "cybergothic": "As gothic cedes to cybergothic, the genre's cultural role in screening off an ultimate, formless horror with familiar figures of fear is turned on its head: gothic shapes

occlude a darker and more destructive romantic flight, a return, not from the past, but from the future" (2008, 58).

2 Some critics have even gone to the extreme of arguing that the early Gothic was anti-modern. For a brief, incisive discussion of this critical debate, see Margaret Carol Davison (2009, 38–46).

3 It should here be noted that the gains of modernity were made primarily among the European elite. However, the British Gothic novels under consideration here were expensive and thus also primarily consumed by that elite (although libraries increasingly made them available to people of other classes). The story looks considerably different if we focus on the British lower class, which remained more wedded to traditional ideologies well into the nineteenth century. It should be of little surprise, then, that the Gothic literature written for the lower class—the chapbooks—was also more ideologically conservative, with the ancient religious enemy of Catholicism playing an even more prominent villainous role than it does in the more famous Gothic novels (Hoeveler 2014).

4 In some years of the 1790s, Gothic novels accounted for about a third of all new English novels published (Miles 2002, 40–42).

5 The ideological crisis experienced by Britons in the late eighteenth century is among the reasons I do not consider the early Gothic as being as far removed from the contemporary Gothic as many critics tend to see it. Steven Bruhm, for instance, focuses on psychological trauma as an explanation for the Gothic's popularity in contemporary literature, with the implication that the twentieth century has experienced such trauma to an unparalleled degree. He writes, "We need [the Gothic] because the twentieth century has so forcefully taken away from us that which we once thought constituted us—a coherent psyche, a social order to which we can pledge allegiance in good faith, a sense of justice in the universe—and that wrenching withdrawal, that traumatic experience, is vividly dramatized in the Gothic" (2002, 273). The loss of a coherent psyche possibly excepted, these "contemporary" traumas were experienced by many Britons in the closing years of the eighteenth century. Like Bruhm, I consider the Gothic to be a literature of trauma, but I believe that the traumas of the eighteenth century are not altogether different from the traumas of the twentieth and twenty-first centuries.

6 See, for instance, Maria Beville (2009, 23–24).

7 Certainly much of the Gothic literature of the nineteenth and early-to-mid-twentieth centuries similarly displayed the ideological and epistemological doubts characteristic of the Gothic literature of the 1790s and today. But a great deal of it did not. Many Gothic writers ignored *Frankenstein*'s warning and embraced modernity, consciously or not, in their fiction. *Dracula* (1897), for instance, is firmly on the side of a modernity threatened by incursions from the pre-modern past and the barbaric frontiers of empire (and if those sources of fear also hold certain attractions, a good Briton should never consciously acknowledge them). Even in the post-nuclear twentieth century, when the potential for annihilation through scientific advancement moved from the realm of science fiction to science fact, the Gothic often continued to advance the project of modernity.

8 Kieran Tranter has similarly argued that *Doctor Who* is "an anti-religious text" and that the Doctor "continually tells an aspiring story of living well within secular universe(s) of matter, energy and time" (2013, 134, 131).

9 In contrast, David Johnson argues that the program is not nearly as committed to the scientific worldview as others have claimed it is, pointing to the episodes that imply the existence of mystical powers and suggesting that the Doctor mediates between science and religion (2013). Johnson's position requires a focus on specific cases rather than considering the totality of the program. Orthia's analysis of the program notes the episodes that present exceptions to her general outline of the show's representation of science, but she does not allow those to distract her from the bigger picture, which is one of positive representation evolving in response to changing public attitudes towards science.

10 There is, of course, nothing impossible about a planet being in orbit around a black hole. Even the "real" science in *Doctor Who* is not always accurate science.

11 The number 666 appears in the Book of Revelation, where it is associated with the Beast of Revelation. See Rev. 13:18 (New American Bible). The Beast is often interpreted as representing earthly servants of Satan.

12 For Davies' public comments on his atheism and its role in his programs, see Balstrup (2014, 145–47). Balstrup's essay also analyses the way in which, under Davies, the program co-opts Christian symbolism in service to the humanistic, atheistic ethical system it promotes. See also Dee Amy-Chinn (2010).

13 Many of the bad faith efforts made to delegitimise science today have taken advantage of the work of these good faith scholars to discredit it. Bruno Latour, a science and technology studies scholar who was one of the major figures who worked to dismantle the idea of science as objective and indisputable, is now working to push back against these bad faith efforts (Vrieze 2017).

14 At times, the Doctor is even portrayed as something of a god himself (Orthia 2010, 123–28). Orthia's dissertation largely concerns itself with *Doctor Who*'s unfortunate tendency, especially in more recent seasons, to render science the purview of elites rather than to democratise it.

Bibliography

Amy-Chinn, Dee. "Davies, Dawkins and Deus Ex TARDIS: Who Finds God in the Doctor?" In *Ruminations, Peregrinations, and Regenerations: A Critical Approach to "Doctor Who,"* edited by Chris Hansen, 22–34. Newcastle upon Tyne, UK: Cambridge Scholars Publishing, 2010.

Balstrup, Sarah. "*Doctor Who*: Christianity, Atheism, and the Source of Sacredness in the Davies Years." *Journal of Religion and Popular Culture* 26, no. 2 (2014): 145–56.

Beville, Maria. *Gothic-Postmodernism: Voicing the Terrors of Postmodernity*. Amsterdam: Rodopi, 2009.

Botting, Fred. "Aftergothic: Consumption, Machines, and Black Holes." In *The Cambridge Companion to Gothic Fiction*, edited by Jerrold E. Hogle, 277–300. Cambridge: Cambridge University Press, 2002.

———. *Gothic Romanced: Consumption, Gender and Technology in Contemporary Fictions*. London: Routledge, 2008.

Brooks, Peter. "Virtue and Terror: *The Monk*." *ELH* 40, no. 2 (1973): 249–63.

Bruhm, Steven. "The Contemporary Gothic: Why We Need It." In *The Cambridge Companion to Gothic Fiction*, edited by Jerrold E. Hogle, 259–76. Cambridge: Cambridge University Press, 2002.

Carson, James P. "Enlightenment, Popular Culture, and Gothic Fiction." In *The Cambridge Companion to the Eighteenth-Century Novel*, edited by John Richetti, 255–76. Cambridge: Cambridge University Press, 1996.

Davison, Carol Margaret. *Gothic Literature, 1764–1824*. Cardiff: University of Wales Press, 2009.

Doctor Who. "Colony in Space." Story 58. Dir. Michael E. Briant. Written by Malcolm Hulke. 1971a. BBC1.

———. "The Daemons." Story 59. Dir. Christopher Barry. Written by Guy Leopold (Barry Letts and Robert Sloman). 1971b. BBC1.

———. "The Impossible Planet/The Satan Pit." Story 174. Dir. James Strong. Written by Matt Jones. 2006. BBC1.

Hoeveler, Diane Long. *The Gothic Ideology: Religious Hysteria and Anti-Catholicism in British Popular Fiction, 1780–1880*. Cardiff: University of Wales Press, 2014.

Johnson, David. "Mediating Between the Scientific and the Spiritual in *Doctor Who*." In *Religion and "Doctor Who": Time and Relative Dimensions in Faith*, edited by Andrew Crome and James McGrath, 145–60. Eugene, OR: Cascade Books, 2013.

Layton, David. *The Humanism of "Doctor Who."* Jefferson, NC: McFarland, 2012.

Miles, Robert. "The 1790s: The Effulgence of Gothic." In *The Cambridge Companion to Gothic Fiction*, edited by Jerrold E. Hogle, 41–62. Cambridge: Cambridge University Press, 2002.

Orthia, Lindy A. "Enlightenment Was the Choice: *Doctor Who* and the Democratization of Science." Australian National University, 2010. https://openresearch-repository.anu.edu.au/bitstream/1885/49358/6/02whole.pdf.

Schmitt, Cannon. "Techniques of Terror, Technologies of Nationality: Ann Radcliffe's *The Italian*." *ELH* 61, no. 4 (1994): 853–76.

Tranter, Kieran. "'Her Brain Was Full of Superstitious Nonsense': Modernism and the Failure of the Divine in *Doctor Who*." In *Religion and "Doctor Who": Time and Relative Dimensions in Faith*, edited by Andrew Crome and James McGrath, 131–44. Eugene, OR: Cascade Books, 2013.

Vrieze, Jop de. "Bruno Latour, a Veteran of the 'Science Wars,' Has a New Mission." *Science*, October 10, 2017. https://www.sciencemag.org/news/2017/10/bruno-latour-veteran-science-wars-has-new-mission.

Chapter Eleven

THE DEVIL'S IN IT: THE BIBLE AS GOTHIC

Brenda Ayres

In the first chapter of this volume, I recounted a history of Gothicism and neo-Gothicism and mentioned some of the key theorists who have written on the genre. There has a been a prolific outpouring of Gothic texts and renditions from the fourth century to the present, but if we can equate Gothicism with horror and terror, then true Gothicism—by any other name—begins with the biblical narrative when Satan rebelled against God, became evil incarnate, vied for power over and against God and brought death and sin into the world. That is when the horrors of life became the text of human life. The first written Gothic tale made it into the early writing scrolls, letters and accounts that would later be canonized into the Holy Bible.

Subsequent to Satan's inclination to become God, we have had Gothic narratives. More recently they have ignited myriad criticism and analysis of the genre, running from disdain to enthusiasm to revelation and insight into the human condition. Nearly every theoretical tool has been used to interpret Gothicism, from psychoanalysis to historicism to Marxism to postcolonialism to structuralism and so forth. Although there is a plethora of literary commentary on Gothicism—whether it be pre-Gothic, old Gothic, new (Victorian) Gothic or neo-Gothic—and although the word "demonic" is thrown about as well as a nod or two made about the Gothic theme of good versus evil, there is very little biblical contextualization of the Gothic. Alison Milbank was astute in placing "God" in the Gothic (in her 2018 *God and the Gothic*), and she mentions Satan/Devil/demons several times but mostly in reference to Faust. Before Milbank, Victor Sage wrote *Horror Fiction in the Protestant Tradition* (1988), addressing religion but saying very little about the devil and his legions.

If, rather, literary scholars insist that the genesis of Gothicism is Walpole's work, then they might concur with Fred Botting that the purpose of eighteenth-century Gothic literature was to "inculcate a sense of morality and rational understanding and thus educate readers in the discrimination of virtue and vice" (1996, 22). "Despite being associated with literary and moral impropriety," he adds, "many Gothic novels set out to vindicate morality, virtue and reason. They were thus caught between their avowedly moral and conventional projects and the unacceptably unrealistic mode of representation they employed" (46). Postmodernism tends to reject any notion of good versus evil and regards morality as relative and rejects anything so absolute as God, disavowing all but the here and now. Nonetheless, given the increase in the supernatural/spiritual appearing in neo-Gothicism, might it not be said that postmodernism has been too hasty to dismiss the beliefs of the past and the present, in particular those narrated in the Bible? By the "Bible," I am referring to the Protestant canonized version beginning with the King James, but not excluding more recent translations. Perhaps literary theory has been illusory and pre-emptively premature in exorcising the Bible as a narrative of universal truth.

Whether or not readers accept or tolerate a conviction that the Bible is *the* Word of God, they cannot deny the impact that the Bible has had throughout history in moulding perceptions and perspectives, specifically about good and evil—about God and the devil. There are millions of people who hold a biblical world view and write, read and view Gothic narratives through that vantage point, so why should there not be a theoretical approach that interprets narratives through a biblical lens? Is it not a theoretical approach as efficacious and valid as any other?

Although more recent Gothicism avoids moralising and asserting any moral absolutes, the Gothic has always and continues to "give[] shape to concepts of the place of evil in the human mind" (MacAndrew 1979, 3), not just in the cerebral and not just in nightmares but through a broader ontological context that includes spiritual (good) and supernatural (evil) beings that interface and interact with humans. To those persons who base their knowledge of truth on the Bible as God's word of truth, evil is a reality: Satan and his league of demons do infest this world, and have done so after God created this world and will do so until God allows Satan to destroy it, and then God will create a new earth and bind the devil and his own for the rest of eternity. That is the full plot of the Bible, wrapped up in the last book, Revelation. If Gothicism, and even more so neo-Gothicism, implicate the spiritual and the supernatural, then would it not be fitting to analyse such narrative through the lens specifically tailored for the spiritual and supernatural, that is, biblical theory?

John Bowen has put such a theory in a time-sensitive context:

Gothic is thus a world of doubt, particularly doubt about the supernatural and the spiritual. It seeks to create in our minds the possibility that there may be things beyond human power, reason and knowledge. But that possibility is constantly accompanied by uncertainty. In Radcliffe's work, even the most terrifying things turn out to have rational, non-supernatural explanations; by contrast, in Lewis's *The Monk*, Satan himself appears. The uncertainty that goes with Gothic is very characteristic of a world in which orthodox religious belief is waning; there is both an exaggerated interest in the supernatural and the constant possibility that even very astonishing things will turn out to be explicable. (2014)

The need for spiritual truth concerning supernatural entities and their functions, limitations and impact on human lives finds expression in the Gothic and even more so in the neo-Gothic. In the nineteenth century, Bram Stocker's *Dracula* (1897) uses biblical language in reference to the vampire: the word "evil" appears twenty times; "Satan," twice; "demon," five times; and "devil," sixteen times. In the twenty-first century Anne Rice, in her *The Vampire Lestat*, explains the existence and the reason for the existence of vampires in biblical terms: "I tell you, you walk this earth as all evil things do, by the will of God, to make morals suffer for his Divine Glory. And by the will of God you can be destroyed" (2014 [1985], 192). Then Mary Going, in her "The Blood Is the Life: An Exploration of the Vampire's Jewish Shadow," locates the origin of the vampire in the Bible (2019, 38), but she is a rare theorist to use the Bible to theorise the Gothic. Regardless of one's theology or attitude towards theology, the true provenance of Gothicism is the narrative of the Christian Bible. One might make the same argument for the Koran. One cannot have the Gothic without the machinations of the devil and his evil minions.

Job is the oldest book in the Bible, having been written 400 years before Moses wrote the Pentateuch (the first five books of the Old Testament), and is therefore the oldest Gothic narrative. The first chapter in Job tells how "one day the angels came to present themselves before the Lord, and Satan also came with them. The Lord said to Satan, 'Where have you come from?' Satan answered the Lord, 'From roaming throughout the earth, going back and forth on it'" (6-7).[1] This verse reveals that Satan is actively cultivating evil on earth; his antics have been the substance of many Gothic narratives ever since. When God pointed out Job as "blameless and upright, a man who fears God and shuns evil" (8), Satan taunts God by arguing that the reason why Job obeys is because God has abundantly blessed him with provision and family. So God gives Satan permission to eliminate these blessings, which he does but Job continues to praise God and will not accuse Him of any wrongdoing (9-22), unlike what most people do. In chapter two, the angels present themselves to God again, and Satan shows up, contending that Job will curse God if his health failed. God grants Satan permission to afflict Job's entire body with sores, but Job still does not sin against God with his mouth (4-10). In the rest of the book, Job is visited by three friends who blame him for all that has happened. It is not long before Job curses the day he was born (3:1). Through the theological debate that follows, Job arrives at a place where he questions the wisdom and love of God (again a common human response to trials), and then in the last chapters, God basically says that He does not need to explain Himself to Job, that no man can fully understand God's ways because no one is God but God. He asks His people to trust and put their faith in Him even when they do not comprehend His will.

If such a good and "blameless" man like Job could be so tested by the devil, then it is very probable that all humans are subject to similar testing. That goes for Christians as well who are told: "for our struggle is not against flesh and blood, but against rulers, against the authorities, against the powers of this dark world and against the spiritual forces of evil in the heavenly realms" (Eph. 6:12). Even Jesus was tempted by the devil when the Holy Spirit led him into the wilderness (Matt. 4:1-11, Mk. 1:12-13 and Lk. 4:1-13). The story reveals that Satan knows the word of God (now written in the Bible) and does quote it to his own advantage. Therefore, in any book or film about Dracula or about an exorcism, either Gothic or neo-Gothic, just holding up the Bible or quoting from it is not going to scare Satan or any demon(s) away. Just by mentioning the name of Jesus is not going to drive off the forces of evil either because Satan is not afraid of Jesus (as shown in Matt. 5), and Satan is arrogant enough to think that he can tempt Jesus to sin, disobey God and serve Satan instead. Satan fails.

Satan was not always evil. His earliest name was Lucifer, which means "light-bringer." Originally, he was an angel who was extremely beautiful (Isa. 14:12). He was "blameless" and "anointed," but too soon full of pride because of his "beauty" and "splendor" (Ezek. 28:12-17). He wanted to "ascend to heaven," "raise [his] throne above the stars of God" and "make [himself] like the Most High" (Isa. 14:13-14). His claim to be God (Ezek. 28:9) seals his fate: He will be "thrown into the lake of fire and brimstone, where the beast and the false prophet are also; and they will be tormented day and night forever and ever" (Rev. 20:10).

Although unsuccessful with Jesus, he is more victorious with the first woman, Eve, who will become the first Gothic victim or passive receptor of evil. He misquotes God to make the restriction sound more unbearable and unreasonable: "Did God really say, 'You must not eat from any tree in the garden?'" (Gen. 3:1). The true wording was "You are free to eat from any tree in the garden; but you must not eat from the tree of the knowledge of good and evil, for when you eat from it you will certainly die" (Gen. 2:16-17). Satan then encourages Eve to fall into the same spiritual pride that got him evicted from heaven in the first place; he convinces Eve that if she eats the forbidden fruit, her "eyes will be opened, and [she] will be like God, knowing good and evil" (Gen. 3:5). Once she takes his advice and disobeys God, to her utter dismay, she does indeed come to know "good and evil" where earlier she knew only good.

The noun "satan" in Hebrew means "adversary" or "accuser" and appears nine times in the Bible, including in Job. In Revelation 12, he is called "that ancient serpent" who will be thrown down and forever bound in the lake of fire. Since the Genesis account describes the serpent as "more crafty than any of the wild animals" (1), does that mean that Satan inhabits the serpent? The medievalists believed that demons either took on the guise of an animal or possessed it. A possessed animal was and is called a familial spirit or animal guide. The most popular has been the black cat, which appears in *Charmed* (for one), the television series from 1998 through 2006, about three sisters who were "good" witches who try to protect innocent people from evil demons.

Despite the dogged idea that there is something called "white magic" and that there are "good witches" in Gothicism and neo-Gothicism, none of this is biblical. Throughout the entire Bible are warnings against consulting witches, mediums, spiritualists, fortune tellers, powwow doctors[2] and anyone else who professes to have supernatural power that is not from Christ through the Holy Spirit.[3] This taboo means that we are forbidden to read fortune cookies and horoscopes, consult fortune tellers and psychics and to think that Glinda in *The Wizard of Oz* movie (1939) and Samantha in *Bewitched* (airing on ABC from 1964 to 1972) were good witches and that Harry Potter is a good wizard, all of which fight evil forces. Other television series with "good witches" and familial spirits are *Chilling Adventures of Sabrina* (2018–19) based on a comic book that began in 2014; *Fantastic Beasts: The Crimes of Grindelwald* (2018–21); *Sugar Sugar Rune*, an anime television series (2004–2007); *The Witch* (2015–16); "The Familiar" and "What We Do in the Shadows" in *The X-Files* (2018 and 2019, respectively); and *What We Do in the Shadows* (2019–20). In addition, the popular game of *Dungeons & Dragons*, first published in 1974, features wizards, witches, warlocks and familial spirits. As of 2015, more than 20 million people have played the game with an estimated 5.5 active users, and it has had "literally thousands of spin-offs" (MacCallum-Stewart 2009, 186).

There have been numerous neo-Gothic works, though, that emphasise how indisputably evil witchcraft and other occult practices can be, such as *The Blair Witch Project* (1999) and *The Conjuring* (2013). No one who consults the supernatural is spared evil consequences; Satan and his demons are incapable of supplying anything but.

According to the Bible, the only one to be consulted about spiritual matters is the Holy Spirit. If someone needs supernatural healing, supernatural deliverance, spiritual baptism and spiritual advice, then he/she is told to turn to the Holy Spirit. Jesus said that after He would die, He would send the Holy Spirit to teach believers spiritual truths (Jn. 14:26) and empower them to effect even greater spiritual acts than the miracles Jesus performed while on earth, like healing supernaturally, delivering people from demon bondage and raising people from the dead (Jn. 14:13-14). The Holy Spirit does not act on His own accord; He speaks as Christ and God disclose for the sole purpose of glorifying God (Jn. 16:13-15). This spiritual power is entirely different from the supernatural power of the occult. Satan's sole purpose is "to steal and kill and destroy" (Jn. 10:10). There is "no truth in him"; he "is a liar and the father of lies" (Jn. 8:44). In direct contrast, God gives this assurance: "For I know the plans that I have for you, declares the Lord, plans to prosper you and not to harm you, to give you a future and a hope" (Jer. 29:11).

Satan does not act alone; he is the ruler over a dominion of demons. "Demons" are mentioned in 19 out of the 27 New Testament books, and the word "devils" appears four times in the Old Testament. He "is a figure amply suited to Gothic mythology, his Miltonic antecedents granting him sufficient nobility, introspection, and perverse attractiveness to accelerate him into a Gothic Hero. As such, he is a brooding offstage presence in works such as *Melmoth the Wanderer* by Charles Robert Maturin; he attains an intrusive role, variously threatening and temptingly debonair, in novels such as *The Monk* by Matthew G. Lewis or *The Sorrows of Satan* (1895) by Marie Corelli" (Hughes 2013, 219).

Still, Moses in the Bible warns to "no more offer their sacrifices unto devils after whom they have gone a whoring" (Lev. 17:7 KJV). The same term is in 2 Chroni 11:15, when Jeroboam murdered all the priests that served the Lord and replaced them with priests that served the devils. The Hebrew word for "devils" here is *se'irim*, translated as "goat idols" in the New International Version or "goat demons" in the New American Standard. Elsewhere translated as "hairy demons," it has evolved into the English word "satyrs." The image may have been associated with Pan who was widely worshipped in the Middle East and considered "the emblem of fecundity" (*Inquiry* 1848, 17), or in keeping with his gender, representative of lust.

"Satyrs" and Pan, of course, do appear in literature; Satyr plays were common among the Ancient Greeks. About the mythological Pan, G. K. Chesterton wrote: "It is said truly in a sense that Pan died because Christ was born. It is almost as true in another sense that men knew that Christ was born because Pan was already dead. A void was made by the vanishing world of the whole mythology of mankind, which would have asphyxiated like a vacuum if it had not been filed with theology" (1986 [1925], 292). Of course, he said this before the appearance of Mr. Tumnus in C. S. Lewis' *The Chronicles of Narnia* (1950–56) and before Guillermo del Toro's *Pan's Labyrinth* (2006).

Unlike the portrayals in these last two works, Satan and many of his demons are highly sexually charged and often perversely so—as will be addressed in the discussion below on *Rosemary's Baby* (1967). Gender, though, was blended in the two occurrences of "devils" or *sheedim* in Deuteronomy 32:17 and Psalm 106:37-39, again an indictment of worshipping and whoring after them. Although the word signifies masculine plural, it refers to multiple breasts and was the Hebrew name for Isis who was worshipped by the Egyptians and Diana (18), associated with fertility, childbirth and the underworld. Hence when studying the Gothic, one can expect some convoluted notions about gender. One can also expect what Ruth Bienstock Anolik calls "horrifying sex" (2007); and Candice Black, in following the theories of the Austro-German psychiatrist Richard von Krafft-Ebing in his *Psychopathia Sexualis* (1886), describes as "Satanica Sexualis" (2007).

In the Old Testament are several warnings that go mostly unheeded by believers and non-believers alike. Inherently, a professing Christian is one who believes in the existence of the Trinune God: God, Christ and the Holy Spirit (also known as the Holy Ghost). All three are spiritual beings. In John 3, Jesus said that "no one can see the kingdom of God unless they are born again" (3). When asked to clarify, Jesus replied, "Very truly I tell you, no one can enter the kingdom of God unless they are born of water and the Spirit. Flesh gives birth to flesh, but the Spirit gives birth to spirit. You should not be surprised at my saying, 'You must be born again.' The wind blows wherever it pleases. You hear its sound, but you cannot tell where it comes from or where it is going. So it is with everyone born of the spirit" (5-8). Paul explains: "The person without the Spirit does not accept the things that come from the Spirit of God but considers them foolishness, and cannot understand them because they are discerned only through the Spirit" (1 Cor. 2:14). In other words, to know God, to see God and to hear God is possible through the Spirit, although Romans 1 and 2 also claim that God has given each person a conscience that craves to know God and should see Him in nature. They often see the spiritual in nature, but then they worship the creation instead of the Creator (Rom. 1:25). We may see leaves scurrying from a wind, but we cannot see the wind and yet that neither means that the wind does not exist nor that we cannot understand from whence it comes (Jn. 3:8).

Most readers will concede that God must be spirit, but many of them are not acquainted with the rest of the spiritual and supernatural hosts described in the Bible, such as angels, demons and Satan. Most neo-Gothic and other modern narratives dispense the same ignorance of the preternatural.

On recurring error is the assumption that when people die, they become angels, like Clarence in *It's a Wonderful Life* (1946), and that they might act as someone's guardian angel and participate in human affairs so that they can earn their wings. This premise is not biblically true. Many people believe or want to believe in angels. When *Touched by an Angel* premiered in 1994, it was the beginning of a nine-year run becoming one of "CBS' highest-rated series, with more than 121 million viewers, and it was nominated for eleven Primetime Emmy awards and three Golden Globe awards" (Benge 2019). Psalm 148 declares that angels were created by God, separately from humans, and this is confirmed in the New Testament (Col. 1:16); angels are supernatural beings—both good and evil— that can come to earth in the form of humans as messengers from God (as they did when the appeared to Abraham in Genesis 18, to Lot in Genesis 19 when Sodomites wanted to have sex with them, to Mary in Luke 1 and to the shepherds in Luke 2; they are separate from the Trinity and in fact worship the Trinity (Heb. 1) and are not, never were and never will be humans (Rev. 7).

Evil beings do interact with humans in corporeal fashion, and Satan does often produce a counterfeit to God's actions, meant to deceive and confuse people so that they will not believe in God. The Old Testament holds over three hundred prophesies of the birth, life, death and resurrection of Christ, the Messiah (Lockyer 1973). Before Mary was impregnated by God, an angel came to tell her what would happen and ask if she would be willing to become the mother of God incarnate (Lk. 1:26-38). God *did not* rape her. He created us with free will and does not force Himself on us (Deut. 30:15-19).

In contrast, in *Rosemary's Baby*, the protagonist is raped by Satan. The 1968 movie was based on the book (1967) by Ira Levin (who also wrote *The Stepford Wives* in 1972), which sold over four million copies, "making it the top bestselling horror novel of the 1960s" (Hoppenstand 1994, 38). A young couple move into an apartment that had been built in the old Gothic Revival-style, by a man who practiced witchcraft and cannibalism. One night she is raped by the devil. Her husband and neighbours are all involved in Satanic rituals, and anyone who gets in their way is moved out of the way; for example, their friend, Hutch, wants to warn Rosemary about the Satanism, but falls into a coma, and three months later, dies, but not before he gives her a book on witchcraft. She gives birth to a child who is to become the Antichrist. The evil in the book and the film are unabashedly biblical. The word "antichrist(s)" is mentioned five times in the New Testament and is prophesied in Daniel 7. There have been many antichrists throughout history as foretold in 1 John 2:18-22, but there is to be one, a great leader who will deceive people and persuade them through signs and wonders to claim him as God. When Jesus defeats him, the earth will be destroyed, Christ will judge all people who ever lived, Satan, the Antichrist and all their followers will be locked in hell for eternity and then there will be a new heaven and earth. This is the prophesy in Revelation, Daniel 7 and 8, and 2 Thessalonians 2.

Since 1968 there were a sequel, a television film in 1978 and a four-hour miniseries in 2014. The director and screenwriter for the first movie, Roman Polanski, also directed *The Ninth Gate* (1999) about the devil, as well as *The Fearless Vampire Killers* earlier, in 1967, in which he also starred alongside a woman he would marry, Sharon Tate. She and four friends would be murdered by the Mason Family in 1969. In 1977 he was charged with drugging and raping a 13-year-old girl, to which he pled guilty, and then escaped to Paris to avoid a prison sentence in America. The moral of this tale is sometimes presented in Gothic fiction, but it is a biblical maxim: "Be of sober spirit, be on the alert. Your adversary, the devil, prowls around like a roaring lion, seeking someone to devour" (1 Pet. 5:8). He is incapable of doing good, and he destroys all humans that serve him, which I never thought was very wise of him.

Good Omens: The Nice and Accurate Prophecies of Agnes Nutter, Witch (1990), a novel by Terry Pratchett and Neil Gaiman, reads almost like a sequel to *Rosemary's Baby*, only it is a comedy about the Antichrist and end times, as if the prophesies in Daniel and Revelation (in the Bible) cannot be taken seriously. The book was made into *Good Omens*, a television miniseries that was first streamed through Amazon Prime Video in May 2019 and is to be broadcast later through BBC in the United Kingdom. The book was a nominee for the 1991 World Fantasy Award for Best Novel and Locus Award for Best Fantasy Novel ("1991 Award Winners" 2019).

Eleanor Beal and Jonathan Greenaway published a collection of essays under the title *Horror and Religion: New Literary Approaches to Theology, Race and Sexuality*. They articulate their mission for the book in their introduction: "to reassess the place of the religious in dominant histories of Horror and reintegrate marginalized theological and religious lines of inquiry into Horror history by considering and examining constructions of religion within the file of Horror literature" (2019, 10). The challenge to such a project is "the sheer scale and heterogeneity of theology and problems of definition—just what theology might mean" (4).

It is true that a plethora of Protestant denominations alone have arisen because of different interpretations of the Bible. But "God is not the author of confusion, but of peace" (1 Cor. 14:33). The dissension that has resulted in not understanding the Bible through the Holy Spirit is human and Satan driven. Beal and Greenaway's work focuses on theology, but rarely does it refer to the Bible, when God has given instructions for its usage: "All Scriptures is inspired by God and profitable for teaching, for reproof, for correction, for training in righteousness" (2 Tim. 3:16).

Judging by the proliferation of zombies, golems, vampires, dragons, humanoids, extraterrestrial aliens, resurrected prehistoric animals and the like in neo-Gothic media, one might conclude that the world needs a lens to discern good from evil and to comprehend a truth perceived beyond the natural senses.

This was certainly true one day after Christmas in 1973 around the globe when *The Exorcist* was released in theatres to long lines of customers willing to stand out in the cold waiting to buy a ticket. It would be the first horror film to be nominated for an Academy Award for Best Picture. A columnist for *Hollywood Report* called it "the most successful and influential horror films of all time" (Barnes 2010). Each year the Library of Congress selects 25 American films that are deemed "culturally, historically, or aesthetically significant." *The Exorcist* was named as one to enter the National Film Registry in 2010 (Barnes).

After *The Exorcist* there has been a steady stream of Gothic tales that iterate the presence of evil in our lives. In fact, on September 26, 2019, *Evil*, created by Robert King and Michelle King, aired on television and on the internet and was watched by 7.96 million people (Thorne 2019). The CBS website describes it as "a psychological mystery that examines the origins of evil along the dividing line between science and religion" (*Evil*). The three major characters are a priest-in-training, a sceptical female psychologist and a carpenter who is also adroit in technology. This team's job is to investigate the Catholic Church's backlog of unexplained mysteries, including supposed miracles, demonic possessions and hauntings. They are to discern whether these occurrences can be explained logically or if they are indeed caused by supernatural phenomena. As of my writing, seven episodes have aired, and throughout, the one thing all three of them seem to miss is that extreme psychological trauma can open the door for demonic oppression and possession[4]; the psychological, the logical and the supernatural can all function in the same space.

David Acosta, the priest-in-training, has been employed by the Catholic Church as a "professional assessor" to discern whether there is demonic activity and whether there are verifiable, supernatural miracles that occur. He is definitely a believer in God, in Satan and in all the spirituality and supernatural described in the Bible. This is Gothic— this belief that the Catholic Church is mystical and that exorcism can be done only by Catholic priests (or almost priests). The show is neo-Gothic because it deals with modern concerns (like the psychologist on the team having four daughters to raise by herself while her husband is off climbing mountains), and the assessor is an African American, when stereotypically African Americans have been associated with, on the one hand, Black churches, Pentecostalism and the Baptist denomination, and on the other hand, Vodun, voodoo and Candomblé. Although he is a mystic, he is very serene and will entertain rational explanations for what appears to the supernatural. Also, he takes hallucinogens in order to see and hear God, and although this may be practiced in some religions, there is no mention that anyone in the Bible who has had visions did so through drugs.

Dr. Kristen Bouchard is the psychologist who has regular sessions with her own psychologist, Dr. Boggs. She is a lapsed Catholic, is not religious at all and adamantly refuses to believe in the supernatural, attempting instead to pose a psychological answer for all human behaviour. David wants her input in discerning whether the behaviour of their subjects can be diagnosed as something psychological. He wants to rely upon her psychological knowledge.

The third member is Ben Shakir, a non-practicing Muslim (another departure from Gothic stereotypes) who works with David as his technical expert and equipment handler; he is the voice of practicality who looks for alternate answers to those items that seem to be supernatural to the viewer and to David. For example, in episode three, titled "3 Stars," a demonic voice comes through a voice-control device (like Siri and Alexa). He is able to track down a hacker who is responsible for this scare tactic, but then he cannot account for the voice that comes through the device at his home that reveals secrets that his sister could know. He and Kristen are each called to be a "devil's advocate," an ironic term, in that Jesus called the Holy Spirit, the "Advocate" (Jn. 14:16).

There are several other regulars who are important to the series' search for truth. Dr. Kristen Bouchard has four young daughters who attend a Catholic school. They are the innocent children who are vulnerable to the evil of occult practices because they are not protected by parents or grandmothers who are unaware of the danger of such things as the Ouija board (ep. 4). In *The Exorcist*, the 11-year-old Regan becomes demon possessed only after she plays with the Ouija board (Blatty 2011 [1971] 39, 79, 80, 83 and 137). In his *The Antics of Satan and His Army of Fallen Angels*, Father Gabriele Amorth reminds us of the First Commandment: You shall have no other gods before me" (Exod. 20:3). He understands this to mean that we are to refrain from turning to "witches, fortune-tellers, occultists, or wizards" (2016, 39). To that I would add tarot cards, crystal balls, horoscopes and fortune cookies while agreeing with his definition of "superstition" from the Latin "superstitio," which "indicates when something is superimposed on another distorting the original sense" (39).

These practices are forbidden in the Bible and can open the door to demon possession.[5] The book of 1 Samuel tells a relevant story about fortune telling. When Saul was anointed by God to become king, he had all the mediums and spiritists removed from his kingdom (1 Sam. 28:3). He relied upon the prophet that God sent to him, to intercede on his behalf and receive direction from God. Disastrously, Saul was notorious about receiving instructions from God and then failing to follow them. One significant example is when he was told to destroy all the Amalekites and their livestock. Knowing that King Saul failed to obey Him, God told the prophet Samuel, "I regret that I have made Saul king, for he has turned back from following Me and has not carried out My commands" (1 Sam. 15:11). Saul lied to Samuel and said that he did follow God's commands, to which Samuel replied, "What then is this bleating of the sheep in my ears, and the lowing of the oxen which I hear?" (14). Saul argued then that he did not kill the sheep and oxen because he planned to sacrifice them to God, thus doing a very religious thing—he wanted to be righteous on his own terms instead of God's.

Moreover, Saul, "being wise in his own eyes" (Prov. 26:5), spared the king and queen, but he did not tell Samuel about the queen. Samuel killed King Agag, but the queen, who was pregnant, survived. The consequences were not just God's displeasure of one king's disobedience; some five hundred years later, Haman, an Agagite or offspring of the Amalekite queen, persuaded King Ahasuerus to eradicate the Jews (Est. 3:5–7:9). If God had not intervened, His chosen people would have disappeared from the earth, which means that Jesus, the Messiah, would not have been born.

Samuel warned Saul with this statement: "For rebellion is as the sin of divination, and insubordination is as an iniquity and idolatry. Because you have rejected the word of the Lord, He has also rejected from being king" (1 Sam. 15:23). After Samuel died, Saul "was afraid and trembled violently" at the prospects of being defeated by the Philistine army (1 Sam. 28:5). He asked God for advice, but God did not speak to him, so he consulted a witch who supposedly conjured up the spirit of Samuel (6-24). Demons that can impersonate dead people are called familiar spirits (1 Sam. 28:3 and Lev. 19). God will never speak through a medium or witch (Deut. 8:10-12 and Lev. 20:27).

Saul was not ignorant of the supernatural, but he refused to obey God. The grandmother in *Evil* is the typical person who is ignorant of the Bible, the supernatural and psychology. She means well but is totally misinformed at how to "raise up a child in the way he should go" (Prov. 22:6) as evident when she gives them virtual reality goggles that enable them to see the monstrous insects and spiders, gruesome ghouls with dripping blood bent on slashing them and a haunted girl ghost. The grandmother represents the secular person who thinks that playing with the occult is a child's game. Then she begins to date Dr. Leland Townsend, a forensic psychologist who, although he looks like a meek and mild man with the eyes of a deer in the headlights behind his glasses, is proven to be a demon in human form in episode seven. He seems to have only one mission and that is to lead people into evil. In an earlier episode, David describes him as a psychopath that encourages others to do evil, but he does not discount that Townsend is 100 per cent evil.

The first episode introduces an incubus by the name of George who looks like something Henry Fuseli could have painted. George visits Kristen while she is in bed. She devises a test to learn if George is just a dream or is real. When George is chopping off her fingers, she confirms that she's in a dream. He appears to her again in episode six. Although she has worked out a plan with her psychologist to take control of her dreams, the incubus has not been told that he is only a dream. The viewer is to understand that George is real; he is an incubus, and incubi really do exist, as authenticated in the Bible.

From the Latin, the word means "to lie upon." Incubi in the Bible are called "sons of God" who conceive with humans and produce progeny known as "Nephilim" (which were renamed as cambions during Medieval times, from the Proto-Celtic *Kamb* or "crooked bent"). In Genesis 6, before the flood, the "Nephilim were on the earth in those days, and also afterward, when the sons of God came in to the daughters of men, and they bore children to them [...]. Then the Lord saw the wickedness of man was great on the earth, and that every intent of the thoughts of his heart was only evil continually. The Lord was sorry that He had made men on the earth, and He was grieved in His heart" (4-6). They are also described in Numbers 13. Besides the Bible, the first incubus mentioned in a narrative is found in the earliest surviving literature, *The Epic of Gilgamesh* (1800 BC): The incubus is Lilu, Gilgamesh's father. The two most famous cambions from fiction are Shakespeare's Caliban and Geoffrey of Monmouth's Merlin.

The television series thus far is accurately reflecting a biblical view of evil. In the first episode, a serial killer is trying to persuade all that the devil made him kill people. When Kristen interviews him, supposedly a demon inside him repeats what was said between her and the incubus. She is quite shaken by his supernatural knowledge of her personal experience. Afterwards, with calm detachment, she remembers that she revealed the incubus visitation to her own psychologist and then discovers that Townsend stole her file thus gaining notes of that and all her sessions. Mystery solved, except how did Townsend know who her psychologist was and that she visited him that day, and how did he manage to steal the file out of a locked cabinet? His wife apparently had emailed her husband, the serial killer, information about how to act demon possessed, which includes speaking in tongues (preferably Latin) and sounding demonic. Yet, how could he break free from his chains, which he did?

In episode five of *Evil*, one of the storylines is that David and Kristen must determine if a woman is demon possessed as she undergoes exorcism by a priest. Caroline Hopkins is bound, sweats blood, vomits, exhibits superhuman strength and speaks in tongues. The two psychologists, Kristen and Dr. Boggs, think all these symptomatic of a schizophrenic and want to send for an ambulance for medical care. Monsignor Matthew Korecki and David believe that she is demon possessed, and despite an earlier exorcism, she is not free. The monsignor and David explain the problem from Matthew 12: "When an impure spirit comes out of a person, it goes through arid places seeking rest and does not find it. Then it says, 'I will return to the house I left.' When it arrives, it finds the house unoccupied, swept clean and put in order. Then it goes and takes with it seven other spirits more wicked than itself, and they go in and they go in and live there. And the final condition of that person is worse than the first. That is how it will be with this wicked generation" (43-45 NIV).

The woman's husband makes the decision that the priest and David should complete the exorcism, while the psychologists look on with concern and scepticism. Caroline has supernatural knowledge of David's visions but lies about their meanings in order to scare him away. David's vision, he learns, is the same vision that Leonardo da Vinci had when he painted *Salvator Mundi* (1500). The three lights in the ball that rests in Christ's hand represent the Trinity. Caroline's demons tell David that his vision is from hell instead of heaven and that the demonic forces are going to kill him. That is when he bargains with them to leave Caroline since it is he that they want. When they do, Caroline visually returns to normal and has peace. The psychologists are amazed.

Mark 5:2-15 (as well as Lk. 8:27-35) tells the story of when Jesus was met by a man "with an impure spirit." This man, like the serial killer and Caroline in *Evil*, had supernatural strength. He was so strong that he could not be bound, even with a chain (Mk. 5:3). He lived "among the tombs and in the hills he would cry out and cut himself with stones" (5). As did the priest in *Evil*, Jesus asked the "impure spirit" his name (9), and the answer was "My name is Legion [...] for we are many" (9). Jesus commanded the demons to leave the man, and they negotiated with him to be sent into a large herd of swine (11). Then the 2,000 pigs rushed down a steep hill into the sea and drowned (10-14). The implication is that demons are real, and they can inhabit animals and people. Demons are subject to Christ, and through Him and the Holy Spirit, they can be exorcised. This is not done through magic or sorcery; Christ has absolute power and divine authority over them (Lk. 4:41).

In the episode scheduled to air on Halloween night, of course, there had to be a ghost, and best of all, a little girl ghost, and she is incredibly malevolent. Ghosts are frequent characters in Gothic and neo-Gothic narratives.

A television series that did not do well was *The Sixth Sense* that ran for two seasons (1971–72), but the movie by the same name in 1999 was the highest grossing horror movie of all time until it was surpassed by *It* in 2917 (Bean 2019). The dates may be indicators of the rise and fall of interest in the supernatural by international cultures. Both the televised series and the movie involved a parapsychology researcher from UCLA who investigated supernatural mysteries and crimes. In 1971, the first episode had a close-up of a quote from Sigmund Freud: "If I had my life to live over again, I should devote myself to psychical research rather than psychoanalysis" (quoted in Williams 2015, 47). Freud did refrain from using "devils" and other biblical or mystical Jewish semantics and instead referred to "repressions" and "complexes" (41). Each opening episode of *The Sixth Sense* began with a quote from the Bible (Joel 2:28): "Your sons and daughters will prophesy, / Your old men will dream dreams, / Your young men will see visions" (Bloch).

More popular was *The Addams Family* (1964–73) with its haunted house, neo-Frankenstein butler, an animated hand (not attached to any body) and a cast of other supernatural beings. It was made into a several movies afterwards, including one in 2019. It was first created as a cartoon by Charles Addams in 1938. The series has won all sorts of awards, been adapted to other media, made into a musical, developed into movies and television shows and featured in video games, and it has probably done more to a promote the Goth culture than any other show. Paradoxically, the 1991 movie was listed as one of "The 50 Best Family Films" by *The Guardian* (2010). This show, along with Halloween and Harry Potter books, is considered innocuous by the culture in general, but all three are very controversial among fundamental Christian and Islamic groups; the founder of Focus on the Family, a large Evangelical Christian group, denounced the Harry Potter series (James Dobson quoted in Jackson 2007). Dobson's chief spokesman said: "[They contain] some powerful and valuable lessons about love and courage and the ultimate victory of good over evil; however, the positive messages are packaged in a medium—witchcraft—that is directly denounced in Scripture."[6]

Unfortunately, many nineteenth-century Gothic narratives could not or did not differentiate evil from good. Beginning with Matthew Gregory Lewis' *The Monk* (1796) and especially through the nineteenth-century Gothic novels by the British, Catholics have been treated as evil beings.[7] Patrick R. O'Malley observes that the anti-Catholic element in Gothic novels ended with the end of the nineteenth century (2006, 33), but the Jew continued to be treated as a figure of Gothic horror well into the twentieth century (192). Nevertheless, stereotypes persist in the neo-Gothic as evident in *Evil*.

Neo-Gothic narratives seem to have the opposite problem: They cannot or do not discern good from evil. Is there such a thing as a friendly ghost like *Caspar* and the like? In the well-known Lazarus story in the Bible, Jesus tells of a rich man who died and went to Hades (or hell) and then begged to be delivered from there. He was informed that there is a "great chasm fixed" between heaven and hell, and "none may cross over" (Lk. 16:26). Upon hearing that he could not appear on earth, the man in hell wanted to come back to earth and warn his relatives that hell is a horrible place and that they should not end up where he is. Surely they would listen to someone "from the dead [and] repent," but the answer was that since they "do not listen to Moses and the Prophets, they will not be persuaded even if someone rises from the dead" (Lk. 16:19-30). According to this passage, God does not permit someone who is in "torment" and "agony" (23-26) to leave hell and come to earth with a message about repentance.

Biblically, then, the ghosts that haunt houses are actually demons in spectral form. In the first century, Pliny the Younger may have been the first to write about a ghost haunting (Cardin 2017, 7), but literally thousands of Gothic tales with haunted houses have followed suit; in fact, it is now considered a subgenre. The Gothic continues to portray ghosts as restless spirits of the murdered dead that haunt either for help to die in piece or else to achieve vengeance. Victor Sage reads the haunted house narrative as a symbol of its owner, one who is restless about the modern world, one who feels as if he/she is buried alive and one whose past life is haunting (1988, 17–18).

Regardless of the reason for the horror, scary Ghost stories have done extremely well in book sales and movie tickets, but usually they were from the point of view of those being haunted. The movies *The Sixth Sense* (1991) and *The Others* (2001) were about "good" people who did not realize that they were actually ghosts. *Casper* (1995) was another film that presented a friendly ghost. It was based on a character created by Seymour Reit and Joe Oriolo in the 1930s, intended for a children's storybook. Then it was made into movie cartoons in 1945 and has continued to be produced through a variety of media. Then beginning with a series of *Ghostbusters* (1984 through 2016), ghosts are presented as comic, obnoxious and mischievous beings that can be discarded as easily as taking out the trash.

Deuteronomy 18 gives this warning: "There shall not be found among you anyone who makes his son or his daughter pass through the fire, one who uses divination, one who practices witchcraft, or one who interprets omens, or a sorcerer, or one who casts a spell or a medium, or a spiritist, or one who calls up the dead. For whoever does these things is detestable to the Lord" (10-11). This is strong language, but the message to avoid the occult is crystal clear. The invocation of biblical demons as "family viewing" in neo-Gothicism may convey the modern family's desperation to find meaning and solutions to modern problems that cannot be found in the family unit. Glennis Byron and Sharon Deans, in their study of the *Hunger Games* trilogy (2008–2009) series, address a desperation in the modern family to find solutions beyond what the modern family is capable of providing. The stories heroise independent adolescents who, once removed from their families and home communities, gain power to bring about change in the world that will benefit their families (100).

Evil does not seem to equivocate about evil, which makes it more neo-Gothic than most of the Gothic that directly preceded it. Just as *The Exorcist* featured two Catholic priests, so there are a Catholic priest and a priest-in-training conducting the exorcisms that follow certain rituals such as the sacrament of Holy Water and the use of the crucifix. Exorcism is different from the deliverance ministries practiced in Protestant and Charismatic churches. Some do use crucifixes, holy water, and anointing oils as well as quotations from the Bible, but those in deliverance ministries believe that the individual must take responsibility and evict the demons from themselves or else the demons will not stay away from him or her.[8]

In *Evil*, when Caroline is being exorcised, Kristen secretly replaces the holy water in one of the bottles with tap water. When the priest throws some of that water at Caroline, just as before, her entire body cringes and she screams as if it were an acid. Kristen has her "Huh-huh" moment, but the priest is not deterred. He says that he believed that the water was holy, and Caroline believed it was holy. To receive a supernatural exorcism, deliverance or healing usually does take faith, although there were times in the New Testament that Jesus performed these miracles on people who had no faith in Him. Jesus said that it is only through witnessing "signs and wonders" that people will believe in Him (Jn. 4:48), and this is one of the reasons that the gifts of the Holy Spirit still operate in the church today (Acts 2). But Jesus also warned that "false Christs and false prophets will arise and will show great signs and wonders, so as to mislead, if possible, even the elect" (Matt. 24:24 NASB).

Kristen and Dr. Boggs are constantly trying to diagnose some mental illness among those who are either demon possessed or prophetic, and those who are experiencing some form of the paranormal. Many psychologists have argued that when people act as if they are demon possessed, in actuality they are experiencing some kind of chemical and/or psychological imbalance, for example, anti-NMDA receptor encephalitis. The NMDA receptor ensures that neurons communicate. If they are blocked, people act as if they have schizophrenia. "Speaking in Tongues" is spiritual phenomenon that is referenced in five places in the Bible: It is understood to be a sign of the baptism of the Holy Spirit (Mk 16:17), a prophetic gift to the church when accompanied by interpretation (1 Cor. 12-14), and a sign to a nonbeliever (Acts 2). Since "Satan himself masquerades as an angel of light" (2 Cor. 11:14), there should be no wonder that the demons counterfeit this spiritual gift, although the tongue of choice in the television series seems to be mostly Latin. Kristen says that this is xenoglossia, for "the deeply religious but highly delusional" (ep. 5).

When someone is delivered of evil spirits, the nonbeliever dismisses it as a delusion, that an individual believed that he/she was demon possessed and then believed that he/

she could be delivered spiritually of evil bondage. As of episode six, Kristen and Ben discount the supernatural, although their confidence in scientific explanations is eroding. In episode five Kristen is told by a prophet that she is to avoid wearing red for a week. The same prophet had warned her neighbourhood that they should vacate their homes because they were going to fall into the earth, and they did; they were swallowed up by a sinkhole. Kristen sees that her daughter is wearing a red sweatshirt, takes no chances and gives her her own tan sweatshirt to wear instead. Jeffrey Burton Russell, an expert on the devil, argues that the colour red has always been associated with evil due to its "hostile hue of the scorching sands" in contrast to black fertile dirt that gives life (1978, 78). Revelation 12:3 calls Satan the "great red dragon"; and 17:3, the "scarlet beast." Significantly, after Kristen's mother sleeps with Townsend, she pulls out of her closet a red dress.

By episode seven, all three assessors are fairly convinced that demons that had possessed a man and woman were responsible for the murder of several little boys.

Maggie Kilgour in her *The Rise of the Gothic Novel* defined the Gothic as "a nightmare vision of the modern world made up of detached individuals which has dissolved into predatory and demonic relations which cannot be reconciled into a healthy social order" (1995, 12).

I say again, why is it so fantastic to believe in God and not to believe also in the devil and demons? One may be skeptical of evil creatures because throughout history there have been charlatans who have taken advantage of susceptible people. In episode 6 of *Evil*, Ben has been invited to appear on a fictitious television program called *Demon Hunters*. Labeled as a "professional skeptic," he means to debunk the whole demon/supernatural business. It does not help that the Toni Pacuci character devises several technological hoaxes to convince Ben, and Vanessa (the show's scientist), that they are seeing a ghost. It is very difficult to know what to believe is truly supernatural versus contrived by humans. That is why it is listed as a spiritual gift, along with healing, effecting of miracles, prophecy, speaking in tongues and interpretation of tongues, but all of them are led by the Holy Spirit and subject to the will of God (1 Cor. 12: 4-11). Furthermore, it is not surprising either that there are so much effort for Satan to disguise his existence and activities in order to convince those who are so logical and who are without belief in the spiritual world that there is no such thing as God or the afterlife. He may think that he is winning. Regardless, if our culture is too sophisticated to accept spiritual truth in the primitive belief systems of times past, then why do we keep writing, reading, and watching the Gothic?

Notes

1 Unless otherwise noted, I will be quoting from the New American Standard because it is most accurate translations from original texts.
2 The word "powwow," coming from the Algonquians and meaning "healer," was adopted by Germans who settled in southeast Pennsylvania (since called the Pennsylvania Dutch) and brought with them their practices of divination, charms and spells based on what they believe(d) to be prescribed through the Bible and grimoires (handbooks of magic and witchcraft).
3 See Deut. 18:10-14; 1 Sam. 15:23 and 22:23; 2 Chron. 33:6; Lev. 19:31, 20:6 and 20:27; Isa. 8:19-22, 19:1-4 and 47:8-14; Mic. 5:10-12; Gal. 5:19-20, 5:19-21; Acts 8:9-13 and 19:17-20; Rev. 18:23, and 21:8.

4 Tobias Hecker, Lars Braitmayer and Marjolein van Duiji are three psychologists who now believe that traumatic experiences can open someone to spirit possession (2015).

5 See Deut. 18:9-12, Isa. 8:19-20, Acts 9:13-19, Gal. 5:20 and Rev. 2:20-28.

6 See "Religious Debates over the *Harry Potter* Series" at *WikiVisually*, https://wikivisually.com/wiki/Religious_debates_over_the_Harry_Potter_series#cite_ref-Harry_Potter_expelled_from_school_15-1. It quotes Paul Hetrick for Focus on the Family (n.d.)

7 See Sage (1988), Griffin (2004), O'Malley (2006), Purves (2009) and Hoeveler (2014).

8 On the Christian deliverance ministry, see *Deliver Us from Evil* (1972) by Don Basham, *Pigs in the Parlor: A Practical Guide to Deliverance* (1973) by Frank and Ida Mae Hammond and *It's Only a Demon: A Model of Christian Deliverance* (2017) by David W. Appleby. See also John Eckhardt's "Why a Christian Can Have a Demon" (2019).

Bibliography

"The 50 Best Family Films." *The Guardian*, October 11, 2010. https://www.theguardian.com/film/gallery/2010/oct/11/best-family-films-kids.

"1991 Award Winners & Nominees." *Science Fiction, Fantasy & Horror Books by Award* (2019). https://www.worldswithoutend.com/books_year_index.asp?year=1991.

Amorth, Fr. Gabriele. *The Antics of Satan and His Army of Fallen Angels*. Manchester, NH: Sophia Institute Press, 2016.

Anolik, Ruth Biestock, ed. "Introduction: Sexual Horrors: Fears of the Sexual Other." In *Horrifying Sex: Essays on Sexual Difference in Gothic Literature*, 1–24. Jefferson, NC: McFarland and Company, 2007.

———. *Property and Power in English Gothic Literature*. Jefferson, NC: McFarland, 2016.

Barnes, Mike. "*Empire Strikes Back, Airplane* Among 25 Movies Named to National Film Registry." *Hollywood Reporter*, December 28, 2010. https://www.hollywoodreporter.com/news/empire-strikes-airplane-25-movies-65915.

Beal, Eleanor, and Jonathan Greenaway, eds. Introduction to *Horror and Religion: New Literary Approaches to Theology, Race and Sexuality*, 1–14. Cardiff: University of Wales Press, 2019.

Bean, Travis Lee. *The Highest-Grossing Horror Movies of All Time*. Forbes, October 3, 2019. https://www.forbes.com/sites/travisbean/2019/10/03/the-highest-grossing-horror-movies-of-all-time/#34bb09eae4d3.

Benge, Dustin. "What Can We Know about Angels? Angels and Demons, Creation, & Worship." *Tabletalk*, March 2019. https://tabletalkmagazine.com/posts/what-can-we-know-about-angels/.

Black, Candice. *Satanica Sexualis: An Encyclopedia of Sex and the Devil*. Bangkok: Wet Angel, 2007.

Blatty, William Peter. *The Exorcist*. Dir. William Friedkin, Warner Brothers. 1973.

———. *The Exorcist*. 1971. 40th Anniversary ed. New York: HarperTorch, 2011.

Bloch, John W. *The Sixth Sense*. Dir. Jeff Corey et al. ABC. 1971–72.

Botting, Fred. *Gothic*. London: Routledge, 1996.

Bowen, John. "Gothic Motifs." In *Discovering Literature: Romantics & Victorians*, May 15, 2014. British Library. https://www.bl.uk/romantics-and-victorians/articles/gothic-motifs.

Byron, Glennis, and Sharon Deans. "Teen Gothic." In *The Cambridge Companion to the Modern Gothic*, edited by Jerrold E. Hogle, 87–104. Cambridge, UK: Cambridge University Press, 2014.

Cardin, Matt, ed. *An Encyclopedia of the Stories That Speak to Our Deepest Fears*, vol. 1. Santa Barbara, CA: Greenwood, 2017.

Chesterton, G. K. "The End of Man." 1925. In *The Everlasting Man*, in *The Collected Works of G. K. Chesterton*, 2: 283–96. San Francisco: Ignatius Press, 1986.

Eckhardt, John. "Why a Christian Can Have a Demon." *CharismaNews*, May 9, 2019. https://www.charismanews.com/marketplace/76293-why-a-christian-can-have-a-demon.

Evil. 2019. https://www.cbs.com/shows/evil/.

Frost, Mark. *The List of 7.* New York: Avon Books, 1993.

Going, Mary. "The Blood Is the Life: An Exploration of the Vampire's Jewish Shadow." In *Horror and Religion: New Literary Approaches to Theology, Race and Sexuality*, edited by Eleanor Beal and Jon Greenaway, 37–56. Cardiff: University of Wales Press, 2019.

Griffin, Susan M. *Anti-Catholicism and Nineteenth-Century Fiction.* Cambridge, UK: Cambridge University Press, 2004.

Hecker, Tobias, Lars Braitmayer and Marjolein van Duijl. "Global Mental Health and Trauma Exposure: The Current Evidence for the Relationship Between Traumatic Experiences and Spirit Possession." *European Journal of Psychotraumatology* 6 (November 9, 2015): n.p. doi: 10.3402/ejpt.v6.29126. https://www.ncbi.nlm.nih.gov/pmc/articles/PMC4654771/.

Hoeveler, Diane Long. *The Gothic Ideology: Religious Hysteria and Anti-Catholicism in British Popular Fiction 1780–1880.* Cardiff: University of Wales Press, 2014.

Holt, Victoria. *The Legend of the Seventh Virgin.* Leicester: Ulverscroft, 1965.

Hoppenstand, Gary. "Exorcising the Devil Babies: Images of Children and Adolescents in the Best-Selling Horror Novel." In *Images of the Child*, edited by Harry Edwin Eiss, 35–76. Bowling Green, OH: Bowling Green State University Popular, 1994.

Hughes, William. *Historical Dictionary of Gothic Literature.* Lanham, MD: The Scarecrow Press, 2013.

Hurd, Richard. *Letters on Chivalry and Romance.* Cambridge, UK: W. Thurlbourn and J. Woodyer, 1762. https://books.google.com/books?id=jUgJAAAAQAAJ.

An Inquiry into the Existence of a Personal Devil. London: Sherwood, 1848. https://books.google.com/books?id=GApmAAAAcAAJ.

Jackson, Kevin. "Dobson Officially Denounces 'Harry Potter.'" *The Christian Post*, July 23, 2007. https://www.christianpost.com/news/dobson-officially-denounces-harry-potter.html.

Kilgour, Maggie. *The Rise of the Gothic Novel.* London: Routledge, 1995.

King, Robert, and Michelle King. *Evil.* New York: CBS, King Size Productions, 2019.

Kliger, Samuel. *The Goths in England.* New York: Octagon Books, 1952.

Krafft-Ebing, Richard von. *Psychopathia Sexualis with Especial Reference to Contrary Sexual Instinct: A Medico-Legal Study.* 1886. 7th ed. Translated by Charles Gilbert Chaddock. Philadelphia: F. A. Davis Company, 1894. https://books.google.com/books?id=9SYKAAAAIAAJ.

Levin, Ira. *Rosemary's Baby.* New York: Random House, 1967.

Lockyer, Herbert. *All the Messianic Prophesies.* Grand Rapids, MI: Zondervan, 1973.

MacAndrew, Elizabeth. *The Gothic Tradition in Fiction.* New York: Columbia University Press, 1979.

MacCallum-Stewart, Esther. "Dungeons & Dragons." In *Encyclopedia of Play in Today's Society*, edited by Rodney P. Carlisle, vol. 1, 186–89. Los Angeles: Sage, 2009.

Milbank, Alison. *God & the Gothic: Religion, Romance, and Reality in the English Literary Tradition.* Oxford, UK: Oxford University Press, 2018.

O'Malley, Patrick. *Catholicism, Sexual Deviance, and Victorian Gothic Culture.* Cambridge, UK: Cambridge University Press, 2006.

Polanski, Roman. Screenplay for *Rosemary's Baby.* Paramount: William Castle Enterprises, 1967.

"Poltergeist-Film Series." *ListArticle.* 2018. https://www.listarticle.com/page/en/Poltergeist_(film_series).

Pratchett, Terry, and Neil Gaiman. *Good Omens: The Nice and Accurate Prophecies of Agnes Nutter, Witch.* London: Gollancz, 1990.

Purves, Maria. *The Gothic and Catholicism: Religion, Cultural Exchange and the Popular Novel, 1785–1820.* Cardiff: University of Wales Press, 2009.

Rice, Anne. *The Vampire Lestat.* 1985. New York: Ballantine Books, 2014.

Rosemary's Baby. Dir. Roman Polanski. Paramount, 1968.

Russell, Jeffrey Burton. *The Devil: Perceptions of Evil from Antiquity to Primitive Christianity.* Ithaca, NY: Cornell University Press, 1978.

Sage, Victor. *Horror Fiction in the Protestant Tradition*. New York: St. Martin's Press, 1988.

Thorne, Will. "Live+7 Ratings for Week of Oct. 7: *This Is Us* Overtakes *Masked Singer*." *Variety*, 2019.

Walpole, Horace. *The Castle of Otranto: A Gothic Story*. 1764. Berlin: Christ: Fred: Himbourg, 1794. https://books.google.com/books?id=YZkLAAAAIAAJ.

Williams, Pat. "Freud." In *Beliefs, Rituals, and Symbols of the Modern World*, edited by Dean Miller, 44–47. New York: Cavendish Square, 2015.

NOTES ON CONTRIBUTORS

Brenda Ayres is the coeditor of this volume and has coedited several additional collections of essays with Sarah E. Maier, the most recent being *Neo-Victorian Madness: Rediagnosing Nineteenth-Century Mental Illness in Literature and Other Media* (2020), *Animals and Their Children in Victorian Culture* (2019) and *Reinventing Marie Corelli for the Twenty-First Century* (2019). She edited *Victorians and Their Animals: Beast on a Leash* (2019) and *Biographical Misrepresentations of British Women Writers: A Hall of Mirrors and the Long Nineteenth Century* (2017). *Betwixt and Between the Biographies of Mary Wollstonecraft* (2017) is her most recent monograph.

Geremy Carnes is Program Director of the English Language and Literature Department at Lindenwood University, Missouri. Carnes' teaching and research focus on eighteenth-century British literature and history. His published scholarship examines eighteenth-century literature in the context of religious conflict and anxiety, particularly with regards to English Catholicism and the development of Gothic literature. He has most recently published *The Papist Represented: Literature and the English Catholic Community, 1688–1791* (2017).

Martin Danahay teaches at Brock University in St. Catharines in Ontario. He has edited the third edition of *Dr. Jekyll and Mr. Hyde* (2015) and *Jekyll and Hyde Dramatized* (2004). Besides several articles, he has published *Gender at Work in Victorian Culture: Literature, Art and Masculinity* (2005) and *A Community of One: Masculine Autobiography and Autonomy in Nineteenth-Century Britain* (1993).

Carol Margaret Davison is Professor of English Literature at the University of Windsor in Ontario. A specialist in Gothic and Victorian literature, African-American literature, women's writing and cultural teratology, she is a former Canada–U.S. Fulbright Scholar. Davison is the author of *History of the Gothic: Gothic Literature, 1764–1824* (2009) and *Anti-Semitism and British Gothic Literature* (2004); editor of *Bram Stoker's Dracula: Sucking Through the Century, 1897–1997* (1997) and *The Gothic and Death* (2017); and winner of the 2019 Allan Lloyd Smith Memorial Prize for Gothic Criticism. She has also coedited (with Monica Germanà) *The Scottish Gothic: An Edinburgh Companion* (2017) and (with Marie Mulvey-Roberts) *Global Frankenstein* (2018).

Jessica Gildersleeve is Associate Professor of English Literature at the University of Southern Queensland. She is the author of *Christos Tsiolkas: The Utopian Vision* (2017), *Don't Look Now* (2017) and *Elizabeth Bowen and the Writing of Trauma: The Ethics of Survival* (2014); and coeditor of *Memory and the Wars on Terror: Australian and British Perspectives* (with

Richard Gehrmann, 2017) and *Elizabeth Bowen: Theory, Thought and Things* (with Patricia Juliana Smith, 2019).

Kate Livett has taught English and Australian literature for many years at a range of universities, particularly at UNSW (University of New South Wales). She is currently a recipient of the Ailsa McPherson Australian Literature Fellowship in the School of Arts & Media at UNSW and is completing a book on class, fetishism, religion and death in Australian women's novels from the nineteenth century onwards.

Karen E. Macfarlane is Associate Professor of English at Mount St Vincent University in Halifax. Her research focuses on zombies and other "monsters" and the Gothic at the turn of the nineteenth and twentieth centuries. She has published "Zombies and the Viral Web" in *Horror Studies* (2018); "Here Be Monsters: Knowledge and the Limits of Empire at the *Fin de Siècle*" in *Text Matters: A Journal of Literature, Theory, Culture* (2016); "Market Value: *American Horror Story*'s Housing Crisis" in *Neoliberal Gothic* (2015) and numerous others.

Sarah E. Maier is the coeditor of this volume and Professor of English and Comparative Literature at the University of New Brunswick. With Brenda Ayres she has coedited *Neo-Victorian Madness: Dediagnosing Nineteenth-Century Mental Illness in Literature and Other Media* (2020), *Animals and Their Children in Victorian Culture* (2019) and *Reinventing Marie Corelli for the Twenty-First Century* (2019). Most recently, she has published extensively on the Brontës, edited special issues on *Sir Arthur Conan Doyle* and *Neo-Victorian Considerations; Charlotte Brontë at the Bicentennial* and published articles on biofiction and neo-Victorian narratives.

Jamil Mustafa is Professor of English at Lewis University, Illinois. He has published numerous articles and chapters on Gothicism, the most recent being *"Penny Dreadfuls'* Queer Orientalism: The Translations of Ferdinand Lyle" in *Entangled Narratives: History, Gender and the Gothic* (2019); "The American Gothic and the Carnivalesque in *Something Wicked This Way Comes*" in *The New Ray Bradbury Review* (2019); "Lifting the Veil: Allegory, Ambivalence, and the Scottish Gothic in *The Bride of Lammermoor*" in *Gothic Britain: Dark Places in the Provinces and Margins of the British Isles* (2018); and "Haunting 'The Harlot's House'" in *Wilde's Other Worlds* (2018).

Ashleigh Prosser is an Early Career Researcher and a Learning Designer at the University of Western Australia. She has a doctorate in English and Cultural Studies from the University of Western Australia. For her dissertation, she studied the Gothic mode in Peter Ackroyd's London-based novels and historical works. Ashleigh's research interests lie with the Gothic and the uncanny in literature and popular culture. She is a Fellow of the Higher Education Academy, the Associate Editor of *Aeternum: The Journal of Contemporary Gothic Studies* and the Social Media Manager for the Gothic Association of New Zealand and Australia.

Nike Sulway is Senior Lecturer in Creative and Critical Writing at the University of Southern Queensland. She is the author of the novels *Dying in the First Person, Rupetta, The Bone Flute, The True Green of Hope* and the children's books *Winter's Tale* and *What the Sky Knows*. Nike coedited (with Donna Lee Brien and Dallas Baker) a collection of essays on speculative biography *Forgotten Lives: Recovering Lost Histories through Fact and Fiction* (2018).

INDEX

Lightning Source UK Ltd.
Milton Keynes UK
UKHW010939130420
361613UK00001B/9